Situation Aesthetics

Situation Aesthetics

The Work of Michael Asher

Kirsi Peltomäki

The MIT Press
Cambridge, Massachusetts
London, England

First MIT Press paperback edition, 2014

This book was set in Filosofia and Helvetica Neue by Graphic Composition, Inc.

Library of Congress Cataloging-in-Publication Data
Peltomäki, Kirsi, 1970–
Situation aesthetics : the work of Michael Asher / Kirsi Peltomäki.
p.   cm.
Includes bibliographical references and index.
ISBN 978-0-262-01368-0 (hardcover : alk. paper)—978-0-262-52608-1 (paperback)
1. Asher, Michael—Criticism and interpretation. I. Asher, Michael. II. Title.
N6537.A8P46 2010
709.048075—dc22

2009019834

Contents

All works reproduced in this book are by Michael Asher.

Acknowledgments

This book has benefited from the help, support, and advice of many individuals and institutions. Michael Asher, first and foremost, showed unlimited generosity throughout my writing process. Beyond opening access to his personal archives, he supported my research by answering innumerable questions about matters the written documents did not clarify. At the same time, his refraining from interfering with my interpretation of his work was the model of artistic and academic integrity. All mistakes that remain are mine.

I first began thinking critically about Asher's work in the Ph.D. program in Visual and Cultural Studies at the University of Rochester. Douglas Crimp's advice remains immeasurably influential for my work, and the sophistication and intellectual scope of his academic practice continues to inspire my own. Grace Seiberling's seminar in museum studies, along with courses led by Janet Wolff and Michael Ann Holly, opened new perspectives for my research. My fellow graduate students in the Visual and Cultural Studies Program were tremendously influential as I formulated the critical framework for this book. In particular, I would like to thank Hanneke Grootenboer, Margot Bouman, Dore Bowen, Reni Celeste, Darby English, Amy Herzog, Alex Miokovic, Nick Newman, and T'ai Smith for friendship and inspiration. While I was in Rochester, my doctoral studies and archival research were funded by a generous grant from the Academy of Finland.

At Oregon State University, a fellowship at the Center for the Humanities enabled me to formulate the first draft of this book. A subsequent faculty release time grant from Oregon State University's Research Office provided time to continue writing. A library research travel grant awarded by the Oregon State University Libraries funded a pivotal visit to the archives at the Van Abbemuseum in Eindhoven, the Netherlands. Reference librarian Loretta Rielly's help was indispensable in tracking down sources. My colleagues at Oregon State University's art department consistently provide a working community that is unparalleled in its openness and generosity. In particular, Barbara Loeb, Jim Folts, and John

Maul have supported my work unwaveringly. And my students keep it interesting, every day.

In addition to Asher's personal archives, my research in this book has benefited from other unpublished sources. I would like to thank Diana Franssen at the Van Abbemuseum, as well as Bart Ryckbosch and Debbie Webb at the Institutional Archives of the Art Institute of Chicago, for facilitating access to documents that deepened my understanding of Asher's projects for these museums. Numerous individuals also took time to discuss their experiences of his work with me. In that regard, I would like to especially thank Brian L. MacNevin and Anne Rorimer. In addition, Claire Copley Eisenberg was particularly generous in allowing me to quote from her unpublished letter written to Asher during his 1974 exhibition in her gallery.

Many illustrations in this book have not been published before. Yoko Kanayama was instrumental in locating images, scanning them, and otherwise facilitating image research in Asher's archives. The permission holders of photographs of Asher's work have been tremendously generous in granting rights to reproduce their images of these temporary situations. I would like to especially mention Valerie Breuvart at the Judd Foundation, who arranged for photographing Asher's 1966 work in Judd's collection. Every effort has been made to trace copyright holders and to seek permission for images, but if any have escaped my notice, I would be happy to hear from them.

Parts of my argument in chapter 1 were previously published in an article entitled "Affect and Spectatorial Agency: Viewing Institutional Critique in the 1970s," which appeared in the Winter 2007 issue of *Art Journal*.

At the MIT Press, Marc Lowenthal, Anar Badalov, and Matthew Abbate have tirelessly answered questions about all matters so necessary for a project of this magnitude. Roger Conover has been the ideal editor, and his support of this book has been nothing less than instrumental.

My family remains my bedrock in this project, as in so many others. My parents, Ritva and Tarmo Peltomäki, have supported me even when my interests have taken me to the other side of the world (twice over). This book is for Mika, both for the time he and I missed, and for what enabled me to finish this project. Ultimately, this book is dedicated to Jillian St. Jacques, whose love, energy, intelligence, and commitment to this project kept me focused each day and year.

Situation Aesthetics

Introduction

The Experiential Matrix

From the outset, Michael Asher designed his work to facilitate human interaction. Even his early experimentations with the production of material art objects in the mid-1960s called for subordinating the art object to its spatial and social contexts.[1] In fact, the material construction of these objects often hinged upon their mimicry of socially recognizable patterns of behavior. An initial case in point might be the minimalist checkers set that Asher displayed in the exhibition "A Collection of Limited Editions by Contemporary Artists" in The Egg and the Eye, the café that later became the Los Angeles Craft and Folk Art Museum, in his hometown of Los Angeles in the fall of 1966. This geometrically shaped game set consisted of round silver and black custom-machined chrome pieces on a cardboard playing surface purchased from a dime store (figures 0.1, 0.2).[2] While on display at The Egg and the Eye, Asher's checkers were spotted by Donald Judd, who had appeared at the Los Angeles County Museum of Art (LACMA) for a speaking engagement.[3] Judd ended up purchasing Asher's checkers set, countersigning his honorarium check to Asher in compensation.[4] It is not difficult to imagine the arch-minimalist Judd appreciating the structurally immaculate repetition of geometric shapes, systematically ordered, one thing after another. Yet Asher's checkers set was not simply an industrially produced compendium of minimal forms; it was also a game intended to facilitate human interaction: come and play, engage with the work.

Now an artist whose site-specific installations connect people with meticulously organized museum and gallery situations, Asher withdrew from the production of material art objects shortly after completing his checkers sets. Since then, he has chosen to work through a process of subtraction, displacement, reemphasis, and replacement. He uses the objects, elements, and relations that pertain to the institutional site that has commissioned work from him. The resulting installations (none of which have titles) have ranged from material gallery interventions to institutional displacements; from highlighting social relations to archival compendia. Typically, Asher's projects—most of them commissioned by

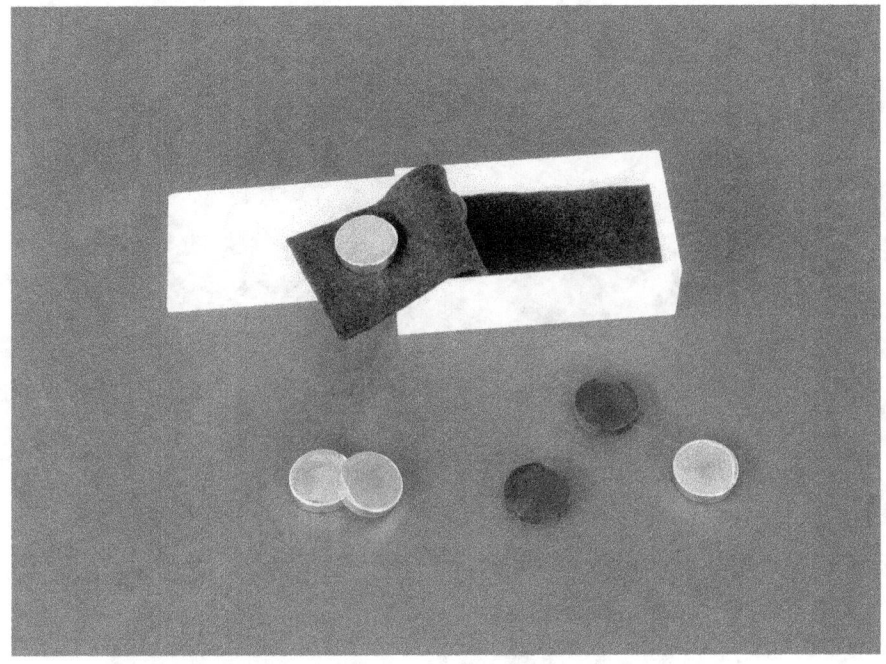

0.1   No title, c. 1966. Steel checkers set plated with a chrome and black-oxide finish
       along with a Plexiglas storage box. Collection of Judd Foundation. (Photograph by
       Craig Rember; courtesy Judd Foundation.)

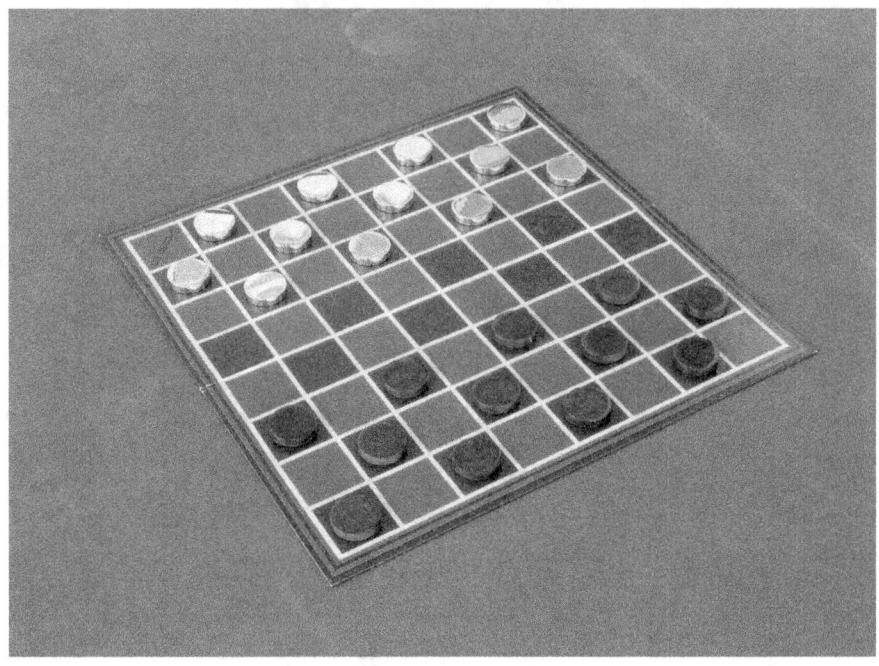

0.2   No title, c. 1966. Steel checkers set plated with a chrome and black-oxide finish, with its standard store-bought checkerboard. Collection of Judd Foundation. (Photograph by Craig Rember; courtesy Judd Foundation.)

museums, galleries, freestanding exhibitions, or foundations—address the given context of their exhibition directly and exclusively. Because his works engage with their existing environments, they most frequently cease to exist at the end of their exhibition, leaving no art object that can be reexhibited, preserved, circulated, or commodified.[5] This exceptional adherence to the 1960s conceptualist principles of dematerialization combines with an approach that Thomas Crow has called "strong site specificity": Asher's installations tend to disable the day-to-day functioning of the host institution, and therefore are barred from permanent material existence.[6] Any notion of permanence within Asher's work is further challenged by his experiential approach to museum or gallery presentation, which addresses the viewer's epistemological and emotional faculties simultaneously. His installations require, and draw from, whatever discursive knowledge a viewer may have regarding the operation of art institutions, while they simultaneously solicit individuated social and psychological responses.

That Asher's experiential site specificity continues to address the ideological debates that surround and influence current museum practices is clear in his project at LACMA in 2000 and 2002.[7] The art museum of the early twenty-first century is a vastly different creature from the 1960s museums and galleries in which Asher started out. In addition to showcasing autonomous art objects, LACMA—along with most American museums—now increasingly centralizes its visitors' experience. In 2000, the museum had founded a division, entitled LACMALab, charged with producing exhibitions designed to reach specific audience groups—in particular, families with children.[8] Extending the museum's pedagogical mission from interpreting singular works of art to producing exhibitions with a clear communicative agenda, the LACMALab initiative addressed the broad sociopolitical imperatives directed at museums by funding bodies and the public to redress past inequalities of cultural exclusivity. In the view of the museum, visitors had lost their claim to uniform art appreciation and had become socially defined individuals whose habits, opinions, dispositions, and reactions—what Pierre Bourdieu would call "cultural competencies"[9]—could be at least partially predicted, and whose particular sensibilities the museum sought to address as part of its core mission.

LACMALab inaugurated its activities in 2000 with an exhibition entitled "Made in California: NOW." Asher was one of eleven contemporary Californian artists invited to make works engineered to "reach" younger museum visitors. Asher's proposal, which involved reinstalling the paintings and sculptures in one of LACMA's permanent collection galleries, echoed the artist's persistent tendency to examine the ideological and contextual dimensions of the art world. Such mock-curatorial artistic projects were common by 2000, having been expeditiously incorporated into the art and museum worlds since the early 1990s.[10] Asher was far more than a casual participant in this museum trend. In fact, his earlier projects, such as the 1979 *George Washington* relocation for the "73rd American Exhibition" at the Art Institute of Chicago, were foundational to it. His reinstallation proposal for LACMA, then, could easily have relied on his seniority in the field by simply reiterating his past, already critically acclaimed, artistic strategies.

Those familiar with Asher's methods—including Robert L. Sain, LACMALab's director, who commissioned the work—cannot have been surprised when the artist chose to strike out in an unforeseen direction. Instead of reprising his own signature approach, Asher paid close attention to the intended audience of the new exhibition—children and teens—by arranging for a group of students from the nearby Fairfax Senior High School to carry out the reinstallation (figure 0.3). This simple gesture of making producers out of a group of intended receivers—without reducing them to subservience or insignificance—gave rise to gallery installations that departed experientially from normative museum presentations. Furthermore, Asher's strategy also called for egalitarian social relations between the students and the museum, which in turn might have influenced the students in their concern for the gallery visitor's affective experience within their installation.[11] As with many other Asher installations, the experiential nature of the production and reception of art trumped the material solidity of standard museum fare at LACMA.

Reconstructing the Asher of Art History

Although Asher has been labeled one of the most significant artists of his generation, the art historical reception of his overall practice has ranged from obscurity to acclaim. The scarcity of critical attention to his work is evident from the fact that there are few extended accounts of his oeuvre. Thus far, there have been no retrospective exhibitions of his work; his commitment to the historical and contextual specificity of each work has led him to consistently decline invitations to reconstruct past projects. In Asher's view, recreating a work would necessitate

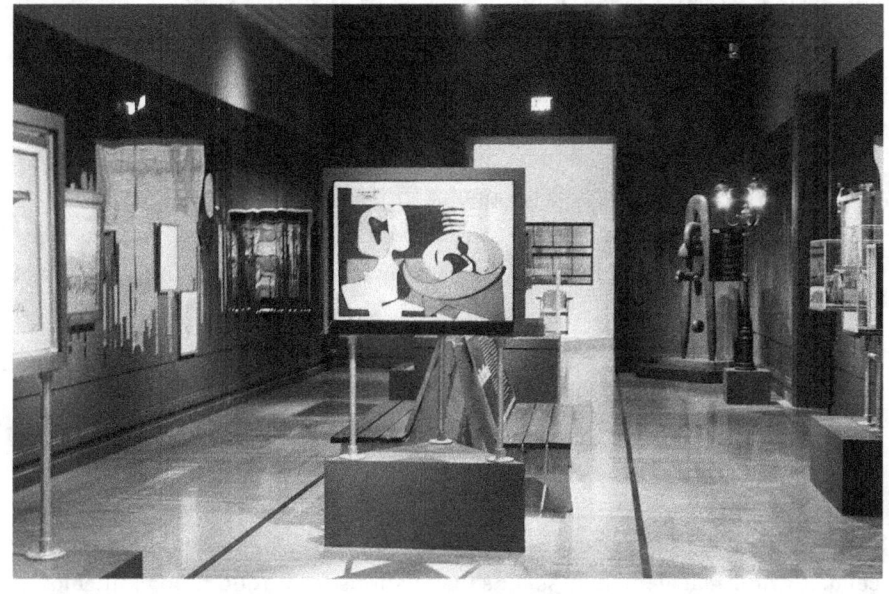

0.3   Los Angeles County Museum of Art, Los Angeles, 2002. Second rotation of the
      reinstallation of the permanent collection in the Modern and Contemporary Art
      Council Gallery by students from Fairfax High School. Viewing west. (Photograph
      courtesy the artist.)

reconstructing the entire historical situation—a task that is, of course, impossible.[12] Hence his participation in historicizing survey exhibitions often involves exhibiting previously unrealized proposals or creating new work.[13] Viewed in the context of the institutionalization of postwar art—which is by now extensive—it is startling to realize that there are no works by Asher in any of the major museum collections in the world, and only a handful of his private commissions have resulted in permanent installations.[14] Although his uncompromising approach to site specificity may have contributed to the dearth of art historical accounts of his work (since critics have had few opportunities to view it), this doesn't explain his inconspicuousness in the art world. Though many of his contemporaries share his temporally delimited approach to artistic production, the difficulty of viewing long-vanished artworks firsthand has not prevented the museological and art historical interpretation of Gordon Matta-Clark's work, for instance.[15]

As if to counter this material obscurity, critics and historians frequently designate Asher's work as vital to major developments in postwar art, in particular minimalism and conceptual art.[16] His early room alterations, such as those made for LACMA in 1971 and Documenta 5 in 1972, have been called "environments" by critics who associated them with minimalism.[17] Because of their perceptually minimal elements, Asher's installations from 1966 to 1976, including the sensory-deprived spaces at the La Jolla Museum of Art in 1969 and the pivotal 1970 MoMA exhibition "Spaces," have been connected with the Los Angeles light and space movement of Robert Irwin, Eric Orr, and James Turrell.[18] The analytic logic of Asher's gallery and museum interventions, such as his exhibition at Claire Copley Gallery in 1974 and his work for the "73rd American Exhibition" at the Art Institute of Chicago in 1979, have been interpreted under the category of conceptual art.[19] From the late 1970s on, his work has been associated with "a critique of institutions" by *October*-affiliated poststructuralist critics such as Benjamin H. D. Buchloh, Craig Owens, Douglas Crimp, and Hal Foster. Indeed, these critics (and others in their wake) have retrospectively designated Asher as one of the founding figures of institutional critique, alongside Marcel Broodthaers, Daniel Buren, and Hans Haacke.[20] Subsequently, Asher's 1990s archival installations, such as the meticulously framed impromptu scraps of paper in his 1991 exhibition at the Centre Georges Pompidou in Paris, have been connected with "the archival turn" in contemporary art, and aligned with the critical scrutiny of museums by artists, critics, and historians in fields ranging from installation art to museum studies and art history.[21]

Alongside its association with art movements, Asher's oeuvre carries critical weight in recent art history. Proceeding beyond a simple renegotiation of formal modernist values—such as opticality, immediacy, authenticity, or the material presence of the object—one finds him mentioned in discussions of institutional critique, site specificity, museum critique, and appropriation. Buchloh considers Asher's work in relation to the limits of modernist sculpture, while for Owens, Asher embodies a shift from "work to frame."[22] Crimp includes Asher among the artists whose practice radicalized the minimalist version of site specificity—and, more recently, Blake Stimson mentions Asher's work as an example of politically progressive conceptual art.[23] Crow's discussion of Asher's "strong site specificity" is complemented by Miwon Kwon's emphasis on the social and ideological specificity of his work.[24] For Anne Rorimer and Martha Buskirk, Asher's practice since the 1970s speaks of tendencies to foreground the context of art.[25]

Yet Asher's critical reception thus far only partially explains the intersubjective dynamics of his 1965–1966 checkers set, or the social interactivity of the 2000 and 2002 LACMA reinstallations by the Fairfax High School students—projects that direct attention to human subjects, such as the viewers, critics, or museum staff members who participate in his situations.[26] In fact, numerous firsthand accounts attest to the centrality of sociopsychological strategies within Asher's work, and there are critics who spend the bulk of their exhibition reviews recounting the experience of a face-to-face encounter with his installations. "As long as I was in possession of only an idea about Asher's contribution, I knew too little about it," wrote one newspaper critic, reviewing his 1979 installation at the Museum of Contemporary Art in Chicago. "My understanding was altered and enlarged by the form of the work. In other words, Asher . . . was most impressive when his concept took on persuasive form, and least so when it did not."[27] A perceptual, material viewing of Asher's work, in other words, remained an important part of the interpretive process for this critic.[28] Similarly, individuals whom he has contracted to play a role in his works often reflect upon their participation by emphasizing their individuated responses. Finally, Asher's written project notes, as well as his published accounts, make it abundantly clear that the artist throughout his career has paid considerable attention to how spectators and participants encounter his work.

Asher's concern for the experiential subject harkens to the lineage of performance-oriented, often participatory projects through which artists have investigated the social relations between artists, viewer-participants, and institutions since the late 1950s. Ranging from task-oriented Happenings and Fluxus events to the conceptual actions of Vito Acconci and the reflexive sculptural work of Bruce Nauman and Dan Graham, postwar artists have long considered how viewers interact with artwork and how the artist's psychological presence affects the work's reception. Like that of Nauman and Graham, Asher's work intersects with both conceptual- and performance-oriented traditions of postwar art.[29] Thus, even though Asher's physically minimal installations of the late 1960s and early 1970s featured solid shapes or architectural forms that aimed at increasing viewers' psychological awareness of their physical space, these installations also attempted to direct viewer awareness toward social factors. True, his early 1970s installations bore a certain resemblance to work of the light and space movement in their use of perceptually subtle phenomena, but unlike Irwin's aesthetically refined spaces, they demurred from posing an opposition between perceptual and conceptual modes of address.[30] Though Asher's works are always based on concepts, he would rarely attempt to eliminate subjectivity from the artwork, as other conceptual artists might have done.[31] Nor does he strive for artistic autonomy, as does Joseph Kosuth. Despite their elegance and precision, Asher's gestures do not rely on poeticity in the manner of Robert Barry.[32] Instead, in a material reticence that Buchloh has termed "ostentatious asceticism,"[33] Asher's installations use the material and signifying conditions of their institutional existence in order to facilitate individuated reflection of those conditions. By focusing on the social and psychological sites of art at the expense of producing autonomous art objects, Asher not only participates in the project of the postwar avant-garde—he does so in order to construct experientially complex situations for individuated human subjects.

The Necessary Status of Experience

The trouble with much critical reception of Asher's work is that it tends to rely on abbreviated sound bites, as if the entire installation could be encapsulated in one sentence. We might know, for example, that he removed the dividing wall between the gallery and office spaces for his exhibition at the Claire Copley Gallery in 1974.[34] But does it follow that by possessing this bit of conceptual information we fully understand Asher's work? Perhaps more important than the architectural cut that divides the gallery space is the social and psychological situation that the missing wall instigated within and between the viewers and the gallerist. What did gallery owner Claire Copley's experience without the wall convey about the effects of Asher's intervention, and how did reactions by gallery visitors contribute to the work?

When examining Asher's critical and archival record, it becomes clear that subjective responses to his installations cannot be reduced to any single position. Documents left by his temporally and materially specific projects include a wealth of information about the experiences of viewers, participants, critics, and institutional representatives. Far from being cognitively uniform, these responses are messy, unpredictable, and individuated; they do not remain detached or disinterested from the work—or their own motives. On the one hand, Asher's reception provides evidence of the analytical work that his viewers and critics undertake by detecting the material clues for displacement or rearrangement and recognizing the changes he had instigated in the exhibition spaces. On the other hand, the tone of the responses to his work extends from the analytical register to an affective one, conveying intensely emotional reactions.[35] "Unnerving," "disconcerting," and "pushing the museum to the edge" are among the phrases that critics have used to describe his projects. In themselves, however, the installations that are described in such loaded terms are not always the most obvious candidates for generating spectacles or public scandals. Indeed, his works tend to be quiet, organized, and tidy—sometimes even self-effacing. What is it, then, that evokes such strong reactions in viewers, participants, and museum staff—reactions that brim with emotions rare in the cool confines of the art world? How do these materially ephemeral, meticulously negotiated works so infuriate, charm, inflame, and elevate the subjects who encounter them? To answer these questions, one needs to further consider the experiential dimension of his work.

The kinds of experience facilitated by Asher's work have changed in concert with shifts in postwar art. For example, his installations in the late 1960s and early 1970s offered viewers opportunities to immerse themselves in sensory experience, corresponding with the phenomenological models that influenced minimalist art and its criticism.[36] However, this paradigm of immediate bodily experience—even when it is understood to produce knowledge rather than reflect it—becomes insufficient when we consider the social turn in Asher's work from the mid-1970s on. While it preserved the individuation of the viewing experience, his careful adjustment of preexisting institutional situations now addressed the social and psychological boundaries between private and public domains by removing gallery walls, for example, or by contracting groups of people to engage in social interaction in the gallery. The social dimension of these situations made specific modes of experience available to his works' viewers and participants. Alongside the material gesture of revealing a gallerist's position at the Claire Copley Gallery, Asher mobilized the viewer's social and intersubjective relations to the gallery visit itself. These relational projects demonstrated the artist's understanding of the more political aspects of conceptual art, requiring the expansion of the "aesthetic experience" into what Buchloh, in his account of conceptual art, describes as "an individual and social investment of objects with meaning [that] is constituted by *linguistic* as well as by *specular* conventions [and] by the institutional determination of the object as much as by the reading competence of the spectator."[37] Asher's attribution of meaning to preexisting art objects is particularly mindful of the social relations within the specific situation. While Barry, Weiner, and many other conceptual artists have challenged the materialization of the art object and the investment of meaning in tangible art objects in general, Asher has consistently sought to reinvest social meaning within particular experiential situations.

During the 1970s and early 1980s, art that seemed especially attuned to viewers' reactions was often called "situational." Victor Burgin had promoted such work with the term "situational aesthetics" in an article in *Studio International* in 1969.[38] Subsequently, the term "situational" was applied to new "impermanent" modes of art that emphasized the experiential, temporary situation over the "stable" art object.[39] Asher had utilized the situational appellation when seeking to distance himself from the ethereal light and space movement in 1974, declaring to a critic, "I don't deal with environments. I do situational work. I'm not interested in manipulating perception."[40] And he further claimed the "situational" concept in 1983 when he defined "situational aesthetics" in his own work as "an aesthetic system that juxtaposes predetermined elements occurring within the institutional framework, that are recognizable and identifiable to the public because they are drawn from the institutional context itself."[41] To Asher, the viewer's epistemological familiarity with the operative institutional norms, or what they already know about the situation, influences the experiential encounter with his work. In this sense, Asher's work makes an articulate intervention in what Jacques Rancière has termed "the given distribution of the sensible," which determines the type of information that is visible, thinkable, or perceivable within a particular context.[42] In calling for viewers to deploy their social and cognitive senses, as well as their sensory and interpretive skills, Asher's situations facilitate epistemological and sensory viewing experiences that, when considered together, have the potential to redistribute the boundaries between visible and invisible aspects of a given institution. In turn, such experiences might lead to what Rancière calls "the formation of political subjects," or new modes of subjectivity.[43]

The process of viewing Asher's experientially specific situations draws from a viewing subject's expectations, active cognition, typecasting, contextual judgments, and social relations. Such modes of temporally intersecting experience draw from the past, even as they affect the future.[44] Numerous visitors to the Art Institute of Chicago, for example, had already passed by the George Washington statue that stood in front of the museum's facade for decades before Asher moved it to a period room inside the museum. Upon its relocation to the museum's lobby after the exhibition, the statue continued to remind frequent museum visitors of Asher's intervention into institutional memory. Rather than take the position that his installations are either exclusively absorptive or phenomenological, it might be more productive to consider the dynamics of experience triggered by his installations through the experiential model that Michel Foucault articulated in his late work.[45] In Foucault's estimation, the temporal horizon of experience is not limited to the immediacy of the present moment; instead, "experience" becomes the crux of a signifying system that combines discursive and inhabited dimensions. Explaining his motives for writing a history of sexuality, Foucault stressed the need to distinguish his project from the more common sociological, psychological, or historical approaches:

I wanted to undertake a history in which sexuality would not be conceived as a general type of behavior whose particular elements might vary according to demographic, economic, social, or ideological conditions, any more than it would be seen as a collection of representations (scientific, religious, moral) which, though diverse and changeable, are joined to an invariant reality. My object was to analyze sexuality as a historically singular form of experience.[46]

The use of "experience" here denotes a temporal condensation of three broad discursive axes, defined by Foucault "as the correlation of a domain of knowledge [*savoir*], a type of normativity, and a mode of relation to the self."[47] This experiential matrix accounts for the collective historical domains of discourses and institutions, as well as for the personal elements that can be interpreted through an understanding of subjectivity as a lived, individuated—yet also unmistakably collective—relation to knowledge, institutions, and events. Considered through Foucault's matrix, "experience" within Asher's work departs from strictly phenomenological, sociological, and psychoanalytical modes. As an interpretative category, "experience" differs from "behavior"—a category one might use to account for observable reactions by Asher's beholders within the museum space, or when considering how institutions react to his proposals, either supporting them or attempting to obstruct their realization. Foucault's model of experience likewise departs from critiques of representation within art history. Applied to Asher's work, such representational analysis might focus on what codes are mobilized in the work, or how it presents the museum. Instead, the Foucauldian experiential matrix focuses upon the shared, recognizable assumptions that the artist, viewers, and participants hold regarding the art institution; it draws from the institutional norms that govern the limits of the social and material relations practiced within the museum and the art world.[48] By including the subject as an ethical formation, this experiential matrix further provides space for a "subject conscious of himself and others" whose relational choices have individually and socially tangible consequences.[49]

Although the experiences that transpire within and around Asher's work gain shape through socially normative, discursive frames of reference, they do not merely reflect the known world back to the work's viewers and participants. Many of the individuals whom Asher has contracted to participate in his work have subsequently connected their roles in the artist's work with their relation to the world in general. For these participants, epistemological accounts—what they knew and what they know now—tend to be inseparable from distinctly emotional, or affective, responses—from how they were moved by their experience within his work. Hence, the "affective" experience that I consider in relation to Asher's reception is not an unmediated outside, a Deleuzian "intensity" or a state of being.[50] Nor is affect a force that wrenches the subject free from its normal disposition, or an ontological sensation per se, an experience that would transcend the epistemological boundaries of discursive representations.[51] Rather, "affect" in this study describes embodied, emotional, socially mediated relations between the self and others, between individuals and collectives, or between individuals and art institutions, within what Sara Ahmed has called "affective economies."[52] The accounts given by Asher's viewers and participants consistently link such affective experiences to the potential of his situations to rupture existing models of interpretation and to reconfigure individual and institutional modes of conduct. Yet it would be misleading to characterize the experiences around his work as liberating, at least in any simple sense of the word; on the contrary, these experiences might foreground the shared or individual limits of conduct by provoking a reckoning of how individuated modes of attention are constituted in relation to the art institution. The experiential result of Asher's work might consist of the gallerist or viewer becoming more aware of the governing social roles within the gallery, for example, rather than exempting themselves from the stronghold of institutional conventions.

Locating Asher's Subjects

This book traces Asher's experiential matrix from his 1960s sensory environments to his twenty-first-century social situations. It delineates his working process through a close reading of the artist's working notes, combining the artist's authorial perspective with institutional responses to his work throughout its planning and realization. My research draws from published accounts as well as previously unpublished archival material regarding Asher's temporally specific events. These accounts include contemporary responses to his installations—by viewers, critics, participants, curators, and museum directors—that both amplify and complicate the artist's perspective concerning his oeuvre. This archival stratum is then related to the critical interpretation and retrospective reception of Asher's work in art criticism and theory. By combining historical and theoretical modes of interpretation, I hope to add a new facet to the art historical understanding of his work, as well as convey some of the intersubjective energy, or sense of possibility, that has animated his arrangements. One of my foremost goals is to connect diachronic accounts of postwar art (in which art is seen as responding to previous art movements and ideologies) with a consideration of subjectivity that contributes to contemporary practice. Such contributions are, after all, integral to Asher's pedagogical influence as the legendary Post-Studio seminar instructor of more than thirty-five years at the California Institute of the Arts.[53]

While "the subject" is a broad area of concern for contemporary poststructuralists, its most discrete meaning in this study relates to human individuals: viewers, participants, museum or gallery staff—and the artist himself. On a discursive level, these subjects are also organized into structural positions that precede any given individual. In the parlance of critical theory, "subject position" refers to a cultural location, a nexus of power and knowledge. Although Asher's subjects are not composed of an essential or fixed set of properties, their role in the work functions as an interface for taking up positions in the world, much like the standpoints Emile Benveniste analyzed in his discussion of linguistic "shifters"—personal pronouns that facilitate context-dependent subject positions.[54] Despite the radical relativism of the linguistic subject position of "you," for example, each "you" has to be inhabited by individuals in any given situation. The social and discursive norms that govern the art world necessitate that one's entry to Asher's work depends on taking up the position of "you," or an interpellated subject.[55] Yet the socially and psychologically constrained subject is not determined in advance. By using the terms "subjectivity" and "subject position," I am not attempting to generalize the attitudes, motives, or affective responses toward Asher's work—nor will I pit interior "subjective" experiences against exterior "objective" facts within the embodied reception of this work. Rather, the intersubjective experiences in Asher's work have both reflexive and potentially affective dimensions. Visitors to the Claire Copley Gallery (sans the dividing wall) entered his work through what they already knew and thought about the art world, but they also were affected by their experience within the work—accounts by critics and Copley certainly attest to that.

These chapters are thematically organized around the subject positions that dominate Asher's work: viewer, participant, artist, and institutional representative. The first chapter, "Viewing Experiences," attends to his sensory and discursive installations, which required the viewer to experience the work within material and social limits the artist had set in place. In contrast with the idealized minimalist spectators who were largely abstracted from particularities,[56] these works experientially located their viewers within the materially and ideologically tangible context of the artist's installation. A viewer's encounter with the installation had both analytical and affective dimensions. I will consider what the viewer's social relationality contributed to the epistemological and phenomenological experientiality of Asher's installations.

After placing heightened emphasis on the viewer's experience in the late 1960s and early 1970s, Asher moved to include participants in his situational works. These participants were typically arts professionals, usually museum staff members or volunteers, who in most cases held positions within the selected museum or gallery. Chapter 2, "Contracted Participation," examines Asher's participatory situations in light of the labor these participants performed within his work—going against the dominant mode of participatory art, in which the participatory function is typically assigned to viewers.[57] His participants, on the other hand, were specifically hired to perform artist-defined tasks, and the limits he had formerly placed upon the physical experience of his viewers became reconfigured as the epistemological and normative dimensions of the social contract he extended to his participants.

In another set of artistic moves, situated within a mise-en-scène of museums and alternative spaces in the 1970s and early 1980s, Asher shifted the lens of social scrutiny from multifarious acts of participation to a tight examination of artistic agency. "In the Name of the Artist," my third chapter, considers the ways in which his performative deployment of the artist's name oscillated between the objectification of the artist within an artwork (as another trope of the institutional order under scrutiny) and the troubling aspect of artistic agency itself, as it attempts to renegotiate the division of administrative and contextual authority within museums—particularly as museums use the act of naming to gain favor with benefactors and trustees by dedicating and designating the museum's material space. A close reading of a cluster of Asher's unrealized proposals from the late 1970s, which led to the artist's 1983 lobby project at the Los Angeles Museum of Contemporary Art, will prove informative for understanding how the appropriation of institutional power structures—particularly in the form of administrative functions—permeates his oeuvre. By proposing to redistribute a museum or gallery's funds, and using his own name to lay claim to a range of administrative responsibilities, Asher teased out the contractual relations between disparate social positions within art institutions (artists, museum donors, and functionaries) in order to investigate the ways in which economic power is exchanged for symbolic power, and vice versa.

The concluding chapter, "Institutional Support," further examines the dynamics of endorsement as they affect institutional authority when the performance of "support" is reciprocated by an artist and offered back to the institution. For Asher, the concept of support includes both a material structure and a social, psychological relation—both of which he appropriated in a number of carefully negotiated works during the 1980s and 1990s. In these projects, he laid claim to the institutional functions of approving and assisting the artist. By reinterpreting institutional situations having to do with funding structures, promotion, ownership, or museum policies, Asher doubled the support received from an institution by simultaneously reciprocating and relocating the institution's gifting gesture. This relocation of power relations within the context of support and endowment created a dialogic relationship between two radically incompatible attitudes toward authority. When, for example, he provided Rudi Fuchs, the artistic director of Documenta 7, with additional walls to hang paintings on, or placed advertisements in art historical journals for the survey exhibition "l'art conceptuel, une perspective," the artist returned to the institution the support he had received—even as the artist's gifting gesture simultaneously teased out the implicit conditions and limits of institutional support, which inevitably centralizes the administrative and economic function of the institution and its financial guardians.

Asher's focus upon the constitutive role of institutional support is paradigmatic of his broader situation aesthetics. Using conceptual, appropriative strategies, the artist underscores the epistemological and often normatizing structures that frame art institutions—as well as the subjects within them. The subtle "affective economies" made possible by his reframing of museum and gallery situations, however, result in highly individuated encounters on the part of viewers and participants.[58] The intimate experientiality of such encounters often tends to implode or fracture the uniformity of ideological institutional edifices that might otherwise seem paralyzing in their efforts to frame the ways in which we perform the viewing of art. The fact that Asher's audience, curators, critics, and institutional "supporters" often remark upon (and in some cases quarrel with) his work's incisive complexity only lends more weight to the critical efficacy of his institutional critique. When speaking about readers' responses to his books—particularly complaints about the works' immobilizing effect—Foucault stressed the practical value of these types of reactions: "It shows that people read [my work] as an experience that changed them, that prevented them from always being the same or from having the same relation with things, with others, that they had before reading it."[59] Asher's situation aesthetics, in its own subtle manner, also works toward achieving such effects. By modifying the perceptual and conceptual givens of exhibition space, his works foreground and generate social relations within art institutions, reformulate history through archival reawakenings, and induce deeply affective experiences that participants view as leading to personal and institutional transformation.

1

Viewing Experiences

"The President and Board of Trustees of the La Jolla Museum of Art Cordially Invite You to Enter the Work of Michael Asher, View Graphics by Edward Ruscha, and See New African Art from the Central African Workshop School, Friday, November 7, 1969, 5:30 to 7:30 p.m." (figure 1.1).[1] This invitation card to the opening reception of Asher's one-person exhibition at the La Jolla Museum of Art—his first solo exhibition—firmly distinguishes Asher's work from that of Ruscha and the Central African Workshop School by its description of the viewer's encounter with the work. The call to "enter" the work marked the expected mode of reception for Asher's installation from the outset. What does it mean to "enter" the work, rather than to "view" or "see" it? "Entering the work" implies crossing a threshold between two environments; it might even promise a passage to an altered state. In other words, "entering" signifies an experience.

Asher's La Jolla installation was a room that had been systematically altered to provide a distinctive visual and auditory experience (figure 1.2).[2] Lighting in the space had been manipulated to be gradually diffused from the center of the room toward the periphery; gallery walls were painted white, the floor was overlaid with white shag carpet, and the ceiling was covered with sound-absorbing material. The natural soundscape that might have resulted from the visitor's movements and other ambient noise was replaced by a single audio tone produced by sound generators and tuned to the shape of the room. The resulting acoustic pattern defined the room spatially by symmetrically canceling and increasing the sound waves that reflected off the room's surfaces. The modification of the room's sound qualities produced an environment in which audio levels were muffled in the center and corners of the room, and subtly increased in other parts of the gallery.[3]

Asher's care regarding the viewer's experience in his La Jolla work is typical of his broader emphasis on individuated reception. The entire installation, which viewers were requested to enter one at a time, was constructed for the sole purpose of facilitating a particular kind of viewing experience rather than explicitly

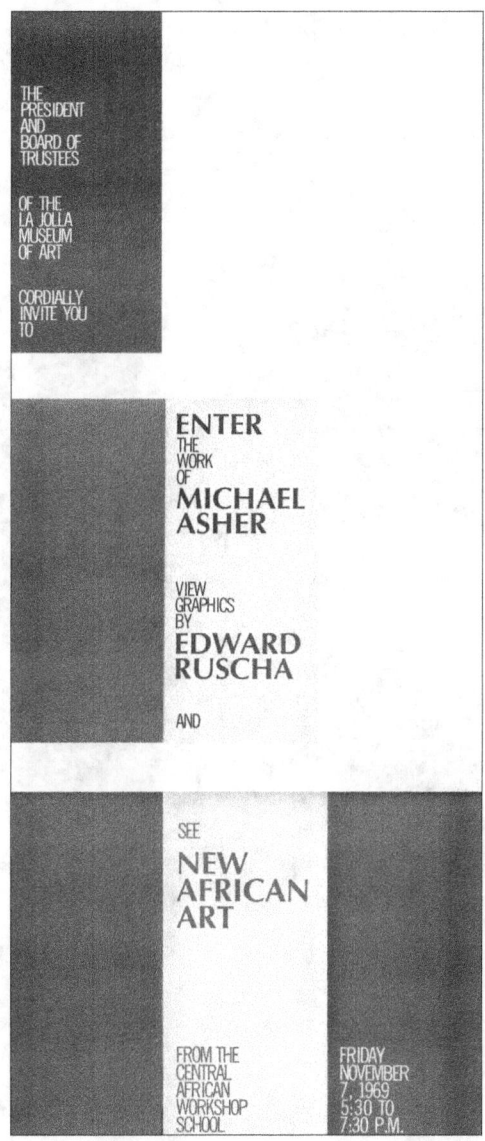

THE
PRESIDENT
AND
BOARD OF
TRUSTEES

OF THE
LA JOLLA
MUSEUM
OF ART

CORDIALLY
INVITE YOU
TO

ENTER
THE
WORK
OF
**MICHAEL
ASHER**

VIEW
GRAPHICS
BY
**EDWARD
RUSCHA**

AND

SEE
**NEW
AFRICAN
ART**

FROM THE
CENTRAL
AFRICAN
WORKSHOP
SCHOOL

FRIDAY
NOVEMBER
7, 1969
5:30 TO
7:30 P.M.

1.1 Invitation card for the opening reception of exhibitions by Michael Asher, Edward
Ruscha, and the Central African Workshop School, La Jolla Museum of Art, La Jolla,
California, 1969. From top to bottom: front of the invitation card, second fold, third
fold. (Courtesy the Museum of Contemporary Art San Diego.)

1.2 La Jolla Museum of Art, La Jolla, 1969. (Photographer unknown; courtesy the artist.)

promoting the artist's worldview, subject matter, formal order, or visual aesthetics. By entering the installation, viewers would ostensibly learn more about themselves than about the artist; the process of artistic production was geared to serve its reception. A similar emphasis on constructing, manipulating, and channeling spectatorial situations reverberates in many of the artist's project notes and statements. Writing about another 1969 installation, this one for the "Spaces" exhibition at the Museum of Modern Art in New York, for example, Asher noted, "experience is all."[4]

The experiential register that Asher's installations occupy has ranged from the intimately sensory to the elaborately conceptual. While his early installations, such as the La Jolla work, revolved around perceptual situations and severely constrained the optical, auditory, and sensory modes of stimulation available to the audience, his later projects have combined perceptual acuity with epistemologically precise references to institutional conventions and norms. In each instance, Asher's installations have engaged both individual and collective aspects of spectatorship, providing viewers pathways to self-reflective situations where they can become intensely aware of their own perceptual and cognitive processes in relation to their social setting as well as to themselves.

That "experience" is a socially as well as individually meaningful category is a notion advanced by Foucault, who sought in his late work to account for how historically particular modes of human experience come into being.[5] For Foucault, experience is a sum of three areas of discourse: fields of knowledge, sets of rules (types of normativity), and the production of meaning (forms of subjectivity). Considered through what he calls "an analysis of 'practices,'" this experiential matrix connects preexisting institutional conditions with individuated encounters.[6] Yet the individuation of experience in this context does not entail singularity or unrepeatability. In Foucault's schema, experience is bound to be a composite of structural and unique elements, what might be called an intersection of collective and individual factors. The museum visitor's experience within Asher's La Jolla installation, for example, might have filtered through structural elements such as the viewer's knowledge about the institution and understanding of the normative viewing conditions at the museum, but the visitor's conduct within the installation would also have been individuated within these epistemological and normative limits.

This chapter addresses the experiential reception of Asher's installations, ranging from the artist's late-1960s sensory installations to his subsequent discursive mappings of institutional history. These visual extremes—from materially blank rooms to relocated statues and functional drinking fountains—are held together by his concerted efforts to address his viewers by presenting them with experientially open (although not unlimited) situations. Although his institutional critique—his investigation of art's institutional framework—is more commonly associated with its epistemological and normative dimensions or with the collective sociopolitical aspects of the art institution, it also evokes distinct modes of subjectivity, what Foucault might call "subject[s] conscious of [themselves] and others," through individuated modes of reception.[7] Accordingly, narrative accounts by critics and other viewers of their experiences within Asher's installations contain a spectrum of sensory, affective, emotional, and psychological registers. Yet even these individual responses need to be contextualized in the collective 1960s and 1970s epistemology of experientiality in the art world, in which minimalist artists and late modernist critics bestowed unprecedented centrality to the viewer's response to the artwork.

The Experiential Turn: From Optical to Sensory Environments

The role of "experience" within the practice of reception, central to late modernist debates about the conditions of viewership in the 1960s and 1970s, was encapsulated by Tony Smith in his 1966 comment on his ride on the unfinished New Jersey Turnpike in the early 1950s: "There is no way you can frame it, you just have to experience it."[8] Although Smith, a prominent New York minimalist sculptor, declined to frame his experience, other artists and critics sought to better articulate how spectators responded to the stimuli provided by artwork. Addressing these issues in relation to his sculptural work, Robert Morris set out to retheorize the viewing experience as a phenomenological relation between the viewer, the artwork, and the material properties of the viewing space in "Notes on Sculpture," a 1966–1968 series of articles published in *Artforum*.[9] For Morris, minimalist sculpture forced the spectator to account for the entire viewing situation, in which the artwork figured as part of ambient conditions rather than an isolated object. To provoke such expanded forms of spectatorship, Morris focused on the perceptual parameters of viewing practice, advocating sculpture composed of whole forms, or gestalts, in order to reduce the primacy of the art object in favor of a wider bodily field of vision.[10] "Every internal relationship," he noted, "reduces the public, external quality of the object and tends to eliminate the viewer to the degree that these details pull him into an intimate relation with the work and out of the space in which the object exists."[11] The viewing experience that Morris promoted posited physical correspondences between the viewer's body and the art objects through the means of scale, gravity, direction (up/down), and the realm of possible actions that determined the relation between the viewer and art object. According to this phenomenological notion of experience, viewing (and making) art was a matter of a lived state of being, or a type of "co-presence,"[12] that in its immediacy preceded (and produced) the viewer's knowledge of the art object and its contingent environment.

Morris's influential theorization of spectatorial experience was prominently challenged by modernist art historian Michael Fried in his 1967 *Artforum* article, "Art and Objecthood." Fried countered the minimalist argument (which for him represented the composite stances of Morris, Smith, and Judd) by unfavorably comparing it to the viewing of late modernist painting.[13] Although Fried drew distinctions between the types of materiality that characterized modernist and minimalist (which he called "literalist") works of art, his contestation of minimalist art ultimately hinged upon modalities of viewing experience. Unlike the modernist beholders who experienced "presentness" in front of art, viewers of minimalist art, according to Fried, were trapped within a theatrical situation that was devoid of the immediacy afforded by modernist art. Such theatricality placed spectators instead "*in a situation . . . that, virtually by definition, includes the beholder*" within a painfully pronounced space-time continuum.[14] In contrast, he argued that modernist art was capable of providing unique spectatorial experiences precisely because it was absorbed in a self-sufficiency that did not address or involve spectators—what Pamela M. Lee, in her discussion of Fried's "Art and Objecthood," describes as "the modernist object's profound antipathy to the beholder."[15] Morris's viewers, on the other hand, would become extremely aware of the sensory variables of the artwork, the space, and their own bodily experience within that configuration. Major differences between Morris and Fried, then, revolve around the scope of the viewer's experiential attention to the artwork and their surroundings.

Yet there were similarities between Morris's and Fried's accounts of beholding. Fried's defense of spectatorial immediacy and Morris's conceptualization of the phenomenological viewing encounter both attributed uniformity to the beholders' response to the artwork. Fried and Morris were not interested in the preexisting qualities of the spectator (who the spectators were before they entered the work) or how spectators differed from each other. Instead, both treated the beholder as a blank slate, without preexisting properties, knowledge, or expectations. The viewer's mode of temporality, accordingly, was centered upon the overpowering sense of the present within the spectatorial encounter, whether that encounter was characterized by immediacy (for Fried) or by duration within but not beyond the gallery space (as Morris argued). Consequently, neither Fried nor Morris considered the social conditioning that beholders brought into the viewing situation. Thomas Crow claims as much when he argues that "the experience of the [minimalist] work remained a matter of voluntary introspection and self-awareness on the part of the sensitive, well-prepared spectator . . . the philosophical terms of phenomenology simply replaced those of modernist metaphysics."[16] In other words, the hypothetical minimalist spectators ignored the institutional framing of their viewing experiences as much as the modernist viewers did.

Asher's treatment of the perceptual aspect of viewing in his sensory spaces of the late 1960s and early 1970s was to some degree comparable to Morris's. In his Documenta 5 installation (1972), Asher optically sliced a specially constructed rectangular space into two halves along a vertical axis by painting one half of the walls, ceiling, and floor white, and the other half black (figure 1.3). The perceptual effects of these rooms evoked stark illusions that interfered with conventional modes of experiencing three-dimensional space. For his 1970 Pomona College installation, Asher reshaped the existing gallery with a new set of seamless interior walls that formed two triangular rooms, intersecting at their apex (figure 1.4). This reconfiguration of the gallery space might have made viewers aware of spatial relationships between the shape of the new space and the environmental conditions of natural light, temperature, and ambient sound, all of which filtered into the gallery directly from the street through the doorway that Asher opened by removing doors for around-the-clock access.[17] Spatial modifications and perceptual effects likewise dominated his exhibitions in three European galleries in 1973. At Lisson in London, Asher cut a one-and-a-half-inch-deep groove into the bottom of the gallery walls where they met the floor, creating a separation that evoked a sensation of floating between the walls and the floor.[18] At Heiner Friedrich in Cologne, he drew a correspondence between the upper and lower limits of the gallery environment by painting the ceiling the color of the floor.[19] At Toselli in Milan, he sandblasted the accumulated layers

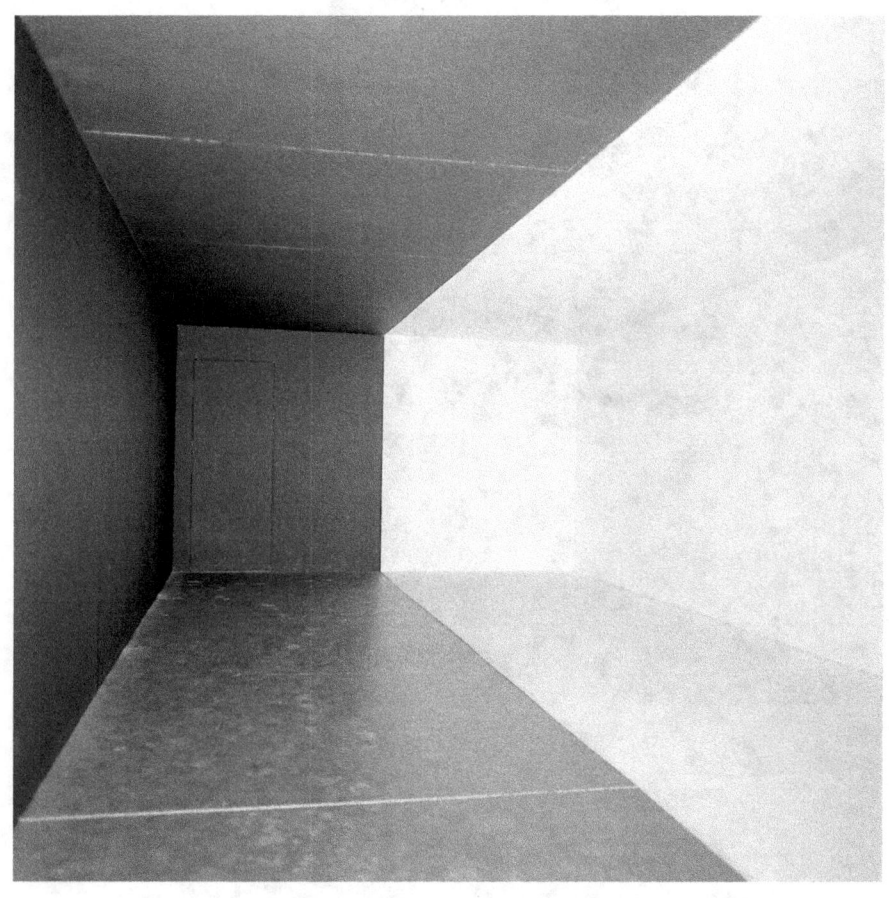

1.3   Documenta 5, Kassel, 1972. Viewing toward southeast corner. (Photograph by Karl-Heinz Krings; courtesy the artist.)

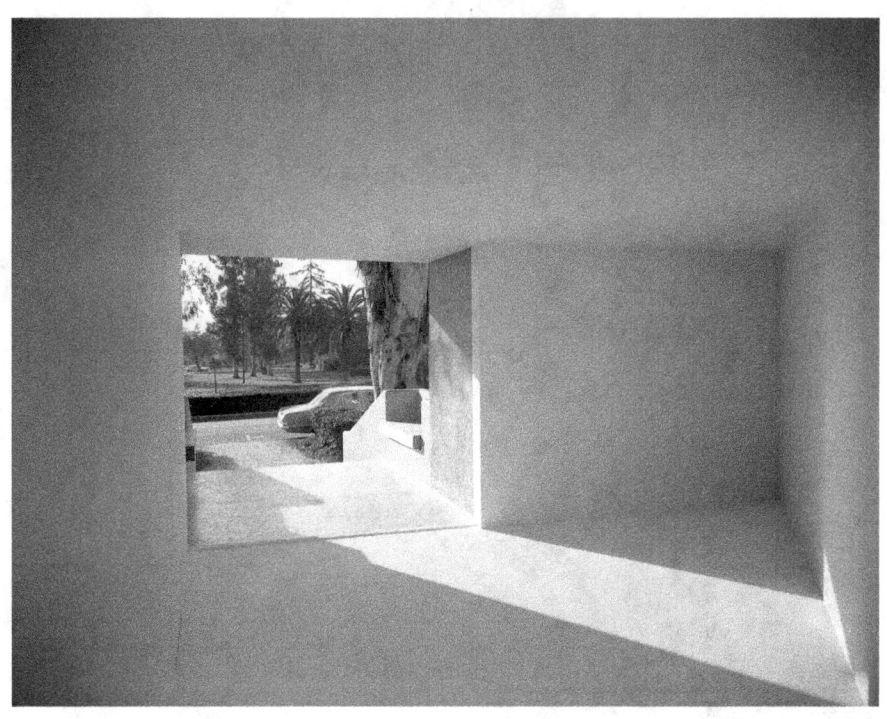

1.4   Gladys K. Montgomery Art Center, Pomona College, Claremont, California, 1970.
       (Photograph by Frank J. Thomas; courtesy of the Frank J. Thomas Archives.)

of paint and plaster from the walls, floor, and ceiling in a gesture of "complete material withdrawal" to reveal the underlying material conditions of the physical space normally hidden underneath the white cube.[20]

Asher's installations at Pomona College, Documenta 5, and the Lisson, Heiner Friedrich, and Toselli galleries attended to the perceptual effects of the gallery space in ways that could be seen as aligning with Morris's argument in "Notes on Sculpture." These installations challenged viewers to measure themselves against the material preconditions of the gallery space, altering the viewing relations between the beholder and the physical environment of the gallery. They were based on the artist's directing the viewer's attention away from the artwork's "internal" relations and toward the "external" viewing space, which was here conceptualized as a set of perceptually experienced relations. With the exception of the work at Heiner Friedrich, these installations were spatially autonomous, comprising an entire room or series of rooms that invited the viewer to coexist with the exhibition space. Asher differed from Morris, however, in what exactly he presented to his beholders within the art gallery or museum. Unlike Morris, whose mid-1960s self-described "phenomenological formalism"[21] had been based on solid whole forms that evoked relational comparisons in terms of shared physical properties, Asher eliminated the object entirely from his installations, directing the beholder's phenomenological attention solely to the surrounding space.[22] Furthermore, he stretched the viewer's scope of perception into the extremes of opticality or materiality. In this manner, the perceptual register of Asher's early installations moved away from Morris's middle ground of intelligible visuality, exemplified by regular geometric shapes inside generic white cubes: instead, Asher's installations in the early 1970s ranged from immateriality (when the artist eliminated the discrete art object altogether) to experiential tangibility (in which the space produced physical effects in the spectator).

The importance given to the viewer's phenomenological experience within cohesive physical environments is one Asher shared with his contemporaries in the Los Angeles light and space movement during the late 1960s and early 1970s.[23] This label was applied to a number of artists, including Robert Irwin, James Turrell, Larry Bell, Eric Orr, and Maria Nordman, whose work had gained national prominence as a West Coast variation of minimalism, albeit one that focused upon perceptual rather than conceptual experience.[24] These artists were known for constructing fine-tuned visual and spatial environments to induce sensory experiences within the viewer.[25] Nordman's and Orr's enclosed installations invited viewers to immerse themselves in spaces with reduced light levels, surrounding them with the minimum amount of visual distractions.[26] Bell's glass cubes and large-scale glass sheet installations reoriented the viewer's reflection into their perception of the material forms themselves, while Turrell's projection experiments from 1966 onward eliminated all external visual stimuli in order to focus the process of viewing upon his light objects, that is, illusions of materially solid objects constructed with projected light. Irwin's paintings from 1962 onward explored deploying minimal visual means to activate the viewers' perceptual process and redirect their attention self-reflectively to their own processes of seeing. For Irwin, this meant wrenching his art away from the ideas and concepts that dominated Western art history.[27] In conversation with Lawrence Weschler in the late 1970s, Irwin described the process of experiencing his own work:

> When you stop giving [my paintings] a literate or articulate read . . . and instead look at them perceptually, you find that your eye ends up suspended in midair, midspace, or midstride: time and space seem to blend in the continuum of your presence. You lose your bearings for a moment. You finally end up in a totally meditative state. The thing is you cease reading and you cease articulating and you fall into a state where nothing else is going on but the tactile, experiential process.[28]

Irwin's description of the experientiality of his phenomenological paintings and installations represents an ideological move seeking to centralize the viewer rather than the artist. Other light and space artists shared this emphasis on the viewer's experience. Turrell's studio experiments, such as the 1969–1974 *Mendota Stoppages*, blocked out all external light and sound sources to create a neutral background for his works of art.[29] Such reduction of perceptual stimuli was taken to its extreme in Turrell and Irwin's collaboration with Dr. Edward Wortz, an experimental psychologist at the Garrett Aerospace Corporation, as part of the LACMA Art and Technology project.[30] Turrell and Irwin conducted a series of experiments on the perceptual limits of human experience within situations from which most sensory (in particular, auditory and visual) stimuli had been eliminated. Although Irwin and Turrell were not the only light and space artists whose interests revolved around anechoic chambers (self-contained spaces from which all sound had been eliminated) and Ganzfelds (continuous visual fields without any discernible points of focus), their experiments within the Art and Technology project allowed them unparalleled access to laboratory conditions under which to test sensory limits, as well as some opportunities to evaluate how other people experienced these sensory conditions.[31] "The works of previous artists have come from their own experiences or insights but haven't given the experience itself," Turrell argued. "They had set themselves up as a sort of interpreter to the layman."[32] Instead of centralizing the artist's own experience, Irwin and Turrell set out to focalize the viewer's sensory experience.[33] For Irwin, "In modern art the artist assumed the responsibilities for the definition of art, forcing an introspective questioning of the how and why of perception. By what he is doing now the artist is placing this *same* responsibility on the viewer."[34] Rather than fabricate objects that would express their own worldviews or respond to art historical precedents, artists now worked to facilitate the beholder's experience, Turrell and Irwin asserted.

Although Asher shared Irwin's and Turrell's interest in the experiential nature of art, he sought to differentiate his work from that of the light and space artists. There are several possible explanations for such a move. Despite their concern with ambient perceptual effects, light and space artists still isolated beholders from their material surroundings to such a degree that the gallery or museum space became at most a backdrop for the viewer's experience. Turrell believed the viewer's attention bypassed the gallery environment in favor of the discrete artwork. "I don't care about 'perfect' walls, surfaces, and edges," Turrell maintained, "I just don't want them to be noticed."[35] By seeking to eliminate the gallery environment, with its distinctive combination of material properties and institutional functions, from the spectatorial experience, Turrell and other light and space artists purposefully excluded the broader sociopsychological sphere from their situations.[36] Instead, light and space environments—what Orr called his "undifferentiated spaces"[37]—veered toward sensory trips undertaken in isolation from the shared social world.

Asher's 1974 comment that he "[was] not interested in manipulating perception" came at the end of his sensory installation period, and served to distinguish his work (which he defined as "situational") from light and space "environments."[38] The viewing experiences with which he wanted to associate his work now aimed to connect the sensory with the social sphere. Whereas Irwin maintained that "[his own] pieces were never meant to be dealt with intellectually as ideas, but to be considered experientially,"[39] Asher's work, even in its most sensory, perceptually focused mode, did not separate intellect from experience.

Asher's differentiation of his practice from Irwin's gained local resonance in the Los Angeles art world, where perceptual experiments were part of the critical mainstream in the late 1960s. In fact, Irwin had exhibited his disc paintings at the La Jolla Museum of Art immediately before Asher's exhibition there in 1969. Besides distancing himself from Irwin's perceptual realm, Asher critiqued the way in which Irwin set aside the social and institutional factors of art from its reception in favor of providing an exclusively perceptual experience. Writing about Irwin's work in the context of his own La Jolla installation, he argued:

> [Irwin's] work's presence as a highly finished object seemed to deny its interdependence on general external conditions. While being interdependent and pretending to be disconnected, it set up a ritualized event which could only be perceived from one position on a bench in front of the presentation, thereby making the presentation more important than the person viewing it. The symmetry of presentation and object were idealized and abstracted from the viewer's perception.[40]

Although Asher rarely comments on another artist's work, in this statement he implicitly (but no less forcefully) asserts the centrality of the viewer in his own project. If Irwin, in Asher's view, "ma[de] the presentation more important than the person viewing it," then Asher must have been promoting the opposite situation, in which the person viewing art was infinitely more important than any material object. Similarly, Asher distinguished his 1969 "Spaces" installation from artistic environments that "attempt to control the viewers' perception . . . creating a hierarchy between the object and the viewers"[41]—another reference to light and space within the context of an exhibition that also featured an environment by Bell.

In a more general sense, Asher's early project notes considered the kinds of effects his installations might have upon their viewers. Early on, he was focused upon the viewer's experience in the present. In contrast with his approach in his later work, he initially thought of the viewer as an ideal figure who would focus upon the installation without being aware of external influences.[42] The reception of Asher's work, however, was never an exclusively optical or visual matter. Instead, the sensory matrix of his viewer spanned from vision to touch, hearing, and bodily sensation.[43] His enclosed room at the La Jolla Museum of Art, for example, addressed the viewer's sense of hearing through the spatial differentiation of sound levels and influenced the viewer's spatiotemporal, kinesthetic experience of moving within the space in order to detect varying levels of light and sound.

Asher's attention to multisensory experience also informed his contribution to the 1969–1970 MoMA exhibition "Spaces." This installation consisted of an enclosed, soundproofed white room with two open doorways and a drop ceiling at a height of less than eight feet (figure 1.5). The only light entering the space came from outside the room, from the corridors that connected Asher's installation with the rest of the museum. The majority of detectable sounds heard within the room emanated from outside because the walls, ceiling, and floor had been acoustically insulated to muffle any ambient sound within the space. This spatial and auditory configuration resulted in an environment within which viewers processed sensory information according to their spatial coordinates in the room. As viewers moved within the acoustically dampened room, with the low ceiling just above their heads, the levels of ambient sound and light would increase or decrease depending on their distance from the doorways. "One is reminded that we rely on senses other than sight for part of our intuition of spatial volume," Carter Ratcliff noted in his review of the work.[44] Asher's multisensory approach in "Spaces" integrated the auditory and visual effects into visitors' kinesthetic mapping of themselves in the spatiotemporal gallery environment. In this situation, the viewers' sense of themselves was produced as a multisensory, spatiotemporal experience.[45]

Even before the La Jolla exhibition and "Spaces" opened in the fall of 1969, Asher had produced situations that literally enfolded the viewer within fields of nonvisual tactility. In two air flow works, which opened one week apart from each other in May 1969, Asher used industrial air blowers to set up "columns of air" that allowed the museum visitor to be immersed in the work in a highly tactile, yet discreet manner. The work for the exhibition "The Appearing/Disappearing Image/Object" at the Newport Harbor Art Museum included a rented Curtainaire air blower that was normally used at meat plants to keep out flies, mosquitoes, and

1.5 "Spaces," Museum of Modern Art, New York, 1969. (Photograph © 2008 Claude Picasso; courtesy the artist.)

other insects. In this work, the air blower covered a doorway into the museum's main exhibition gallery with a wall of air that was at its most forceful near the ceiling and gradually spread and diminished in force toward the floor, to the point of being undetectable.[46] For "Anti-Illusion: Procedures / Materials" at the Whitney Museum of American Art, Asher set up a similar doorway structure but reduced the amount of air flowing from the blower in the interest of "strengthen[ing the] conceptual dimension" of his work within the exhibition's premise of "anti-illusion."[47] The invisibility of his air curtain challenged the museum visitor's accustomed means of viewing artwork, since Asher's work did not include any visible elements. Instead of seeing art, the viewers were asked to *feel* the faint breeze against their skin. Appropriately, "Anti-Illusion" co-curator James Monte placed Asher's piece in the context of late-1960s postminimalist investigations that were fundamentally experiential. Monte characterized Asher's field of air as a work in which "[f]eeling and therefore knowing replaces the cycle of seeing and hence knowing the sculptural presence."[48] In other words, "feeling" allowed for bodily relations between the museum visitor and the artwork.

The haptic intimacy of Asher's air curtains set up permeable relations between museum visitors and their environment. The air flow descending from the blower was experienced, as Monte noted, as caressing their skin. It further entered the viewers with every inhalation they took within the doorway, instigating a fluidity of boundaries between museum visitor and art object. Porosity, though perhaps in a less physiological sense, is a development that Rosalind Krauss has ascribed to the viewer's relations with minimalist art. Aiming to rescue minimalism's art historical interpretation from idealization and perceptual formalism, Krauss makes a case for the minimalist loosening of boundaries around the viewer and the work of art. She asserts that minimalism ultimately paved the way for the subsequent understanding of art's contextuality as a broad sociopolitical category:

> Th[e] issue of contingency that Minimalism had forced into the open, the permeability of both subject and object to what goes on in the space in which both coexist, became the basis of a series of interpretive rewritings [by artists] in the decades that followed the 1960s. Since "what goes on in the space in which both coexist" could be . . . understood to include the institutional construction of that very "space": the legal and financial

"arrangements" that shape and control it, the discursive practices that make possible what can become visible within it.[49]

For Krauss, this artistic "rewriting" of the minimalist legacy included practices such as Asher's. My account above has focused upon the differences between Asher and the East Coast minimalists, on the one hand, and the Los Angeles light and space artists, on the other. I want to conclude this comparison, however, by calling attention to the connections between Asher and the kind of minimalism that was premised upon the contingency of experience that Krauss calls the "permeability" of the viewing subject. What "Anti-Illusion" co-curator Monte described as the "feeling" of Asher's work was one manifestation of this permeability. In Asher's case, it meant exposing museum visitors to multisensory experiences rather than appealing primarily to their vision. These experiences were set up to challenge the distance between the viewer and the work. Asher's viewers stepped into his installations only to become "engulfed" by the environment: they found no art object, no focal point to divert their attention onto or distance themselves from.[50] Asher's description of his "Spaces" installation stated as much by comparing the process of viewing to an evenly disseminated field of experience, noting that the work "created a continuity with no singular point of perceptual objectification, unlike phenomenologically determined works which attempted to fabricate a highly controlled area of visual perception."[51] While Morris, who exhibited alongside Asher in "Anti-Illusion" and "Spaces," critiqued modernist art for relying on the intimacy of viewing situations in which viewers were pushed into close contact with the internal relations of the artwork, Asher explored the intimacy implicit in a viewer's contact with the work of art, which was not merely seen but felt—and could be felt even when it could not be seen.

Asher's interpretation of intimacy in his installations of the late 1960s and early 1970s resulted in spaces that Italian critic Germano Celant described as "deprived." Within these works, Celant maintained, "the visitor must take himself as the subject, enter his own body and make it an object with active and creative characteristics."[52] This description stresses the introspective relations that Asher's perceptually constrained installations might have stimulated within their beholders. Although these installations straddled thresholds of perceptibility (to the degree that they might have been mistaken for spaces void of any artistic intervention), many viewers experienced them as distinctly unsettling, sometimes unendurably so. Ratcliff described the experience of entering Asher's "Spaces" room as one "of benign oppressiveness."[53] The multisensory reduction in Asher's installation at La Jolla provoked even more extreme critical responses. "As the room neither 'showed' anything nor 'did' anything some spectators suffered an immediate esthetic collapse and left at once," wrote Thomas H. Garver. "Those who entered the room without being prepared to perform—even for themselves—were acutely embarrassed."[54]

Such descriptions of "oppressiveness" and "embarrassment" may sound excessive when used in relation to Asher's subtle, almost imperceptible sensory installations. Yet psychologically intense reactions to his early work demonstrate the destabilizing complexity of these viewing experiences. Tactile and auditory elements joined visual stimuli in calling for multisensory modes of response, and the purposeful minimization of sensory elements caused beholders to become even painfully aware of their own modes of sensory reception. These viewing experiences were described by critics in emotionally and psychologically charged terms as intimate, deprived, uncomfortable, and embarrassing. These affective aspects would become more pronounced in Asher's work from 1973 onward, when the artist's multisensory approach expanded to deploying "normal" or conventional social situations.

Affective Viewing Experiences: On the Threshold of Normalcy

In the early 1970s the experiential matrix of Asher's installations shifted from multisensory environments to investigations of "normal" and even normative viewing experiences. This shift did not mean that he now ignored the bodily relations between the beholder and the space; rather, he sought to heighten the intensity of such relations by investigating the ways in which viewers were positioned against the phenomenological certainty of spatial givens. The porous, battered, sandblasted surfaces of Asher's 1973 Toselli work, for example, suggested correlations between the skin of the beholder and the skin of the space, which was rubbed raw of its protective layers of plaster and paint (figure 1.6). The destabilization of the external gallery space might then have become internalized if the beholder identified on a bodily level with the material givens of the gallery space. Although Asher described the effects of his Toselli installation as "[a]

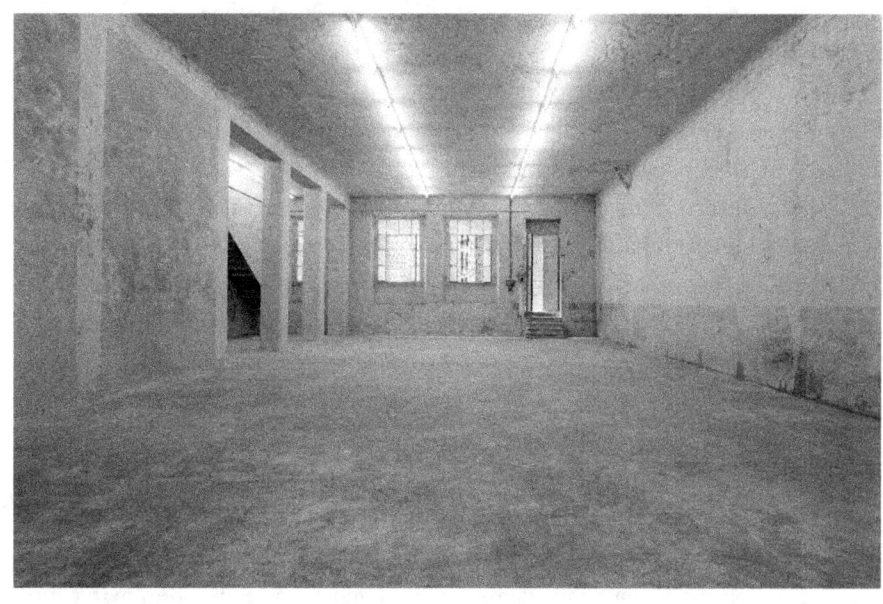

1.6   Galleria Toselli, Milan, 1973. Viewing west. (Photograph © Giorgio Colombo, Milano; courtesy the artist.)

feeling of relief, resulting from the recognition of traditionally suppressed visual elements,"[55] I propose a different model for viewing this work: one in which proximity replaces distance, and intimate identification overtakes detached recognition. Sensation, which Asher described as "feeling," undoubtedly was central in the reception of the Toselli work. But did the viewer's awareness of self and viewing relations necessarily produce Brechtian distantiation, or cool reflection? Could the spectator's heightened sense of the self within the installation instead have functioned to engender an intimate sense of panic, collapse, even "acute embarrassment," to return to Garver's description of Asher's La Jolla exhibition, or other distinctly affective forms of response to this environment that challenged the normal configuration of gallery space?

Asher produced a particularly intense set of emotionally and psychologically resonating situations between 1973 and 1976 at locations ranging from American commercial galleries and alternative spaces to a television station in Portland, Oregon. His exploration of normalcy was evident even in projects—rare for Asher—that were based on moving images rather than three-dimensional spaces. In 1973, Asher produced a film for a screening at an alternative space called Project, Inc., in Boston.[56] This film was a gray monochrome that minimized perceptual variation to its extreme. The film stock was run through developing chemicals to produce a uniform medium gray, without prior exposure (figure 1.7). The projected version of the film had no discernible images, distinctive scratches, or other evidence of individuation (figure 1.8). For Asher, the purpose of this work was to turn the viewers' awareness away from the projected image and onto themselves as well as the technological and material context of the screening.[57] He chose the medium gray tone of the image to avoid the spectacular and metaphoric connections easily made with degrees of light and dark, even in the absence of images or other identifiable visual markers.[58]

Three years later, in January 1976, Asher explored the affective thresholds of normalcy by devising a television program that literally turned the camera back onto itself by filming the scene of production in the control room of the television station, and broadcasting the footage of the backstage activities to viewers at home (figure 1.9).[59] Produced with the support of the Portland Center for the Visual Arts in Portland, Oregon, as Asher's contribution to the exhibition "Via Los Angeles," the program aired as an episode in the regularly scheduled arts program *Eight Lively Arts* on KGW-TV at one o'clock on a Sunday afternoon. "Andy Warhol should have been in Portland Sunday," declared the local newspaper *The*

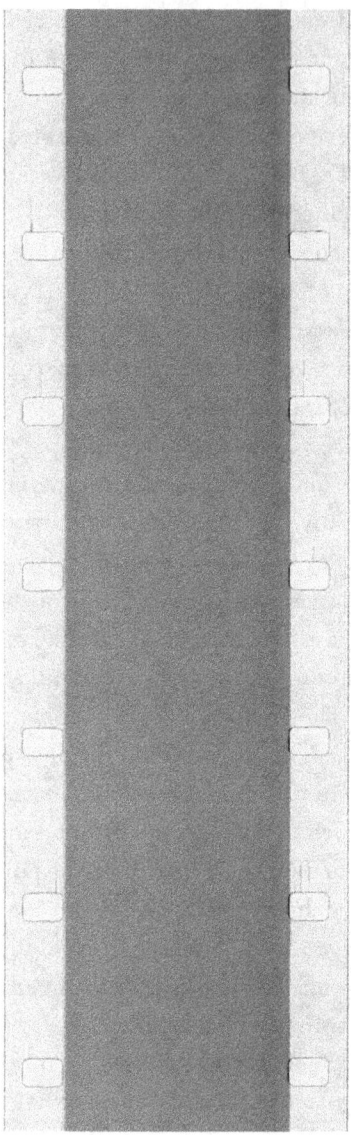

1.7 Fragment of filmstrip produced for Michael Asher's screening at Project, Inc., Boston, 1973. (Photograph courtesy the artist.)

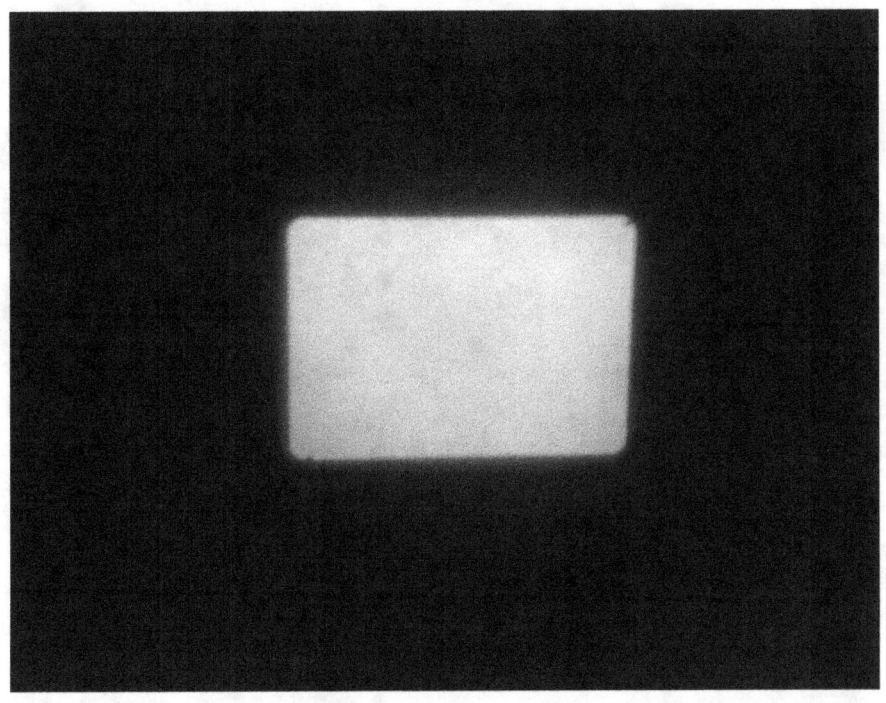

1.8   Project, Inc., Boston, during film screening, 1973. (Photograph by Paul McMahon; courtesy the artist.)

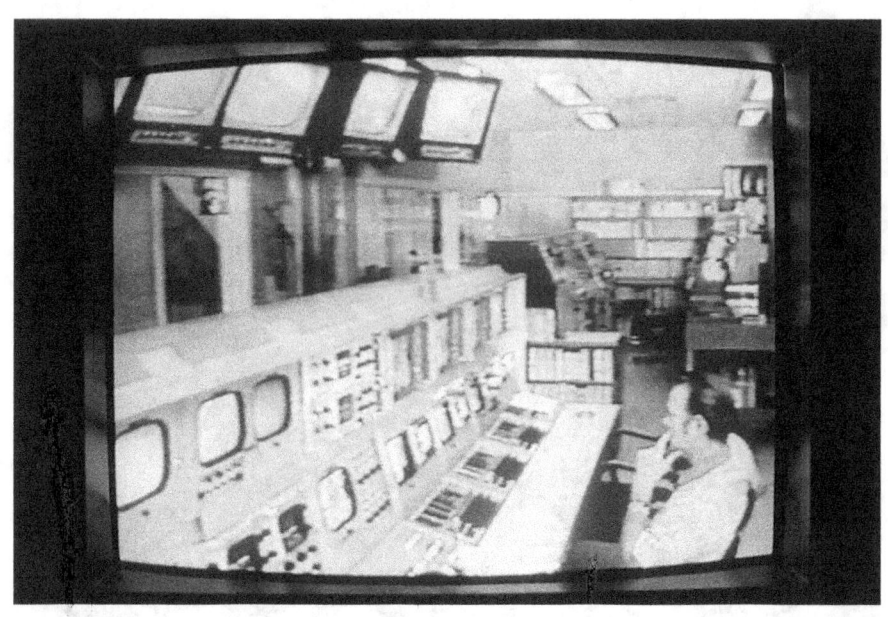

1.9   "Via Los Angeles," Portland Center for the Visual Arts, Portland, Oregon, 1976.
Documentation of the live feed of the control room at KGW (radio and television).
(Photograph courtesy the artist.)

Oregonian on its front page the following day. "He would have appreciated the Michael Asher 'visual art' presentation on KGW-TV. Numerous viewers didn't. They thought it was 'an accident.'"[60] During the Asher broadcast, the station's telephone feedback line received around 140 phone calls about the program. Some of the callers, disturbed by the situation, wished to alert the station to the fact that there were technical problems with the broadcast.[61] "[O]ne call came from a television technician . . . who, thinking there was a faulty transmission, called the station to let us know that there was a camera in the master-control area," Asher recounted. "A number of other callers . . . also communicated the same observation, some of them noticeably upset."[62] Although the act of calling KGW-TV to notify it of a perceived problem might have been an altruistic deed resulting in no immediate personal gain, it might also have been prompted by a more acute psychological need. The tone of the calls underscored the viewers' urge to protect the television station from error—as they perceived Asher's back-stage view to be—and their desire to prompt the station into restoring normalcy to the broadcast.[63] Ultimately, this impulse might have been linked to the caller's own identity, to the degree that the caller's sense of normalcy was affirmed by recognizable television content.

Although it would be easy to stereotype the Portland callers as cultural dupes who were naive or ill-informed because they missed the point of Asher's project, such a reading would miss the power of personal response that Asher's program unleashed within the callers.[64] The callers were perfectly aware of the normative boundary that the project unseated when it crossed over the lines of conventional broadcasting. Immediate feelings of anxiety became more than ambient affective states when these reactions turned into acts of calling the station. The perceived irregularity of Asher's program moved these television viewers into attempts to correct the situation and restore normalcy to what they considered normatively irregular television content. Their experience of the project was based upon particular forms of cultural knowledge, assumptions, and rules, but these collective aspects were modulated by individual response. The experience of the work mobilized in these viewers what Foucault might call relations to self and others, relations that were articulated in the emotional and practical care these viewers demonstrated in attempting to remedy the situation.

While Asher was developing his Portland project, he was also investigating the emotional threshold between experientially normal and unusual viewing conditions in an installation for the Clocktower Gallery in New York City. This project was conceived before the work at the Portland television station but was exhibited shortly after, in March and April of 1976.[65] The Clocktower was an alternative space run by the Institute for Art and Urban Resources, situated on the top three floors that had been added during the early twentieth century to a nineteenth-century building. As an exhibition venue, the Clocktower was clearly not the typical white cube. The gallery rooms were dotted with windows positioned high on the walls and punctuated by doors, columns, and staircases. Asher chose to address the material perforation of this space in his site-specific installation by eliminating the material boundary between the inside and outside; accordingly, he ordered all windows and doors to be removed from the three gallery spaces (figure 1.10).

The effects of Asher's window and door removal were distinctly sensory. Upon entering the gallery, the viewer stepped into a series of materially bare rooms that lacked any discernible art objects. There were no strong, reassuring, or recognizable gestalts or discrete forms for the viewer to apprehend and absorb— yet visiting the space provided unmistakably bodily experiences. Analogous with the 1969 air curtain works at the Newport Harbor Art Museum and the Whitney, in which viewers were enveloped by Asher's work, the physicality of outdoor air flooded the Clocktower rooms. In late March and early April, when the Clocktower exhibition took place, New York weather presented viewers with a forceful discrepancy between indoor and outdoor ambient climates. Fracturing the boundary between inside and outside, architecture and nature, climate control and climate, the situation worked the threshold of visibility to disintegrate one's phenomenological certainty about the stability of a gallery visit.

However commanding, Asher's gesture seems understated when compared with another 1976 intervention in a New York alternative space involving a superficially similar act of letting air into the gallery space: Gordon Matta-Clark's *Window Blowout* for the Institute for Architecture and Urban Studies. Instead of executing his characteristic cutting-out of neat sections of dividing sheetrock wall (the proposal that the exhibition organizers had approved), Matta-Clark made it a project of shooting through each of the windows lining the gallery space.[66] As a result, outside air entered the gallery through shattered glass. In this respect, Matta-Clark's *Window Blowout* was analogous to Asher's Clocktower installation: the sheltered interior was exposed to the natural conditions of the outside world. Yet the artists' gestures were diametrically opposite in other ways. In Asher's case, the meticulously organized and commissioned removal of the windows erased

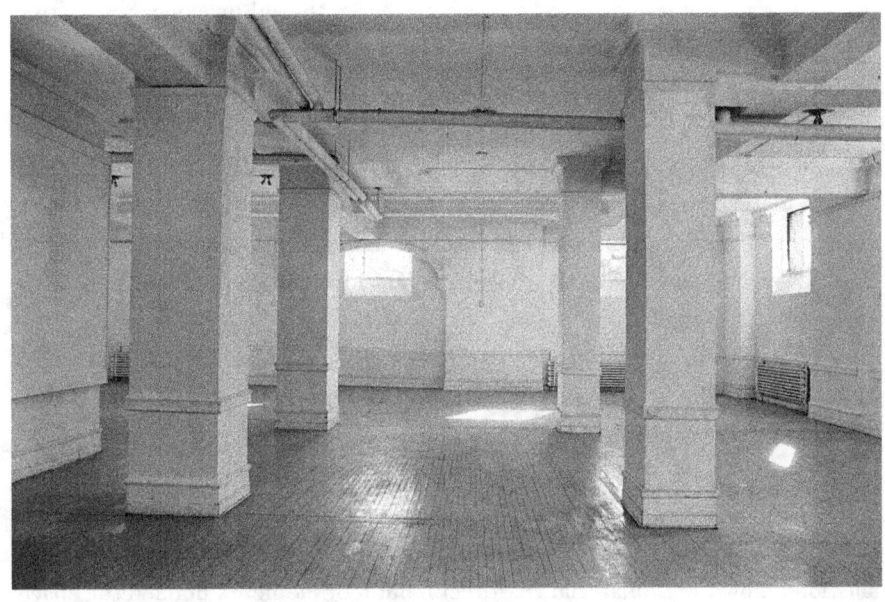

1.10   The Clocktower, New York, 1976. Thirteenth floor, viewing south. (Photograph courtesy the artist.)

the visible marks of the artist's gesture, and the material fact that the window-panes were absent seems less important than facilitating a subtle sensory experience for the gallery visitor. In Matta-Clark's installation, the visible traces of the artist's act would more likely have suppressed the subtly experiential atmospheric effects that signaled the erasure of the inside/outside boundary, and the violent connotations of the act of shooting might have overpowered his desire to draw an analogy between the hermetic windows of the rarefied Institute and the perpetually broken windows of the Bronx.[67] Whereas Matta-Clark's broken windows remained two-dimensional surfaces, however unconventional, that viewers might have encountered had the work remained open to the public, Asher's Clocktower work enveloped the viewer as a multidimensional environment to be experienced gradually.[68]

Nancy Foote's *Artforum* review of Asher's Clocktower exhibition described one such self-reflective viewing experience. The physical environment of the gallery was the first aspect of Asher's installation that Foote noticed. She remarked on her acute awareness of the attention she paid to the conventionally established boundaries of the space, observing that she immediately wanted to cross them: "My first inclination was to go out and walk around the balcony."[69] Next she noted how the immaterial yet forceful outdoor elements flooded the space: "Coming back in, I noticed the sun streaming in through the paneless window, felt the breeze and heard the sound of the traffic below."[70] Rather than a distanced survey through which the critic analytically weighed the success of an artwork, Foote's viewing experience became a self-reflective account of spectatorial conditions, her scrutiny of the material division between the gallery's inside and outside becoming reconfigured into a dialogue between the physical environment and one's psychological relation to it.

Foote's viewing experience at the Clocktower was framed by her anticipation of Asher's alteration of the gallery space: she knew beforehand what kind of art Asher made. This a priori acknowledgment of Asher's oeuvre granted agency to the installation before Foote ever entered the gallery. Foote commented on this agency when she noted, "Viewers don't like to feel they're being reviewed by art; it's a presumptuous switch in roles that gets under the skin." She thus associated her "irritation" at being under observation by the artwork with a sense of anxiety concerning the adequacy of her performance as a viewer. She found herself thinking about "how one ought to be reacting, and . . . if one is really 'getting it.'" Although Foote's sense of being observed seemed to disappear during the course of viewing the installation, it was replaced by an urgent need to view and interpret the work (to "get" it), along with a nagging desire to be assured of the adequacy of her interpretation. Asher's installation compelled the critic to reflect on her own process of viewing, interpreting, and "getting" the work, and to consider how the artwork was constructed to facilitate such reflection:

> The art is pushing you around, sending you scrambling for its subliminal effects without having the courtesy to provide adequate cues. Once you make the outside/inside connection, you think you've got it. Then it dawns on you that the work is also about the process of making that connection. It comments on awareness itself by forcing you to think about how it ought to affect you.[71]

The psychological effort Foote directed toward viewing Asher's Clocktower installation thus turned back on itself to become self-reflection.[72] Affective or emotional responses, such as irritation, annoyance, frustration, and even a sense of being manipulated, inflect Foote's review.[73] Such responses might affect the ways in which viewers perceive themselves in relation to the world. This interpretation would be in line with Asher's statement that ideally his practice "demands the receiver to take a critical position within the material world."[74] To take a critical position on something requires knowledge of existing conditions and the use of judgment regarding them. It requires understanding the cultural rules and norms that govern the situation at hand. And it requires a subject who, like Foote, responds to the artwork. In that sense, Asher's spectatorship aligns with Foucault's characterization of experience as a combination of "understandings of a certain type, . . . rules of a certain form, . . . certain modes of consciousness of oneself and of others."[75] Within Asher's situations, beholders know what gallery spaces usually look like as well as how they should behave in them. Foote's irritation and the alarm demonstrated by Portland television viewers did not spring from thin air: they were influenced by specific formations of knowledge (how indoor spaces are separated from the outdoors) and cultural norms (what television broadcasts should contain). Of equal importance to the normative limits, however, is the multiplicity of responses to Asher's work. Foote's account is hardly the only reaction to his Clocktower installation. And some of the Portland callers even "congratulated" (to use Asher's word) the television station for this innovative project.[76] Such individuation of viewer responses reflects the range of "critical positions" available to Asher's viewers.

Almost as soon as Asher had established his multisensory paradigm in the late 1960s, his installations branched out to investigate perceptions of normalcy as well as the embedded cultural norms. When Portland television viewers were disturbed by his project to aim the camera backstage, for example, they perceived his broadcast as a technical malfunction because it deviated from the normative mode of transmission. Sensory and affective modes of experience nevertheless remained integral to these explorations. Asher's installations of this period seemed to invite reflective relations between the viewer's self, the environment, and other subjects within the situation. When Foote stalked the freshly aired space at the Clocktower, her experience became a relational encounter that turned her attention onto the environment, then back to herself. This particular viewer was not only acutely aware of but emotionally and intellectually implicated in, and individuated by, Asher's situation. In the course of the 1970s, his work invited such reflective viewing experiences by asking viewers what they already "knew" about art museums and about appropriate forms of conduct within shared social spheres.

Subject and Knowledge in the Art Institution

Since the late 1970s, Asher's works have attended to formations of knowledge within art institutions. The viewing of the artist's situations is to some degree influenced by the viewer's knowledge of institutional practices. While much of this knowledge preceded and informed the viewer's engagement with the work, Asher's spectatorship also produced experiential knowledge of the museum site and the individual's relation to the broader social world.

Take, for example, the museum visitors who entered Asher's work for the "73rd American Exhibition" at the Art Institute of Chicago (1979). In this well-known act of displacement, Asher had moved a weathered statue of George Washington from its traditional perch in the middle of the Art Institute's facade to a period room that contained eighteenth-century European fine and decorative arts (figure 1.11).[77] As these museum visitors approached the Art Institute, they might or might not have noticed the absence of the *George Washington* at the museum's exterior.[78] In the Morton Wing galleries housing the "73rd American

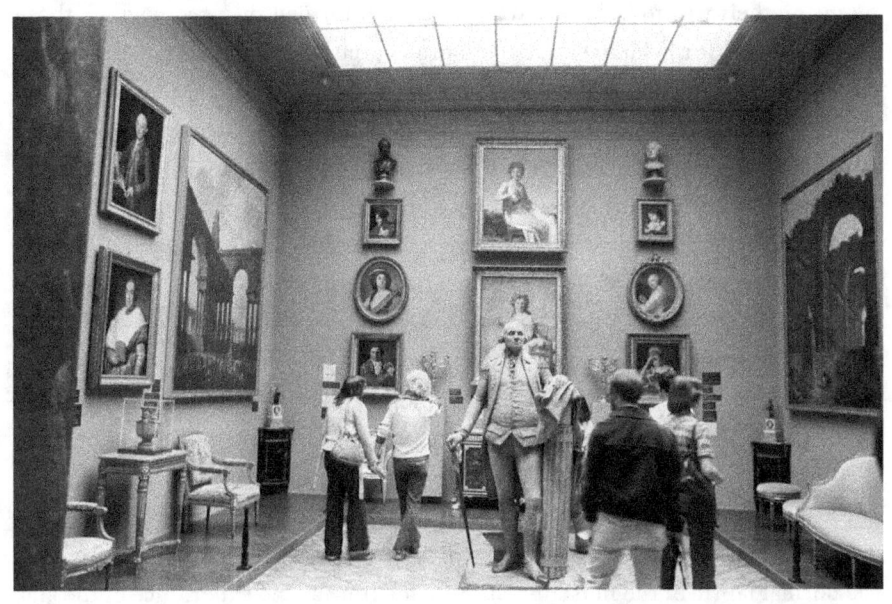

1.11 "73rd American Exhibition," Art Institute of Chicago, 1979. *George Washington* in Gallery 219. (Photograph courtesy the artist.)

Exhibition," these visitors might have glanced at an information sheet on the wall that indicated that Asher's work was located in Gallery 219, another part of the Art Institute. The passage through a number of other European period rooms on their way to Gallery 219 might have informed the way in which these visitors looked for evidence of Asher's project, possibly leading them to reflect on the epistemological and normative relations that Asher's relocation of the George Washington statue evoked. These relations ranged from the historical (contemporary exhibition/eighteenth-century museum context) to the national (American/French), museological (decorative object/conserved sculpture), art historical (a cast reproduction of the original marble statue/original paintings on the gallery walls), and the aesthetic (covered in patina/color matching the gallery walls).

This narrative of spectatorship is, of course, only one possible viewing scenario. For many Art Institute visitors, Asher's work no doubt slipped by unnoticed. The unobtrusive placement of *George Washington* in the period room made it entirely possible to completely bypass the project, since nothing in Asher's approach forced the viewer to confront the artist's message. For those who knew that the statue's placement was Asher's project, however, his work stood out from the normal fabric of the museum, at the same time as the experience of the statue's relocation drew from the discursive field of knowledge that the Art Institute of Chicago articulated. These viewers already knew that *George Washington* was, in Crow's description, "an impostor" in the period room of Gallery 219.[79] Their viewing experience was produced by and productive of knowledge: it was affected by preexisting assumptions, rules, and social conventions that were then extrapolated by individual museum visitors into experiential situations. These viewer preconceptions were then tested against the perceivable difference that Asher made to the exhibition site. A statue normally present outside the museum was now absent. The same statue on display in an unusual location (the period room) was coded against its normative placement in the museum's exterior. Connections that were not obvious were made visible and even necessary through metonymical relations between discursive elements (such as the museum facade and the period room). All this specialized information was now displayed to a wider public. The viewer here could not be innocent, a blank slate, likely to believe anything he or she saw. Instead, viewers were presented with a situation that drew from what they already knew. Asher's viewing situation, then, allowed for spectatorial agency by subtly demanding a response, while the viewer's moves, options, and modes of interpretation were constrained by the range of specific material, textual, and intentional elements for reception.

Within this experiential matrix, Asher's recreation in 2005 of the 1979 Art Institute project called attention to changes in the art and museum worlds (figure 1.12).[80] In 1979, he had brought in the weathered *George Washington* from outside the Art Institute, keeping the work's context within the art museum. But in 2005, the same "George" (as the project staff referred to the statue) arrived at the Art Institute from the Chicago mayor's office, where it had resided since 1984. The expansion of the sociopolitical context of *George Washington* is clearly outside the artist's sphere of influence, and thus could not be returned to the artist's intention. Precisely for this reason, Asher's situation in 2005 called attention to the ways in which twenty-first-century museums participate in the broader public sphere.

The type of knowledge production engaged by Asher's relocation of *George Washington* at the Art Institute had also changed between 1979 and 2005. His 1979 exhibition statement discussed the functionality of sculpture in different contexts within the art institution.[81] In that statement, the statue was coded as a readymade, an object that acquires meaning from authorized placement within an institutional context. In 2005, Asher accompanied the statue's presentation with a separate archival display in the Art Institute's Ryerson Library reading room, featuring an extensive collection of original documents on the statue's history within the Art Institute (figure 1.13). In this instance, an archival discourse had replaced the primacy of the readymade, replacing the epistemology of modernist avant-garde with the epistemology of the museum.

Arrangements of institutionally specialized knowledge were prominently featured in Asher's practice following the "73rd American Exhibition." His 1990 exhibition at the Renaissance Society, for example, highlighted two kinds of relation to early-twentieth-century industrialization: the writings of social scientists on the mechanization of labor, and the patent numbers of industrially produced architectural fixtures of the exhibition space (a window pull chain, sash lock, and radiator cover).[82] All of the quoted academics had been affiliated with the University of Chicago, the institutional crux of the exhibition, which operates the Renaissance Society. In his exhibition, Asher displayed the writings of these academics (silkscreened on the walls) along with stenciled patent numbers of the architectural fixtures. The discourse of individual fulfillment through arts and crafts was thus juxtaposed with standardized mass production. Asher's exhibition at the Palais

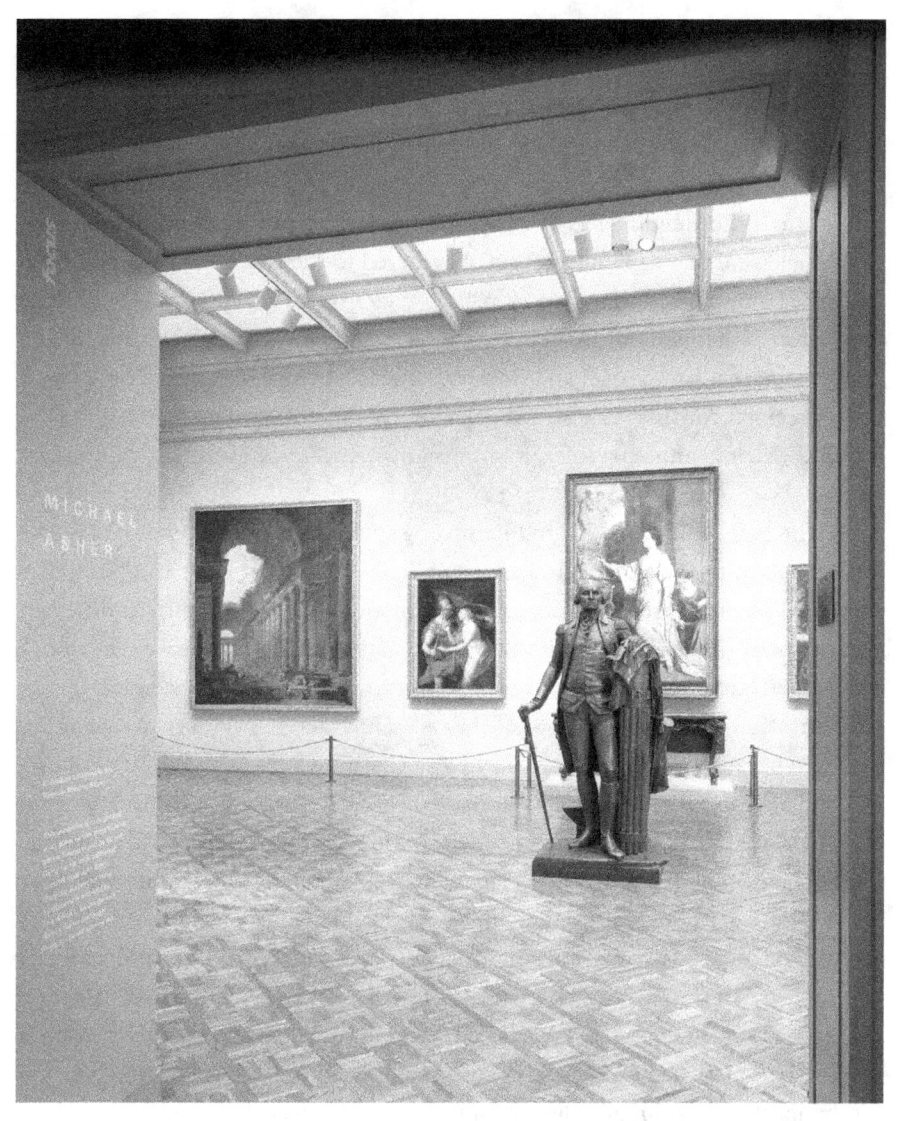

1.12 "Focus: Michael Asher," Art Institute of Chicago, 2005. *George Washington* in Gallery 220. (Photograph by Michael Tropea, Chicago; Photography © The Art Institute of Chicago.)

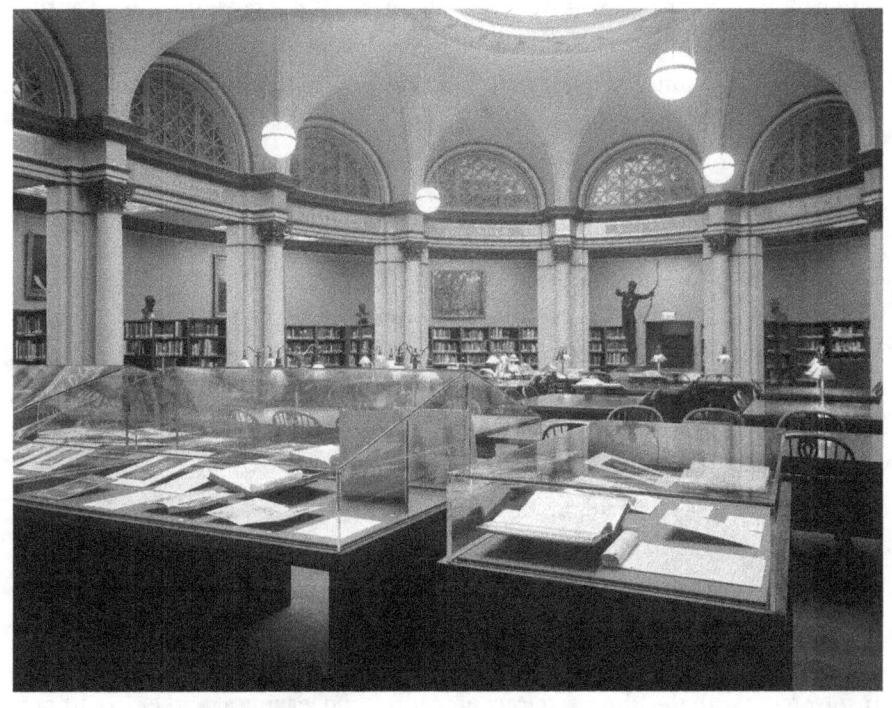

1.13 "Focus: Michael Asher," Art Institute of Chicago, 2005. View of the reading room of the Ryerson Library. (Photograph by Michael Tropea, Chicago; Photography © The Art Institute of Chicago.)

des Beaux-Arts in Brussels in 1992 was another example of his use of institutionally specific knowledge.[83] This exhibition centered on two historical figures, the art nouveau architect Victor Horta, who designed the building in which the exhibition took place, and the Los Angeles water baron William Mulholland. For this exhibition, Asher researched and displayed exhaustive amounts of information about Horta and Mulholland, tracing historically possible connections between the two figures. Both the Renaissance Society and the Palais des Beaux-Arts exhibitions relied on information that pertained to the exhibition site, making the viewing experience a function of knowing as well as looking.

In his 1991 archival project for the Centre Georges Pompidou in Paris, Asher further individuated the institutionally informed practice of spectatorship. In preparation for this exhibition, he removed all the paper fragments that he found lodged within the books in the psychoanalysis section of the Centre Pompidou's Bibliothèque publique d'information, or Public Reference Library. He then mapped the location of these paper fragments on the pages of these books, and exhibited the fragments under glass along with each book's bibliographic entry, silkscreened on the wall. The size of the glass, and the placement of the paper fragment under it, corresponded with the size of the book in which that particular fragment was found by Asher (figure 1.14).[84] These place markers ranged from random scraps of paper to advertisements for professional counseling. In Asher's exhibition, they functioned as traces of the reader-subject's involvement with the library (the act of reading and leaving a marker in a library book), representing a material trace of the reader's literal insertion into the discursive order of the library. Asher presented these individual reading practices and the library's classificatory system as visually and epistemologically parallel systems. The material objects—the paper fragments—in Asher's exhibition functioned primarily to point to the discourses they were embedded in.

Asher's procedure in his Pompidou Center exhibition drew out two sets of subjects in relation to the discourse of psychoanalysis: the library users who had left the paper fragments in the books, and the exhibition viewers. The viewing might then have proceeded by relating the practices of individual marking and collective classification to one another, effecting, Birgit Pelzer has argued, "comic surprise" through the juxtaposition of the mundane pieces of paper with the authority of the book.[85] The museum visitor's response to these individual reading and collective classificatory practices remained inseparable from the library's normative frame of reference. Asher wrote that his Pompidou Center

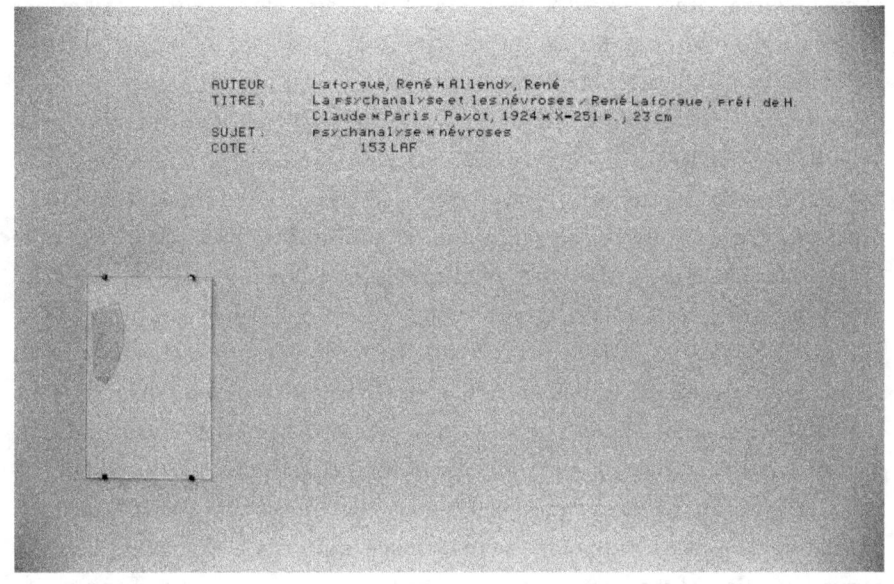

AUTEUR : Laforgue, René ⋈ Allendy, René
TITRE : La psychanalyse et les névroses / René Laforgue, préf. de H.
Claude ⋈ Paris : Payot, 1924 ⋈ X-251 p. ; 23 cm
SUJET : psychanalyse ⋈ névroses
COTE : 153 LAF

1.14 Musée national d'art moderne, Centre Georges Pompidou, Paris, 1991. Detail view of installation, one of sixty-seven paper fragments accompanied by the library citation for the book where the paper fragment was found. (Photograph courtesy the artist.)

exhibition addressed "the function of the museum and the viewing subject's role within that institution."[86] The artist's juxtaposition of the knowledge contained in books, on the one hand, and the knowledge communicated by discarded scraps of paper, on the other, served as the overarching frame of reference that viewing subjects encountered in his exhibition against their preconceived understanding of museums, libraries, and practices of reading.

Asher's 1991 project for the Stuart Collection further articulates relations between individuated modes of viewer behavior and their epistemological frames of reference. This work, one of Asher's few permanently installed projects, joined the Stuart Collection arrangement of public sculptures placed throughout the campus of the University of California, San Diego. It consists of a fully functional drinking fountain, constructed from stainless steel and two types of granite (figure 1.15). Custom-manufactured after the design of the ubiquitous, industrially produced mid-twentieth-century water fountain, Asher's work is located on an aisle of grass between two streets and their adjoining parking strips (figure 1.16). The placement emphasizes the symbolic value of two preexisting markers on the site, a functional flagpole and a monument constructed out of a natural boulder. The boulder, with its inscription label, commemorates the former function of the UCSD campus as a military training ground. Through its placement, Asher's fountain evokes an implied axis between the flagpole and the boulder geographically (by mirroring the position of the boulder in relation to the flagpole) and metaphorically (monumentalizing the current educational use of the former military site).[87] Alternately nondescript and out of place, the drinking fountain in the midst of a walkway solicits further attention. Robert Storr, for example, notes that the fountain "stands out over time in inverse proportion to the degree that it begs to be overlooked on first inspection."[88]

Asher's drinking fountain has rich metaphoric significance. On the one hand, it co-opts the classic form of a public monument: the grand water fountain. Formally, Asher's fountain conforms to the monumental tradition of public sculpture: it is crafted of the same traditional sculpture materials and polished to a deep glow. Yet the fountain's claim to conventional monumentality is counterbalanced by the fact that it is not strictly decorative but resolutely practical. Asher's fountain also flirts with the art historical legacy of the readymade in terms of its relationship to its 1917 cousin, Duchamp's *Fountain*. But these fountains differ in two respects. First, Asher's fountain is custom-made, as opposed to Duchamp's mass-produced object. Second, Asher's fountain remains prosaically

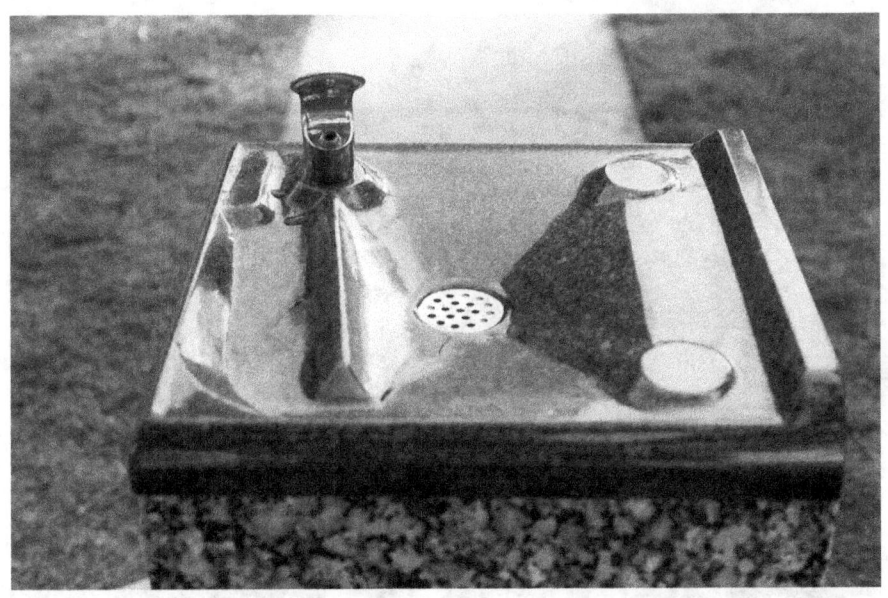

1.15　Permanent work for the Stuart Collection at the University of California, San Diego, 1991. Detail view of granite basin and stainless steel water bubbler. (Photograph courtesy the artist.)

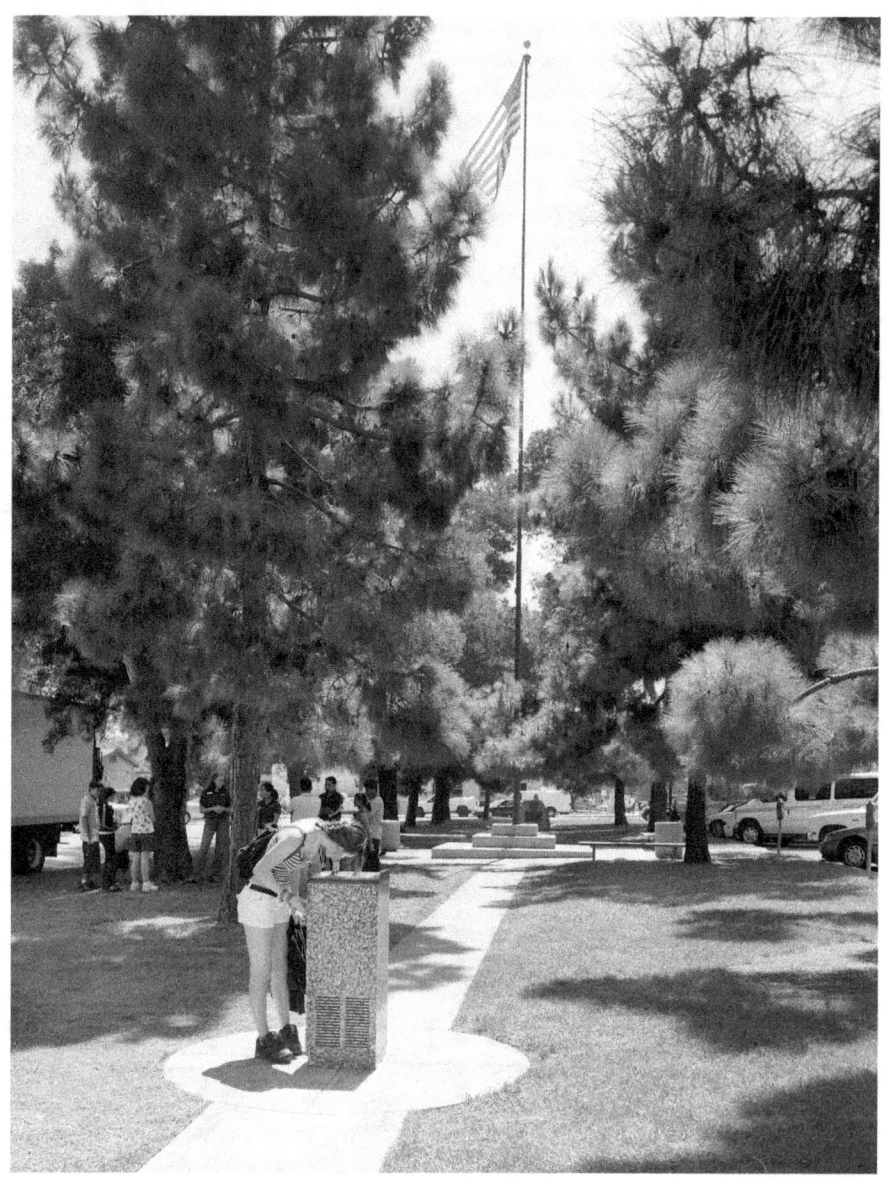

1.16   Permanent work for the Stuart Collection at the University of California, San Diego,
        1991. (Photograph by Philipp Scholz Ritterman; courtesy the Stuart Collection.)

functional, producing its own filtered and treated water in a manner comparable to any drinking fountain placed in offices, schools, museums, or other public facilities.[89]

The associative qualities of Asher's water fountain support the artist's objective of avoiding the "represent[ation of] abstract forms that would immediately individuate [his] work in public space."[90] In other words, upon encountering Asher's work, passersby might take notice of a drinking fountain rather than "an Asher," or a generic public sculpture. Such a challenge to the art object's individuation might sharpen the way in which viewers perceive an object in relation to its environment, allowing the object to function as connective tissue between viewer, situation, and the practices of everyday life. In this sense, the familiar form of Asher's water fountain individuates the site and the knowing subject instead of the object. This recognizability further reconfigures the act of viewing into as an experiential practice that engages the viewer's relation to self and others within a socially normative situation.

The media reception of Asher's fountain called to light one such set of social norms. Television news crews, covering the opening of Asher's work, treated the fountain as a joke.[91] This mass-media interpretation presumed a recipient who agrees with this slant, which the network anchors then seem to channel rather than construct. Thus, the television coverage was aimed at a specified viewer whose agreement with the news anchor was assumed and enforced by the unquestionable clarity of the media's own viewpoint.[92] In the media reception of Asher's fountain, the specified viewer was a statistic, an anonymous audience member. As if caught in a trance, this viewer might align with the view of the mainstream media, encountering the fountain and reenacting its preconceived interpretation of the work.

Through his insistence on the functionality of the fountain, and by inviting contact, Asher sought to challenge such specified modes of reception.[93] His fountain calls for viewers to engage with the work based on their a priori knowledge of this particular fountain and its properties. In fact, according to UCSD campus lore, students should drink the fountain's "smart water" before taking exams.[94] The very existence of this tradition underscores the quality of Asher's work as a special kind of fountain and its substance as special kind of water. Such individuated viewing experiences are produced in the intersection of Asher's situation and each viewer's decision to make use of it and to assign meaning to it, by interacting with the fountain. In addition to reconfiguring its site materially,

Asher's work recontextualizes and advocates epistemological practices for institutionally situated viewers: students, staff, faculty, and Asher aficionados. Their relation to the fountain is based on their interactions with it during the course of their everyday life; thus, the fountain reiterates the artist's intent for the work to "hav[e] the potential to bring together the viewing subject and the object for something other than transcendent renewal."[95] Although the fountain might resist immediate individuation as an art object, it becomes individuated through epistemological situations that specific viewers experience when they literally draw from the fountain in the context of their daily practice of living.

Conclusion: The Experiential Viewer

From deceptively empty rooms to reconfigured and recontextualized institutional situations, Asher's installations present their viewers with intellectually and emotionally nuanced experiential conditions. Even his early multisensory environments of the late 1960s and early 1970s were built upon defining and engaging an experiential matrix in which multiple epistemological and normative layers were embedded in viewing situations. In these projects, he summoned viewers to consider what they knew about a given institutional situation and what social and discursive norms applied to it. Such viewing situations are often described through their collective dimension, drawing from bodies of shared knowledge and rules. Yet the viewing conditions of his situations also become individuated through a combination of sensory, social, and psychological modes of reception. This experiential complexity stands out, for example, among the accounts Asher's viewers have given of their encounters with his installations.

The experiential tone of these viewer accounts was echoed once again in the reception of Asher's 2008 exhibition at the Santa Monica Museum of Art. His conceptual approach to this project will seem familiar: he reconstructed the wall studs of all forty-four exhibitions that had been held in this exhibition space over the past ten years, the length of time the museum had occupied its current location.[96] The outcome of this mapping operation comprised a dense maze of galvanized steel and wood studs (figure 1.17). In a small adjacent gallery, Asher displayed the key to the placement of the wall studs in the form of tear sheets that detailed the previous exhibitions and their configurations. Yet no matter how prominent the organizational armature, critics associated the physical structure

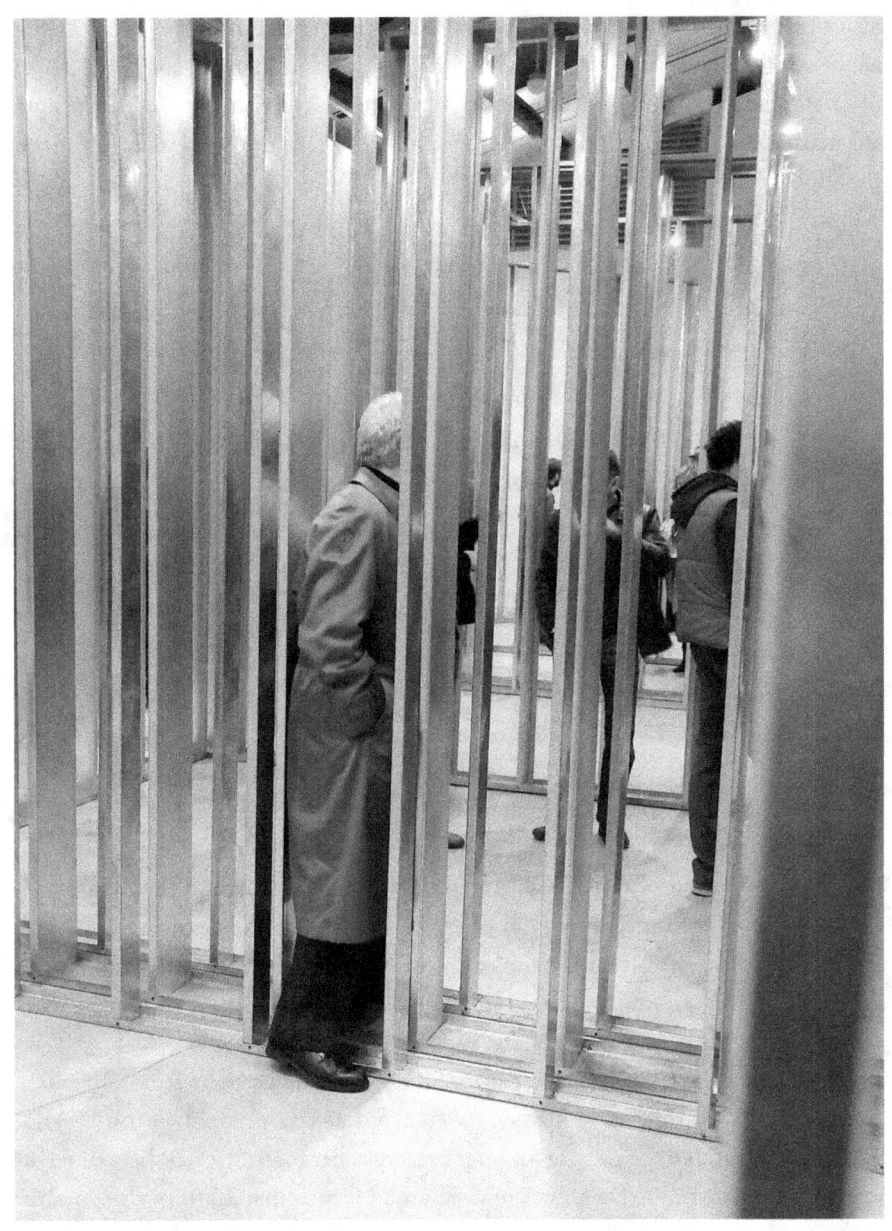

1.17 Santa Monica Museum of Art, Santa Monica, 2008, detail view of installation.
(Photograph by Bruce Morr; courtesy the Santa Monica Museum of Art.)

also with experiential qualities.[97] Walead Beshty remarked that he experienced "a sequence of disquieting perceptual transformations" in Asher's space.[98] Kirsten Swenson noted that "bodies interacting with this disorienting space . . . became the main event."[99] Mark Godfrey's description likewise attends extensively to the process of viewing the work:

> You entered the space and signed a waiver, and then found yourself confronted by the armatures' bars. You could move to left or go forward, but from there on in there was no obvious route to follow: it was a labyrinth without a centre. For the larger viewers it became quite uncomfortable to squeeze through the gaps and step over the ridges on the floor. Some walls were close by others, elsewhere space opened up unexpectedly; moving from end to end of the museum felt relentless. . . . Sometimes you thought about imprisonment; but most of all there was the illusion that you were walking through a hall of mirrors.[100]

Godfrey's description recounts his process of "entering" Asher's Santa Monica installation as a combination of the bodily, social, and discursive facets of the viewing experience. Just as the La Jolla Museum of Art had invited viewers to "enter the work of Michael Asher" in 1969, the 2008 Santa Monica project required a threshold crossing with psychological and bodily effects that were "disquieting," "disorienting," and "uncomfortable." The fact that the Santa Monica Museum of Art required visitors to sign a waiver before entering the space, for example, indicates that the museum was well aware of the potential effects Asher's installation might have, and the museum elected to withhold bearing legal responsibility for those effects.

Of course, much had changed between 1969 and 2008. Most obviously, Asher's concentration on sensory experience that was present in the La Jolla work had expanded to include an engagement with institutional discourses of art. The spectatorial experiences of the Santa Monica installation were analytical and affective. But both the La Jolla and Santa Monica exhibitions, spanning Asher's career from the late 1960s to the twenty-first century, were realized as situations that used collective institutional conditions to provide for an individuated experience.

The position of the viewer in Asher's work is intrinsically extended to anyone. There are no preconditions for this spectatorship, nor are viewers threshed and gleaned into preconceived categories based on their identity—though the knowledge viewers bring with them to the institution (including their knowledge about his practice) certainly inflects the meanings garnered from his situations. Such equality, though now enclosed within a contractual structure, is also characteristic of the participatory projects that I consider in the following chapter. In these projects the artist asked specific individuals to execute particular tasks within his work. Unlike the general viewers, these participants—gallerists, museum staff, or students—were individuated even before they entered the work. Yet what Asher's participants will share with his viewers is the potential for experiential transformation through their encounter with the artist's work.

2

Contracted Participation

Participatory approaches to art have increased both in number and scope since the Happenings and Fluxus events of the 1950s and 1960s; this is particularly true for the types of works Claire Bishop describes as embracing "the collective dimension of social experience."[1] In their zeal to account for diverse social situations and activities, many recent participatory works require a high degree of commitment from their audience and supply them with a demanding set of instructions. During the course of a museum or gallery visit, viewers might be asked to consume a meal in the company of the artist, contribute to a wall drawing, or take a taxi to a different side of town. These situational works often contextualize the request for participation as an invitation to engage in voluntary activities, ostensibly for the purposes of expanding a "passive" mode of viewer engagement toward a more active involvement with the piece. In this schema, and particularly when the viewer's acts are heavily scripted, participating in a work of art becomes a form of labor, in which viewers are summoned to work out a tangible set of activities in pursuit of material outcomes.

The notion of labor is also central to Asher's approach to participation, but with material and structural nuances that probe the multifarious, socially discursive conditions of viewing art within the institutional milieu. In a range of projects completed since the early 1970s, Asher has contracted participants to perform tasks that question the institutional distribution of authority as it bears on the production and reception of art. In most cases, his contracted participants have been arts professionals—gallery directors, museum staff members, or students—requested to carry out labor consistent with their everyday occupations, whether these involve guarding a gallery, installing an exhibition, or engaging in new artistic processes.[2] In most cases, these participants receive compensation in the form of money or educational credit. Consequently, professional participation in Asher's work does not constitute a leap into "unknown" social or experiential territory, which could describe the participatory experience of regular museum patrons in other viewing situations. Instead, his participants are often conscripted into complicity well in advance of the project's execution. This a priori contractual agreement tends to bind the participants into Asher's artistic agenda; if formed in good faith and under appropriate institutional circumstances, J. L. Austin reminds us, contracts have tangible consequences, particularly when they involve performing one's "familiar" or "authorized" professional duties.[3]

Yet participatory labor within Asher's work is differentiated from its everyday institutional context by virtue of its inclusion within the artist's premeditated plan, as Asher's conceptual guidelines for participants clearly affect the behavior of his contractees. Moreover, he tends to leave the specific details regarding his work's realization open to participant interpretation. Contractees might be requested to conduct themselves as "regular viewers" when they gaze at a painting, for example—although he refrains from offering participants an indication of what specific behavioral codes signify "regular" museum conduct.[4] These open-ended experiential situations require his participants to assume personal accountability for the way in which they carry out their institutional tasks within the artist's designated framework. The individuation of participatory behavior that results from such broad contractual arrangements is evident in participant accounts. Many responses imply that labor within Asher's work has contributed to a reconfiguration of professional roles and intersubjective relations, as well as to an institutional change capable of transforming singular systems into internally conflicting domains that allow for distinct forms of spectatorial and participatory agency. Such effects are already discernible in the earliest responses to Asher's participatory works of the 1970s, in which the artist contracted gallery workers to carry out everyday activities in plain view of gallery visitors—and, in one instance, even engineered the removal of the ubiquitous gallery guard.

Social Contracts, Individuated Effects: Gallery Labor in the 1970s

Asher first deployed the tactic of formally contracting participants during two chronologically overlapping gallery projects in 1974. At the Claire Copley Gallery in Los Angeles, the artist removed the dividing wall that separated the exhibition space from the gallery's office quarters, and removed one of the gallery's light tracks. He then refinished the gallery walls and ceiling to conceal any traces of his structural alterations (figure 2.1). Two weeks after opening at Claire Copley, Asher

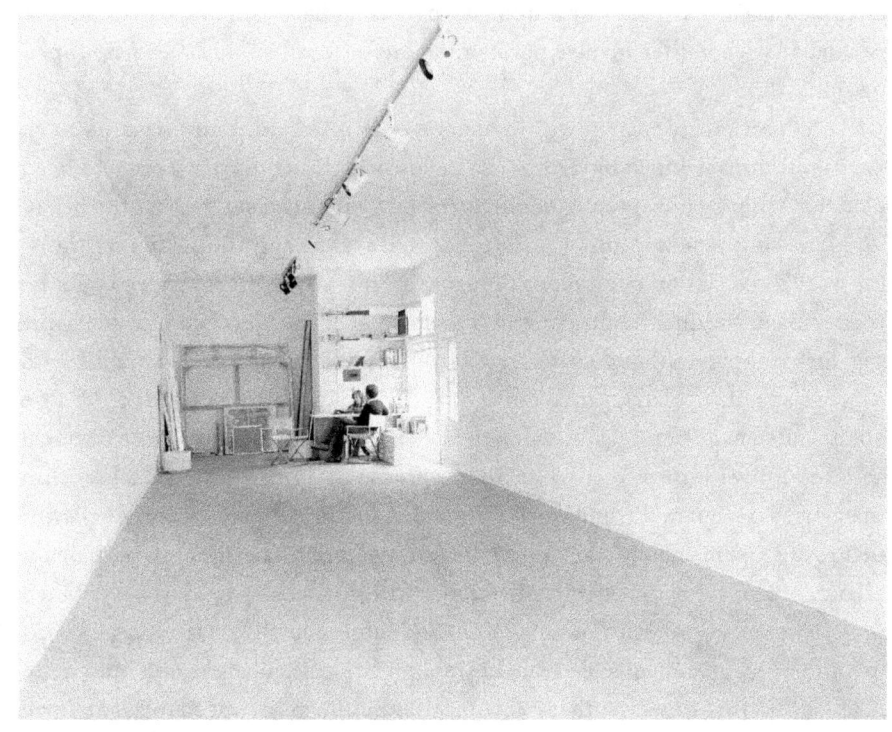

2.1   Claire Copley Gallery, Inc., Los Angeles, 1974. View toward gallery office. (Photograph by Gary Krueger; courtesy the artist.)

launched another installation at the Anna Leonowens Gallery at the Nova Scotia College of Art and Design in Halifax, Canada, where he was working on a book project with Kasper Koenig, the editor of the school's press.[5] In this instance, Asher's alterations to the gallery space were truly minimal, and consisted of simply removing sunscreens from the uppermost parts of the transparent glass walls and turning off the gallery lights (figure 2.2).[6] The evanescence of his installation at Anna Leonowens was amplified by the artist's request that the gallery guard "not be present every day."[7] This artistic move left the gallery unattended, devoid of the socially restrictive checkpoint that visitors to the gallery, located in a lobby of a classroom building, would otherwise encounter.

There were a number of similarities between the Claire Copley and Anna Leonowens projects. Both were based on subtle, almost intangible material adjustments Asher made to the gallery space—although the removal of the gallery wall at Claire Copley had a more striking effect upon the architecture than the understated modification of light quality at Anna Leonowens. The similarities between the two exhibitions served to underscore the artistic purposes behind the physically concrete gallery alterations: in both cases, Asher's material staging of a situation served to centralize the social relations within the gallery at hand. The elimination of Claire Copley's wall turned the viewer's attention upon Copley's everyday administrative gallery activities. At Anna Leonowens, on the other hand, his request to remove a normative human presence reversed the intensified social visibility of the Claire Copley situation. In other words, instead of subjecting visitors to the additional social scrutiny of gallerist Copley, subtracting the guard from Anna Leonowens displaced whatever administrative and social restrictions the students, staff, and visitors at the Nova Scotia College of Art and Design might have faced when they passed through the gallery space on their way into the building. Yet both installations bore a striking similarity, inasmuch as their critical effects relied upon the artistic rearrangement of institutional relations and modes of authority—at once structural and deconstructive.

It was not long before Asher returned to investigating the social relations of the gallery. In late 1976, Copley extended him a second invitation to exhibit in her gallery in February 1977. Because this invitation coincided with a concurrent offer from Santa Monica gallerist Morgan Thomas, Asher opted to combine two exhibitions into one project schema. In a dual situational move, he proposed that Copley and Thomas switch galleries for the duration of the project. Asher's intention was to use the gallery-gallerist switch to foreground the geographical

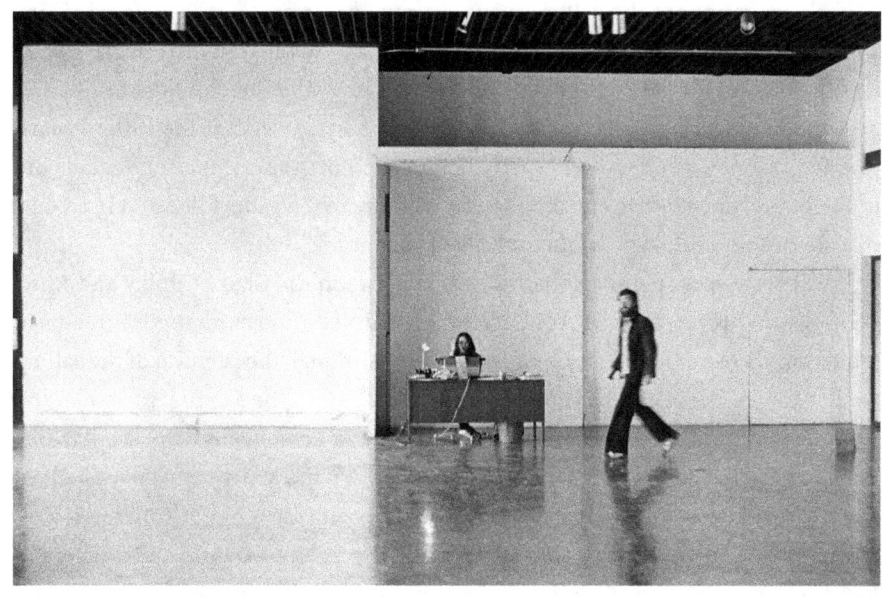

2.2   Anna Leonowens Gallery, Nova Scotia College of Art and Design, Halifax, 1974.
Viewing east in gallery toward the gallery attendant's desk (photograph taken prior
to Asher's exhibition). (Photograph courtesy the artist.)

location of each venue within the Los Angeles gallery economy.[8] In the weeks to come, Copley and Thomas shifted their regularly scheduled exhibitions and gallery operations to their counterpart's premises. For the duration of three weeks, Copley operated out of Thomas's relatively quiet Santa Monica location, showcasing works by Daniel Buren, On Kawara, and William Leavitt (figure 2.3).[9] At the same time, seven miles away—and closer to the center of Los Angeles—Morgan Thomas carried out work at Copley's space on La Cienega Boulevard, in the heart of LA's gallery district, exhibiting Raul Guerrero, Doug Metzler, Peter Alexander, David Bungay, James Hayward, and Gary Krueger (figure 2.4).[10] Like the earlier 1974 exhibitions at Claire Copley and Anna Leonowens, Asher's 1977 project targeted the sociopolitical structure of the Claire Copley and Morgan Thomas galleries.[11] The exhibition of individual artworks by Buren and Alexander in "different" gallery spaces, for example, seems to be of less significance to Asher than the attention he focused upon the gallery at large, highlighting its institutional frame as a sum of aesthetic, operational, and social attributes—from the types of exhibitions each dealer carried to the design of their office and gallery facilities—and, ultimately, to the professional practices of both Copley and Thomas.

This focus on the art gallery as sociopolitical entity differentiated Asher's 1970s gallery projects from his predecessors' nouveau réalisme and conceptual empty gallery scenarios, which centralized the figure of the artist and their designatory act of negating the material art object. While Yves Klein's white room in *Le vide* (1958) at the Galerie Iris Clert was a particularly showy authorial move, Robert Barry's literal barring of spectators from the physical space of the gallery in *Closed Gallery Piece* (1969) equally emphasized the authorial power of the artist.[12] Asher, however, reduced the visibility of the artist in his antimaterial gallery interventions by effectively obliterating any physical or temporal evidence of his intervention.[13] Before the 1974 Claire Copley exhibition opened, he smoothed over any residual marks of the gallery reconstruction, such as abrupt carpet edges, scratches, or ridges of accumulated paint—as these might have pointed to the previous existence of the dismantled partition wall. And his intervention at Anna Leonowens was so materially subtle that visitors might have missed the installation altogether as they strolled through the gallery (the only indication of the exhibition was a posting on a bulletin board outside the entrance).[14] In a similar manner, Asher's 1977 exhibitions of presentations by Morgan Thomas at the Claire Copley Gallery and by Claire Copley at the Morgan Thomas Gallery did not reveal any visible evidence of Asher's authorship, with the exception of a

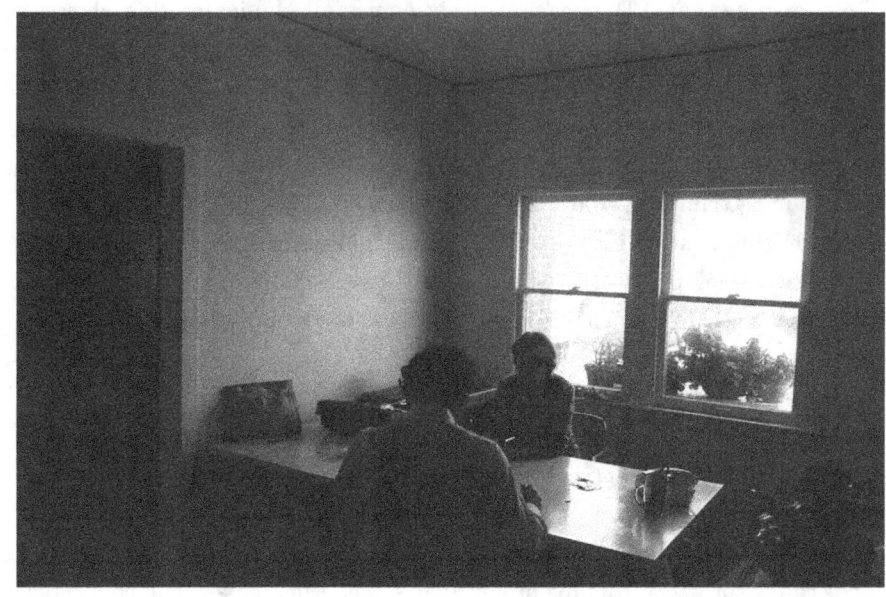

2.3   Claire Copley Gallery, Inc., Los Angeles, and Morgan Thomas Gallery, Santa Monica,
      1977. Photograph of Claire Copley in Morgan Thomas Gallery. (Photograph courtesy
      the artist.)

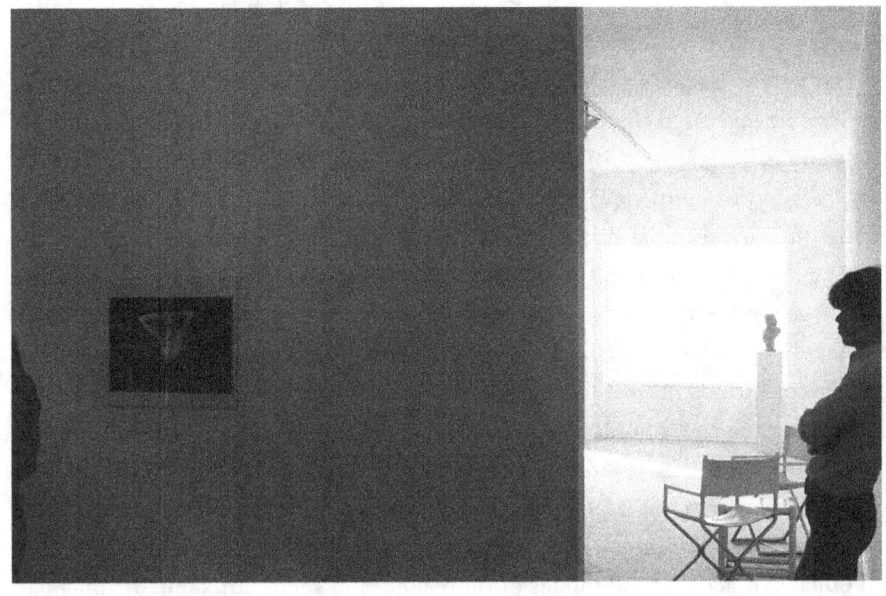

2.4   Claire Copley Gallery, Inc., Los Angeles, and Morgan Thomas Gallery, Santa Monica,
       1977. Photograph of Morgan Thomas in Claire Copley Gallery. (Photograph courtesy
       the artist.)

joint informational announcement card that was presented to visitors as external or tangential to the project—rather than an artistic gesture in itself.[15] Such withdrawal of authorial markers kept Asher's individual gesture from acquiring primacy in these gallery situations: there were no spectacular declarations after Klein's example, nor were there designations in Barry's transcendental mode.

Instead, Asher's authorial demurral within his series of materially sparse gallery arrangements aided in highlighting the typically muted social relations between gallerist and gallery visitor, as such relations tend to be perceived as exterior to the act of viewing art. To the same extent that Asher insisted upon using the already existing material features of the gallery—walls, lighting, carpeting—he focused upon the familiar social presence of the gallerist working in the gallery. In this context, the professionally appropriate and institutionally situated labor that gallerists Copley and Thomas performed became a central feature of Asher's project. These gallerists did nothing they would not normally do during the course of a typical workday—indeed, the context of their activities seemed familiar to both visitors and gallerists alike. These performances of labor were articulated through what French philosopher Jacques Rancière might call a "distribution of the sensible," or the way in which a limited number of objects, practices, and modes of representation seem thinkable within a particular society or culture.[16] For Rancière, this distribution of the visible, sensible, and thinkable has profound political value because it contributes to upholding the current arrangement of societal order and distribution of power. Accordingly, Rancière argues that shifts in visibility are inseparable from shifts in what is possible within aesthetic and sociopolitical fields when political and cultural acts and utterances "modify . . . the ways in which groups of people adhere to a condition, react to situations, recognize their images."[17] In that sense, the labor that Asher contracted Copley and Thomas to perform within his project produced a shift in institutional context and meaning, in which both gallerists and visitors recognized themselves within a new set of social relations.

In Asher's 1974 exhibition at the Claire Copley Gallery, where his removal of a dividing wall reconfigured the visible space of the gallery, viewers encountered precisely such a relocation of social relations. For a visitor familiar with the gallery's architectural layout, the Copley Gallery's subtly altered topography might have looked different, as the office area was exposed to reveal a space and an activity previously shielded from public view: Copley sitting at her desk, facing front. Instead of the anticipated collection of paintings or sculpture, there were no conventional art objects in sight—nothing to deflect the viewer's attention from Copley's office area at the rear of the gallery. Furthermore, while gallery-goers had no visual distractions to keep them from noticing Copley at her desk, neither could Copley ignore her exposed visitors, creating a reciprocal viewing situation that local critics described in vivid detail. "Standing directly in front of Copley," Melinda Wortz observed, "it is almost impossible not to confront her and ask the inevitably embarrassing questions about the show. The viewer does not have the option of anonymously viewing the exhibition and leaving, nor can Copley feign ignorance of your presence."[18]

Faced with this pointedly personalized encounter, viewers might have wished they could avoid the confrontational situation that Wortz and other critics described.[19] Yet the embarrassment that Wortz felt was not entirely singular or individual. Rather, her response stemmed from—and was mediated by—the socially specific gallery context. At Asher's 1974 exhibition, visitors did not merely "confront" the gallerist as a unique, isolated personality, but found themselves viewing the structural condition of a gallerist at work within her own gallery. In a similar vein, the gallerist did not greet viewers as private acquaintances (even when she might have known them well) but rather as potential clients or customers. The psychological charge of the situation was symptomatic of, and firmly framed by, the institutional context of structurally preexisting social relations between gallerists and visitors.

This institutional context did not entirely determine what transpired between Claire Copley and her audience, though—or between Morgan Thomas and her visitors. Critical accounts describe these gallery situations as shaped by Asher's refusal to dictate how participants should behave. Critic Nancy Marmer, for example, commented on his 1977 arrangement with Claire Copley and Morgan Thomas in theatrical terms:

[O]nce the players are in place and the scene is set, the artist steps back; as dispassionate, nail-paring observer, he permits the situation, with all its uncertainties and variables, to work itself out as it will. . . . He provides few props, no scripts, no schedule of activities, no themes, no conclusions, no documentation, and, once they are installed, no guidance for the participants.[20]

Asher's abnegation from controlling the behavioral situation within the gallery, which Marmer extends from preparatory "themes" to final "conclusions," made the resulting social situation profoundly unpredictable in a manner the gallerists could have experienced as frustrating or unnerving. Yet it was precisely Asher's refusal to furnish "guidance for the participants" that seems to have provided an affective space for Copley and Thomas to gain new insights into their cultural and social practice. According to Marmer, the gallerists "appeared to find the exchange disruptive, but also exciting, informative, and (they claimed) personally revelatory."[21] Copley had referred to such "personally revelatory" effects in a letter to Asher written from inside the work, while she watched over her gallery during Asher's 1974 exhibition.[22] This letter expressed Copley's insights regarding the way in which Asher's situation had tangibly embedded her in the overarching gallery apparatus:

> Really, you have created something here that is unbelievable. You have eliminated any possibility of anonymity, evasion, neutrality, or shelter, and not only for me, but for all those who walk in the space, pass by the window, or in any way approach the space. This space and I have become a unit, indivisible, and it's amazing. Direct contact is mandatory and so natural.[23]

On the one hand, Copley's response to Asher's work acknowledges the constraints of the artist's schema: the removal of the wall between the gallery and office makes interactions between Copley and the gallery visitors "mandatory," thus structurally anticipating the way in which she would relate to visitors. Yet Copley simultaneously recognizes that her own labor within the gallery is inseparable from the material conditions of the space. Along with the floors, walls, and the storage shelving, *she* is part of the gallery apparatus. In this context, interactions with viewers are not only necessary—they are "natural" inasmuch as they are grounded in her "normal" modes of professional labor.

Further accounts of Asher's 1974 Copley exhibition, however, indicate that the critical reception of this work was also highly individuated. Wortz's review for *Art News* emphasized the socially restrictive elements of Asher's situation, pointing out that "[Asher] virtually forces social interaction, robbing both Copley and the viewer of their sense of privacy and psychologically limiting their freedom of action."[24] Wortz, then, considers the structure of Asher's situation to be emotionally oppressive for gallerist and viewer alike, whereas Copley ascribes substantial transformative significance to her involvement within the same situation.[25] Reflecting on how the social relations in her gallery were transformed by Asher's situation, Copley bears witness to the affective potential set in motion by her own participation in Asher's work:

> I begin to recognize that more than being a contending element in the conception/construction of the piece, I am also an element in the working of it, and in the realization. It is amazing too that every minute I am here I am dealing with this piece and its implications. It is unavoidable. I find what is happening within these walls and within my walls to be quite fantastic. Aside from the art aesthetics, and business, you have given me something that is continuing and just wonderful and for which I feel very special and I thank you for. There is something, a part of this, that goes from you to me and back again. I wonder if I have ever understood a work of art this completely. And something new, which makes it even more important. It is completely satisfying and moving and I am sure you know how much more by the degree to which I am carrying on. This is very important to me.[26]

In contrast to the constrained psychological space described by Wortz, Copley's letter discloses transformative elation about her professional yet individuated experience within Asher's situation. On the one hand, Copley's presence within the installation falls in line with the structural specificity of Asher's project: she performs the professional role of the gallerist in her gallery. On the other hand, her participation exceeds the limits of her solely professional involvement in the work as a "contending element" who might affirm Asher's piece in her gallery without specifically supporting it. Instead, Copley's labor within the project provides the gallerist with a complex, "completely satisfying and moving" experience. The individuation of the gallerist's participation transforms her professional role within and beyond Asher's work.

By reconfiguring visible—and conceivable—social relations, the individuated experiences that emerge through accounts by Copley, Wortz, and Marmer give a sense of how Asher's participatory gallery projects of the 1970s contributed to the types of shifts within the distribution of the sensible that Rancière theorized.

These shifts were based on understanding the institution of the art gallery as a sociopolitical totality, the experience of which was nevertheless individuated—and invested with meaning—through the psychologically and emotionally charged interactions between gallerists and visitors. In this context, Asher's description of his work as "situational" (rather than "environmental") to a critic who was reviewing the 1974 Copley exhibition emphasizes the social elements of his work.[27] "Environments," for Asher, were associated with specific material alterations to the exhibition space that were meant to be experienced phenomenologically.[28] "Situational work," on the other hand, would engage the social relations of the gallery. In the case of his projects at Claire Copley, Anna Leonowens, and Morgan Thomas galleries, the participating gallerists and visiting critics attribute profoundly transformative, rather than simply affirmative, effects to these social relations. In that sense, Asher's gallery projects experientially redrew the conditions of possibility for the social world that the gallerists and visitors shared. Considered through Rancière's theory of visibility and thinkability, the labor of Copley, Thomas, and the critic-visitors "modif[ied] . . . the ways in which [they] adhere to a condition, react to situations, recognize their images."[29] Furthermore, these psychologically intense effects of the interactions between the gallerist and visitors seemed to extend beyond the duration of Asher's exhibition—certainly this is what Copley alluded to when she described her experience within Asher's work as "something that is continuing."

Yet the fact that Copley described a transformative experience "within these walls and within my walls" did not mean she abandoned her regular professional role in the gallery. On the contrary, it would be more accurate to note that Copley and Thomas doubled their "normal" gallerist identity by folding their role in Asher's project into their everyday activities, which they continued to conduct with visitors whose business in the gallery might have been entirely separate from viewing Asher's work. Indeed, the only procedural condition Asher charged Thomas and Copley with—a request for each gallerist to pass along whatever business communications were intended for the other—was to assure that the everyday business of running these galleries would not be disrupted by his artistic translocation.[30] The fact that Copley and Thomas retained their professional identities might have contributed to their finding their participation in Asher's work both "revelatory" and "exciting." These gallerists were not haplessly "exposed" to gallery visitors—because they had not been hidden from them in the first place. Asher's reluctance to explicitly lay claim to "exposing" previously "hidden" truths resonates with Rancière's disinclination to claim "hidden" substructures beneath visible "surfaces." In Rancière's way of thinking, focusing on lateral "systems of possibilities" might provide a more accurate method of examining the redistribution of the sensible within a given situation.[31]

Most visitors to Asher's exhibition were almost certainly familiar with the social conditions of the art gallery, and aware of the gallerist's existence before Asher's intervention. But the visitor's and gallerist's lateral familiarity with the social elements of the gallery encounter did not preclude the profound rearrangement of these social elements within Asher's situation aesthetics. The gallerists' recontextualized social interactions with visitors prompted them to reconsider their own institutional positions within their professional framework. The importance of including professionally appropriate labor within the social interactions at the Copley, Anna Leonowens, and Morgan Thomas galleries is distinctive when these projects are compared with Asher's 1977 work at the Los Angeles Institute of Contemporary Art (LAICA), in which he did not contract participation in a professional capacity, but set up an open laboratory situation. In fact, the artist's decision not to give instructions for the conduct of contracted participants in the LAICA project perhaps paradoxically increased some of the participants' tendencies to define and maintain preexisting social boundaries.

On the Labor of Social Relations: Asher at LAICA

Asher had been invited to LAICA by curators Tom Jimmerson and Helen N. Lewis, whose 1975 proposal for the recently established nonprofit space sought to exhibit Asher's work within the context of related artists, in order to further local understanding of his oeuvre.[32] As if to respond to the curatorial goals of promoting his work to Los Angeles at large, Asher proposed promoting and advancing LAICA's own institutional mission within the community. His first LAICA proposal, had it been accepted, would have convened an "advisory board" of experts in fields such as urban planning to discuss LAICA's upcoming relocation from the ABC Entertainment Center in Century City to South Robertson Boulevard in Culver City.[33] After the exhibition's organizers determined that the budget was insufficient to properly compensate the professionals who would sit on Asher's hypothetical board, the artist modified his proposal so that it retained a participatory discussion format but removed any set of predetermined conversation topics from the agenda. Hence, Asher stuck with his situational strategy of providing a hub for social exchange, but did not focus with such immediacy upon LAICA's institutional identity.[34]

In its modified state, Asher's final proposal for LAICA departed from his previous participatory projects in that it did not call attention to specific professional activities. Instead, he sought to employ on average four participants at a time to occupy the LAICA gallery space during the hours it was open.[35] "Nothing was required of the participants," he later stated, "other than their presence within the actual installation area or within the confines of the LAICA exhibition space."[36] The social function of the contracted participants was left open to the point of ambiguity: there were no clearly defined tasks for them to execute, no institutionally appropriate functions to embrace—Asher's participants were merely required to show up at LAICA for their shift.

Asher's LAICA exhibition was accompanied by installations from Richard Long and David Askevold. In an adjacent room, Long's *California Wood Circle* was a floor installation made of driftwood, while Askevold's *Video Bar Installation* consisted of a bar counter with a video monitor playing a tape of an improvised singing performance by Askevold's student John Todd. Compared with the works of Long and Askevold, Asher's repositioned gallery space might have seemed more of an informal meeting environment than a structured installation. Situated just beyond the LAICA lobby, a book display, and the museum director's desk, the most visible evidence of Asher's work was his arrangement of furniture: a sofa, folding chairs, and a table. Within this venue, about four participants were ensconced at any given time (figure 2.5). The participants were individuals Asher had solicited based on their "categories of professional activity."[37] Most were already engaged in art at least semiprofessionally, as artists, critics, curators, or students. All participants were compensated four dollars per hour from the grant LAICA received for the exhibition from the National Endowment for the Arts.[38]

Even though Asher did not charge his LAICA participants with carrying out professional tasks, he had an underlying ideological objective for the situation. "It was hoped," he later remarked, "that this installation would serve as a model for a locus outside of academic, commercial, or private social situations, where discussion and study could take place."[39] Within that framework, Asher acknowledged that he had some expectations for the participants' behavior, mentioning in his notes that he had "blind trust that [the participants] will not abuse the

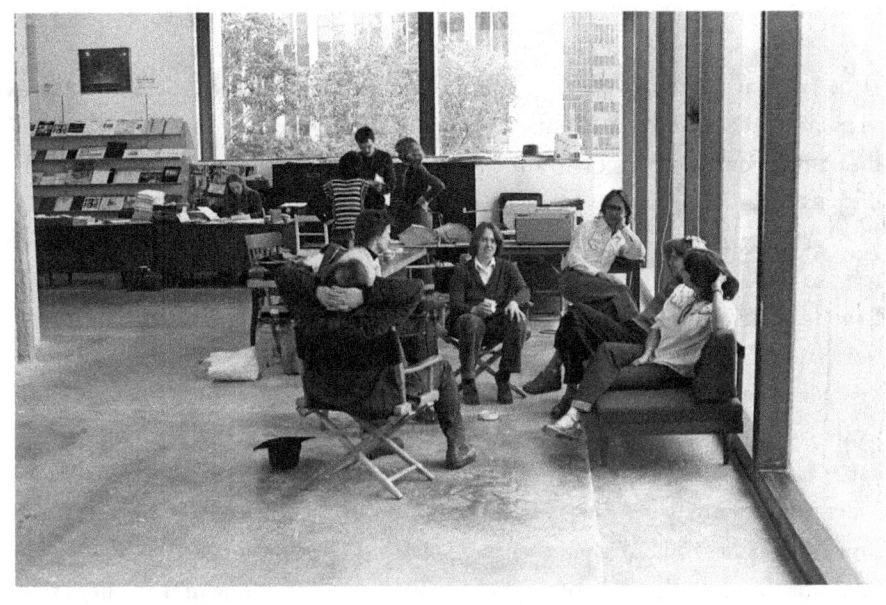

2.5 Los Angeles Institute of Contemporary Art, Los Angeles, 1977. (Photograph by Robert L. Smith; courtesy the artist.)

work."[40] Apart from this general stance, he refrained from giving his participants any instructions on what to do with their time at LAICA. Unlike Claire Copley, who continued to supervise her gallery during Asher's 1974 exhibition, the LAICA participants did not perform specific professional roles—nor was their presence at LAICA framed as an extended act of performance art. Rather, according to Asher, "[t]he paid participants were free to pursue their day-to-day activities as usual in as much as the context of the situation would allow them to do so."[41] And indeed the context, or the social constraints, of the exhibition affected the ways in which his participants experienced the situation at LAICA.

At the time of the 1977 LAICA project, the notion that works of art could refer to activities rather than material objects was commonplace in the art world. In general, projects that proposed to create a shared space for social relations were still often tinged with utopian connotations, as in Barry's Marcuse-derived 1970 statement that an art gallery is "[a] place to which we can come and for a while 'be free to think about what we are going to do.'"[42] To describe a gallery space as an alternate universe that shelters individuals from the demands of the social world while granting them freedom to think requires drawing a distinction between art and nonart spaces; separating the ostensibly constrained social relations that occur outside of the gallery from those relations in the gallery that Barry envisioned as exempt from normal social restrictions.

Asher's LAICA project also set up a space for social discourse within the art space. Unlike Barry, who at least hypothetically addressed any visitor entering the gallery, Asher sought to promote dialogue among a group of specifically contracted participants. In their comments on the LAICA work, Asher and some of his participants, however, distanced the LAICA situation from utopian notions of discursive freedom. Rather than experiencing freedom from social constraints, many of these contracted participants testified to the ethical and emotional complexity that the social relations within an art gallery shared with those of the everyday social world.[43]

Some of Asher's participants explicitly questioned their social roles at LAICA. Although these contractees were situated a mere ten or fifteen feet away from the LAICA director working at his desk, they could not legitimately consider themselves as LAICA employees with a sanctioned list of duties. What, then, was their function in the space? Although some of the participants took it upon themselves to engage in activities ranging from semiprofessional to purely social—editing film, reading, studying, eating, conversing with one another—

others also felt the pressing need to critically examine their participatory role in Asher's schema.[44] One participant, identified as "Sally," described her part in Asher's work as "a simple contractual agreement (time in exchange for wages hourly)."[45] For Sally, the remuneration she received from Asher "assuage[d] any guilt or other emotional complication that might arise from a more conditional exchange i.e. friendship or volunteerism."[46] According to this rationale, Asher's contractual structure served to absolve Sally from a sense of personal responsibility, allowing her to separate her participation in his work from more personally defined modes of relationships which she associated with "friendship" and "volunteerism."

If Sally found absolution in the fact of her paid status, another participant, artist Dorit Cypis, felt emotional discomfort due to Asher's offer of monetary compensation. "He asked me if I would participate, and said he would pay," Cypis later recalled. "Actually, the latter presented more of a problem to me than the former. Why a money involvement? Would that make me an employee and add some assurance of proper conduct on my part? . . . Should I act a certain way? Why so paranoid? Does money equate responsibility?"[47] Cypis's concerns about Asher's expectations, as related to the artist's system of monetary compensation, underscored her individuated sense of responsibility as a participant worried about properly fulfilling the terms of a prospective employer's contract. Moreover, her concerns reflected the broader dilemma these participants faced: without explicit instructions from the artist—which might have enabled them to complete their contractual obligations in good faith—the contractees needed to make their own decisions regarding "proper conduct," and to negotiate the social situation at LAICA as best they could—without recourse to the artist's authority.

Asher took notes on the situation at LAICA while it was unfolding in order to think through the critical implications of the work.[48] These notes, which corroborate participants' accounts of efforts to resolve the overall ambiguity of the project, indicate that he was well aware of some of the participants' struggles between their own responsibility toward the artist and their freedom to determine their activities within the work. Asher commented: "With no orders . . . [my project] is modeled . . . to become restrictive for the paid participants in their decision-making capabilities for some are not sure as to how responsible they must be towards [my] work. This lessens their immediate freedom until they become used to the work."[49] He thus contrasts freedom of conduct with "proper" conduct, or participatory behavior that demonstrates responsibility toward the artist's agenda. It is precisely this chasm between practical freedom and responsibility that Asher situates as the source of the social conflicts that manifested at LAICA between some of the participants and gallery visitors.

According to the artist's notes, certain participants sought to confront gallery visitors as a means of clarifying their participatory status in the project, and "stop[ped] every audience [member] to make them conscious [of their] participant [status] and actively point out or draw them near to the area of other participants." In contrast, Asher also observed some of his contractees avoiding regular gallery patrons by "retreat[ing] into talking amongst themselves or reading or anything else which seems to take their mind off the audience."[50] Both reactions toward gallery patrons resulted from participant efforts to differentiate themselves from the visitors, and to seek recognition of that differentiation by engaging in particular forms of *social conduct*. These modes of direct confrontation or studied disregard by Asher's contractees affected gallery patrons, whose behavior adopted a corresponding tone. According to Asher's notes:

> The audience seems different. Some settle in for several hours, while others walk up to request what is going on while [even] others walk towards the participants then shy away or walk past the area as rapidly as possible only to escape back into whatever they wanted LAICA to provide them. A loaded area seems to be that the audience doesn't know what the paid participants are perceiving and the paid participants don't know what the audience is thinking except for that part of the audience who join the participants.[51]

In other words, the contact zone between the contracted participants and gallery visitors was riddled with intersubjective uncertainty, resulting in heightened modes of identificatory relations: the urge to unequivocally locate oneself as *either* participant *or* visitor, and the attendant need to distinguish oneself from others (defined against one's institutional role). The tendency of some of the LAICA participants to confront gallery visitors, for example, might have contributed to consolidating their own sense of identity within Asher's situation. In this sense, the social interactions within the situation functioned as technologies, or modes of conduct, that participants and visitors seized to substantiate their social identities. Foucault evoked such "technologies of self" in his late work, describing them as sets of historically specific practices that individuals use to shape themselves by "act[ing] upon [themselves]."[52] The labor of forming a relation to oneself might seem an internal pursuit (inasmuch as it requires a degree of observation and self-reflectivity), yet Foucault emphasized the importance of practices, or concrete acts, in shaping one's self.[53] At LAICA, these modes of conduct were fueled by some of the participants' ethical qualms about their institutional roles (such as Cypis's concerns about "proper conduct"), but they were manifested in the participants' acts of purposefully confronting or ignoring the gallery visitors. The tension between participants and gallery visitors seems to have been relieved only when the members of each group had clearly acknowledged their status as distinct from one another, separating the participant from the spectator and the labor of participation from that of spectatorship.

The psychological milieu stirred up by the instability of social relations within Asher's LAICA project became evident in some participant responses to the situation. Sally, for example, withdrew from the project "[a]fter spending approximately seven and a half hours under [Asher's] employment."[54] In her resignation letter, she voiced discomfort at the effect of her semi-ambiguous position within the LAICA exhibition space on her everyday behavior: "'Social interaction,' you say: big concept—encompassing at the least. . . . As a physical actualization, in this case, such interaction seemed aggressive in a convoluted kind of way."[55] Sally's attribution of "aggression," or a distinctly emotional charge, to the participatory social relations at LAICA seems a further indication that the relations between participants, gallery visitors, and artist did not discard but rather amplified social and psychological constraints that might otherwise seem everyday—even familiar. For some of Asher's contracted participants, the affective spectrum of the LAICA work ranged from aggression and violation to paranoia and liberation. The socially and psychologically demanding situation, which the artist later described as "a host of contradictions,"[56] led to substantial ethical and emotional conflicts for some of the participants. The various outcomes of Asher's LAICA project were far from utopian in Barry's Marcusian sense, in which participants would have been released from the constraints of their daily lives. On the contrary, these participatory experiences provided grounds for participants and viewers to rethink the consequences of their actions within the constrained social relations that they already occupied.

Although the participatory structure of Asher's 1977 LAICA project resembled the artist's earlier situation at the Claire Copley Gallery, in that the artist had contracted arts professionals, the two projects also differed significantly—particularly if we consider the status of professional labor within the work. Copley, sitting in her gallery, continued to carry out her everyday gallerist's duties, whereas the LAICA participants were placed in a less-than-familiar environment without any specified activities to occupy them. The LAICA situation stands out among Asher's participatory projects precisely because it lacked the element of professional labor. And although Asher continued to execute projects that hinged upon the interaction of gallery visitors with contracted participants, only at LAICA were the outcomes of the project so dynamically fractious. Indeed, Asher's next participatory project after LAICA—the Claire Copley and Morgan Thomas gallery exchange—returned to contracting the labor of participating gallerists in their professional capacity. The productive role of labor would continue to occupy Asher even in those participatory projects that foregrounded art's reception over its production, as in his work for the "74th American Exhibition" at the Art Institute of Chicago in 1982.

The Work of Museum Reception:
Contracted Viewers at the "74th American Exhibition"

Although its central focus was on the labor of museum reception, Asher's project for the "74th American Exhibition" was once more based on a prearranged contractual arrangement. For this work, Asher hired participants to view two paintings on display in the Art Institute's Gallery 226, a permanent collection space showcasing early-twentieth-century European painting and sculpture (figure 2.6). These participants, about six at a time, were divided between Pablo Picasso's *Daniel-Henry Kahnweiler* (1910) and Marcel Duchamp's *Nude Seated in a Bathtub* (also 1910). The viewing shift for each of Asher's contractees lasted thirty minutes and took place daily, from 12:15 to 12:45 p.m.

Textual information was available in several locations at the Art Institute to alert regular museum patrons to the contractual status of Asher's spectators. In the Morton Wing, for example, where most of the "74th American Exhibition" was housed, a neatly typed handout in a wall-mounted Plexiglas holder outlined Asher's project, while a wall label (placed next to the handouts) encouraged them to visit Gallery 226 to actually view the work.[57] There were also supplementary labels in closer proximity to the contracted viewers, and adjacent to the Picasso and Duchamp paintings, tucked discreetly below the paintings' permanent

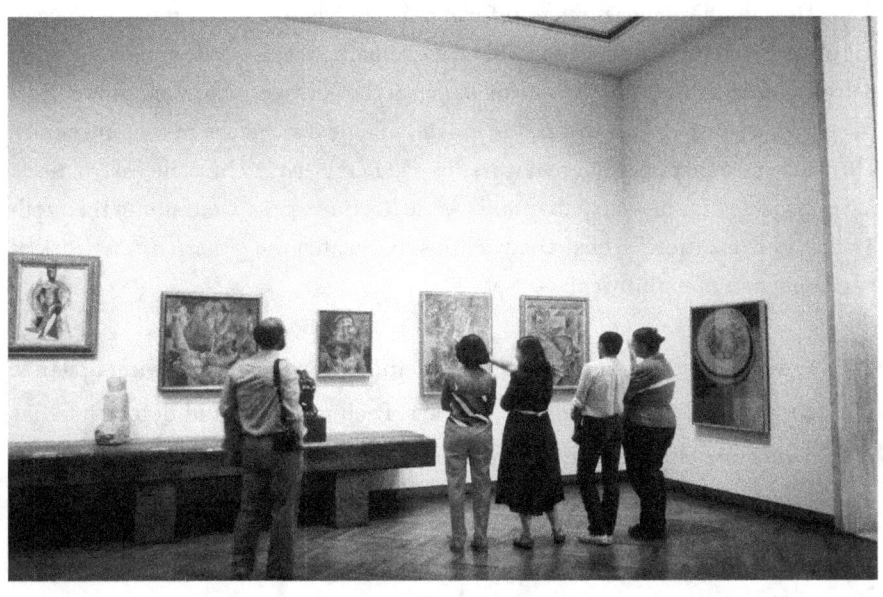

2.6   "74th American Exhibition," Art Institute of Chicago, 1982. Asher's viewers in front
       of Pablo Picasso's *Daniel-Henry Kahnweiler* in Gallery 226. (Photograph by Anne
       Rorimer; courtesy the artist.)

information (figure 2.7). These supplementary labels notified visitors that the adjacent painting was "[o]ne of two works viewed as part of Michael Asher's work in the 74th American Exhibition (June 12–August 1, 1982)."

Despite these measures to inform museum visitors about the existence of the project, Asher's installation might have remained invisible for many museum patrons, so accurately did the performance of the contracted participants reflect the typical visitor's place within the epistemological structure of the museum.[58] This close mimicry of regular viewership had been written into the instructions Asher provided for his participants via Anne Rorimer, the co-curator of the "74th American Exhibition." These instructions delineated the generic framework of participant responsibilities:

> Viewers should stand facing their painting at a normal viewing distance in a natural position for viewing art. Each group should define itself as a separate cluster with each person not more than about 2 feet from the other person. . . . Viewers should not be posed as performers, but rather as regular museum viewers.[59]

For the most part, Asher's request for contractees to behave "as regular museum viewers" adequately discouraged them from interpreting their labor of viewing as something that could be seen as a performance. These contracted participants were not meant to stand out from the crowd or call attention to themselves beyond occupying the familiar, broadly recognizable institutional role of the museum visitor. Beyond issuing these broad guidelines for his participants, Asher refrained from mapping out what "regular" viewing behavior might entail or specifying any desirable mode of attention, behavior, or response. The artist's reluctance to dictate what "regular" meant within the epistemological framework of the museum implied that each of the contractees needed to individually *and* socially resolve his or her own mode of conduct within the work. The ensuing participatory activities, then, were shaped by each participant's personal interpretation of what "regular" museum viewing meant.

This personal freedom of conduct manifested itself in the ways participants performed the labor of viewing. Documentary photographs of Asher's contracted viewers show them interacting with each other, gesturing and looking at each other to the same extent that they face the paintings (figure 2.8). They fold

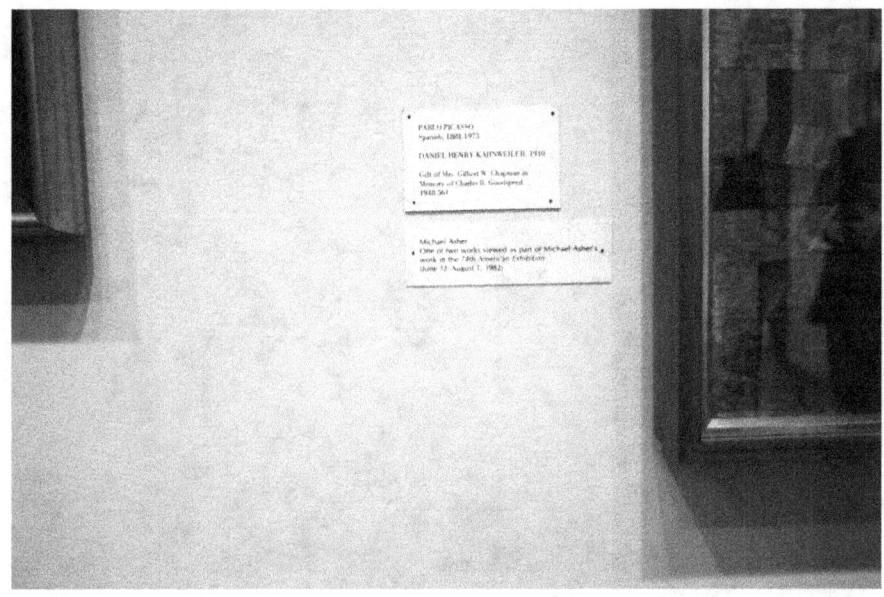

2.7 "74th American Exhibition," Art Institute of Chicago, 1982. Asher's label containing information about his contribution was placed below the Art Institute's wall label for Picasso's *Daniel-Henry Kahnweiler* in Gallery 226. (Photograph by Anne Rorimer; courtesy the artist.)

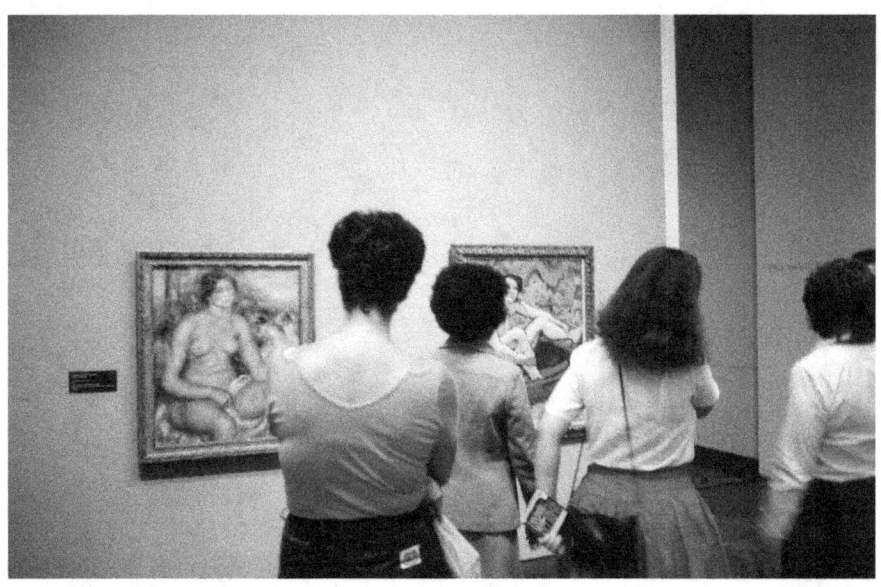

2.8   "74th American Exhibition," Art Institute of Chicago, 1982. Asher's viewers in
       front of Marcel Duchamp's *Nude Seated in a Bathtub* in Gallery 226. (Photograph by
       Anne Rorimer; courtesy the artist.)

their arms, lean toward a painting or each other, step closer or further away from the wall. At some moments they stand intimately close, blocking other passersby from obtaining a frontal view of the painting. Then, as if on cue, the contractees move apart, expanding their command of the gallery space. The physicality of their viewing practice inflects the nuanced quality of their attention; a hand-bag slung over the shoulder might slip, or the participant might thrust her body weight from one hip to another. Occasionally, a second group of viewers forms behind the contractees, seeing the Picasso or Duchamp painting *through* the con-tracted activity; actual museum visitors reach—obliviously or not—into the space of contracted insiders through the shared epistemological practice of museum conduct, that of viewing paintings in a museum.

What were the regular museum visitors to make of *Asher's* work, though? The Morton Wing handout and the additional label, placed near the contracted viewers, explained the artist's project—for those who paid it any notice. This supplemental information split the temporality of viewing into two related responses: the experience of one's own museum visit, followed by an observation of Asher's situation. Martha Buskirk identified such a doubling between "experi-ence" and "explanation" in her analysis of conceptually oriented performance art in the 1960s and 1970s, in which an act performed by an artist within a public space was later documented by an artist's statement regarding the significance of the act.[60] According to Buskirk, such a temporal split between "absolute imme-diacy and significant delay" characterized the street projects of Adrian Piper and Vito Acconci—particularly Acconci's *Following Piece* (1969)—in that "an unsus-pecting public" encountered the artist in the streets in the context of an act left intentionally incomprehensible to that same accidental public.[61] Only later did these artists provide conceptual (and intent-driven) frameworks for their acts—and often in an exhibition context that differed from the original encounter.

Although Asher divided the reception of his work at the "74th American Exhibition" into two strata—one primarily experiential, the other explanatory—in the manner of Piper and Acconci, he allowed for the possibility that the same public might benefit from access to both modalities of experience. While, as Buskirk illustrates, the reception of early Piper and Acconci projects was char-acterized by "[a] delay . . . in the dissemination of knowledge about the work to an audience that has access to the activity only through the accounts and docu-mentation the artist decides to provide,"[62] Asher's audience at the Art Institute had almost simultaneous access to both modes of knowledge: the experiential activity of viewing and the artist's account regarding its logic. The act of looking by regular visitors to the Art Institute combined these two elements of spectatorship when their individual viewing of the Picasso and Duchamp paintings and of Asher's contracted viewers of those paintings was framed by the artist's explanation. In this manner, the regular Art Institute visitors were invited to connect their individual modes of looking at art to the museum's ideological framework. The superimposition of the "explanatory" upon the "experiential" mode of reception within Asher's "74th American Exhibition" project further refined the contracted viewer's role at the Art Institute into a tool or mechanism that allegorically reproduced the social relations of art appreciation for the benefit of the regular museum visitor.[63] Asher suggested this interpretation in his exhibition handout, in which he stated that his viewers "[were] paradigmatic of museum visitors."[64] While this contracted act of viewing was individuated according to the participant, it was thus also framed by the sociocultural conventions of the viewing act, or the historically and institutionally specific formations of knowledge, conduct, and social relations that structure museum visits.

If, as Asher argued in his exhibition handout, "the viewers serve to demonstrate the museum visitor's role at the point of presentation,"[65] then regular museum visitors found themselves viewing themselves viewing art through the contracted participants. In other words, the contracted viewing labor modeled, imitated, and doubled the everyday viewing relations at the Art Institute. Craig Owens links similar instances of intertextual proliferation, when "one text is doubled by another," to critical allegories in which "supplementary" texts stand to take over the established meaning lodged within the primary source.[66] Through its doubling of viewing relations, Asher's "74th American Exhibition" viewing situation might have generated such new meanings that could affect the practice of looking at art in museums. Not merely a simple replication of existing viewing relations at the Art Institute, Asher's situation sought to engage museum visitors in experiential, individually negotiated, and self-reflexive modes of epistemological insight that remained distinct from regular modes of museum reception— even when they reflected those paradigmatic museum viewing conditions.

When Asher first proposed his viewing work to the Art Institute of Chicago, he mentioned Walter Benjamin's argument in "The Work of Art in the Age of Mechanical Reproduction" as a basis for his investigation of museum reception.[67] In a 1980 letter to A. James Speyer, the Art Institute's curator of twentieth-century painting and sculpture, Asher cited Benjamin's theory as a context for his own use of labor. In this classic 1936 essay, Benjamin argues that historically specific modes of production—in particular, the modern industrial techniques that enabled the reproduction of images—inescapably affected a viewer's relationship to the image. Benjamin points out that, before the advent of mechanical reproduction, relatively few, socially privileged individuals were able to view artworks firsthand, but recent techniques had made images of these works accessible to large numbers of people. Yet Benjamin distinguishes the experience of viewing a mechanical reproduction of a masterpiece such as Leonardo's *Mona Lisa* from the experience of beholding the original painting because the public's exposure to reproductions, along with the new frequency of such encounters, had changed the experience of viewing art. Indeed, reproduction transformed the reception of art to such an extent, Benjamin argues, that the art object itself seemed to have changed. The original artwork, when faced with a barrage of reproductions, had lost its aura.[68]

In his letter to Speyer, Asher envisioned his proposed installation as "a response to [Benjamin's] article," and enumerated the ways it addressed both the embodied and socially conditioned processes of reception: "[p]erhaps [the loss of 'aura'] is possible, but I also feel that the original experience of a painting or sculpture is mediated by the context the receiver finds himself in while intimately viewing the work with other people."[69] Here Asher describes reception as a social and experiential practice centered upon the recipients or viewers of an image or object. Rather than assuming that museum viewers would completely reproduce the collective social relations of museum spectatorship, he stresses the unmistakably "intimate" effects produced by the museum's social situation.

By definition, intimacy is a relational affect, an emotion or sensation that one feels toward other subjects—or objects, including paintings. Sara Ahmed sees intimacy as an emotion that participates in "affective economies" perpetually circulating between social subjects.[70] The relationality of emotions, Ahmed argues, accounts for their power to actively shape (rather than passively reflect) individual experiences and identities.[71] Thus, the social aspect of a museum viewing situation might produce feelings of intimacy—rather than reflect individual, self-contained viewing experiences. This relational understanding is emblematic of Asher's characterization of intimacy in the museum. In Asher's Art Institute viewing situation, "receivers," or museum visitors, were not observing the artworks in isolation; instead, they were subject to affective and psychological pressures by their viewing companions, other visitors, and museum staff.

By proposing to hire viewers to perform the labor of looking at two paintings in the Art Institute's collection—paintings that were found in their usual location within the museum—Asher sought to position the experiential processes of spectatorship in relation to Benjamin's scenario in "The Work of Art in the Age of Mechanical Reproduction." Just as Benjamin's modern observers had been repositioned in relation to mechanically reproduced art objects, Asher's audience encountered original works of art that they might already have seen as mechanical reproductions—as prints, illustrations, or in the form of the ubiquitous museum postcard. According to Asher's handout, his strategy in selecting which paintings his contracted viewers would gaze at was to run an experiment on the viewing of two paintings reproduced in varying degrees.[72] Having chosen to set his project in Gallery 226, one of the Art Institute's permanent collection galleries, Asher sought to identify the most and the least reproduced paintings in that gallery. Using sources in the museum's Ryerson Library, he determined that images of Picasso's cubist Kahnweiler portrait had been disseminated extensively in a number of art journals and exhibition catalogues, whereas Duchamp's Cézanne-styled painting had not received broad public exposure.[73] The question Asher posed to all Art Institute visitors was whether one's previous familiarity with reproductions of a given painting determined the way in which one viewed the original painting as well.[74] Would the museum visitor pay more attention to the typical, more familiar Picasso than to the atypical, unfamiliar Duchamp? Did the collective viewing relations within the museum somehow replicate the reproduction and circulation history of individual paintings, in which the stereotypical Picasso basked in the limelight while the obscure Duchamp painting languished in the shadows? Asher's question applied Benjamin's argument about the historically vanished aura to the contemporary social institution of the art museum dedicated precisely to the cultivation of original, "auratic" works of art, asking whether "originality" in the museum was mediated by the constant barrage of reproductions, on the one hand, and by the "intimacy" of the social practice of museum-visiting, on the other.

During the early 1980s, Asher was hardly the only artist or theorist drawing from Benjamin's work. Poststructuralist art historians Benjamin H. D. Buchloh, Douglas Crimp, and Craig Owens made frequent references to Benjamin to theorize both the historical role of photography in relation to art and the allegorical appropriation so prevalent in the practices of the 1970s and early 1980s.[75] Buchloh even used Benjamin as a means of approaching recent works by Asher in a 1982 *Artforum* article, "Allegorical Procedures: Appropriation and Montage in Contemporary Art." This article included three illustrations of Asher's "74th American Exhibition" project.[76]

Benjamin's "aura" was clearly a social category for Buchloh, Crimp, and Owens; it provided an analytical approach for rethinking the politics of representation as well as the production and reception of art. Asher's Benjamin-related work mostly pertained to this latter set of concerns. Having focused on museum reception in his 1980 proposal for the Art Institute and its subsequent realization at the "74th American Exhibition" two years later, Asher moved on to consider the material production of art. Saying that he considered the material production of art does not mean that the artist personally fabricated material art objects. Instead, he once again contracted the labor of arts professionals or students to produce the objects on display.

For his 1981 exhibition "Vocation/Vacation" at the Banff Centre's Walter Phillips Gallery, Asher requested that six fiber artists in residence at the Banff Centre each manually replicate a sixteen-by-sixteen-inch section of the gallery's industrially produced carpet. For the 1986 exhibition "Extension" at Occidental College in Los Angeles, Asher directed undergraduate students to make paper that was indistinguishable from its machine-made counterpart. In both cases, the contracted producers applied either their skills as fiber artists (at Banff) or the craft of papermaking they were learning as college students (at Occidental College). In a twist upon conventional (and Benjaminian) causal relations, in which reproductions mimic "originals," Asher instructed his contracted producers to invert the qualities of original and reproduction, so that handmade replications explicitly imitated machine-made originals. Both the rug-hooking and paper-making processes aimed at a functional mimicry of a mechanically reproduced product (carpet or paper) that assigned use value to the original, as the handmade products were ultimately subjected to the same wear their industrial counterparts habitually encountered. For "Vocation / Vacation," the six handmade carpet squares were installed on the gallery floor after a corresponding ninety-six-by-sixteen-inch section of the industrial original had been removed (figure 2.9). The displaced segment of the industrial carpet was hung on the wall. On the right, it was accompanied by six matted and framed color photographs of the handmade carpet squares, placed above those same carpet squares on the floor. To the left of the swatch of the industrially made carpet, the viewer found a similarly matted and framed photograph of that industrial carpet piece (figure 2.10). Each photograph included the name of its producer, either the industrial carpet manufacturing company or one of the six fiber artists. In an analogous manner, Asher used the paper produced by Occidental College students for printing the exhibition catalogue. In fact, the printing of the catalogue was accomplished by running the meticulously crafted paper through a photocopy machine rather than a professional press, showing that the handmade paper produced by the students differed very little from commercial products.[77]

Asher's installations of carpet at the Banff Centre and paper at Occidental College further emphasized the human labor involved in material production. The Banff installation featured three text panels with extracts from Benjamin's essays "The Work of Art in the Age of Mechanical Reproduction" (1936) and "Doctrine of the Similar" (1933). The text display was flanked on both sides by audio speakers running a sound track with a male and a female narrator alternately reading passages from the same Benjamin essays (figure 2.11). Asher punctuated the recitation of Benjamin's essays with excerpts of rug-hooking instructions taken from a recent rug-making manual.[78] At Occidental College, Asher's installation highlighted student labor by displaying a selection of documentary photographs of the students at work, accompanied by a glass vitrine that contained papermaking materials and samples of paper from various stages of the process (figure 2.12).[79] The Occidental College work further connected the historically specific relation of production and reproduction with the institutionally specific relation of teaching and learning, when the pedagogical discourse of learning a craft and then deploying the results of that knowledge was superimposed upon the historical relation between handmade ("original") and mechanical ("replicated") modes of production. Here, in place of the contemporary fetishization of the handmade object that accounts for the place of papermaking within the art school curriculum, Asher revived the historic goal of papermaking: its *use value* as a ground for printed—reproduced—material.[80] Finally, by using craft as

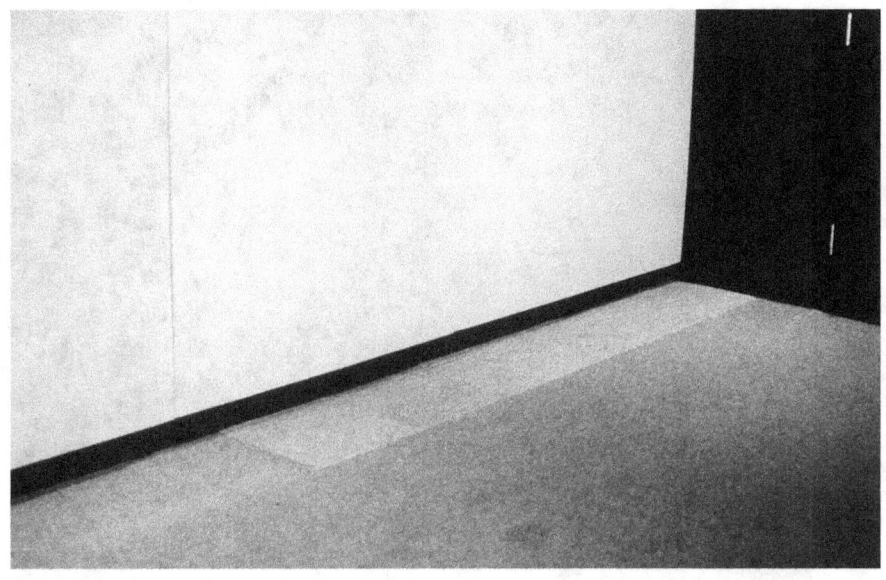

2.9 "Vocation / Vacation," Walter Phillips Gallery, Banff Centre School of Fine Arts, Banff, Alberta, 1981. Handmade carpet squares, made by artists in residence in the fiber art department, installed on the floor of the gallery. (Photograph by Brian L. MacNevin; courtesy the artist.)

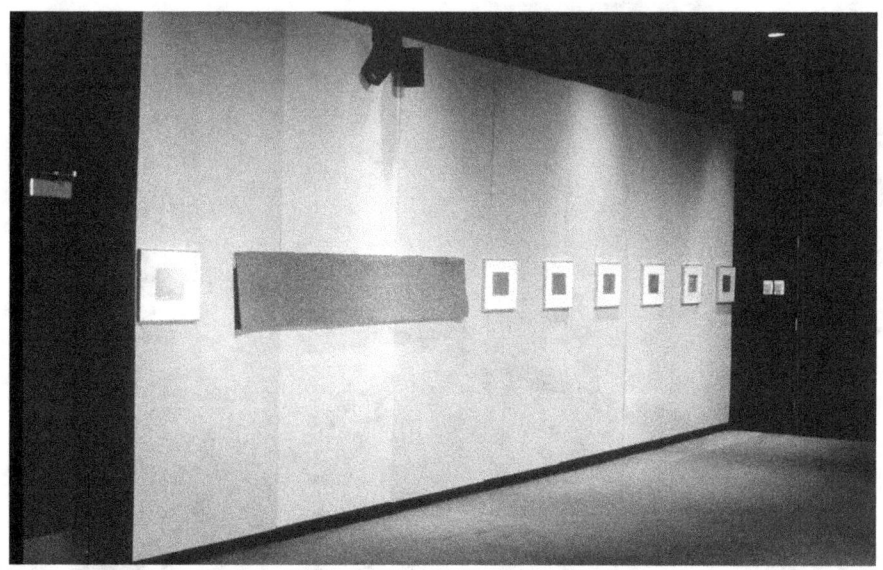

2.10 "Vocation/Vacation," Walter Phillips Gallery, Banff Centre School of Fine Arts, Banff, 1981. From left to right: photograph of the industrial carpet from the floor of the gallery, a section of the same industrial carpet, and photographs of handmade carpet squares installed on the wall. (Photograph by Brian L. MacNevin; courtesy the artist.)

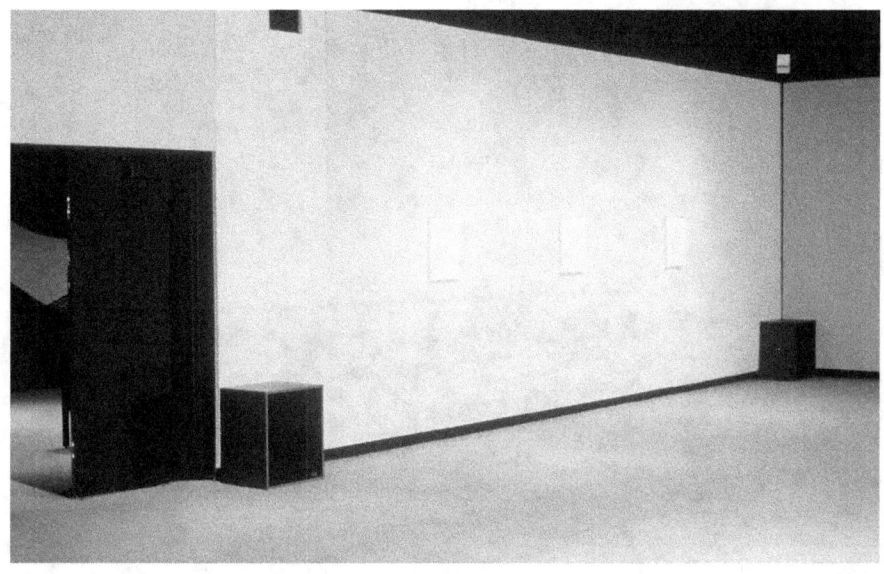

2.11 "Vocation/ Vacation," Walter Phillips Gallery, Banff Centre School of Fine Arts,
       Banff, 1981. Text panels and audio speakers, installed opposite the display of carpet
       and photographs. (Photograph by Brian L. MacNevin; courtesy the artist.)

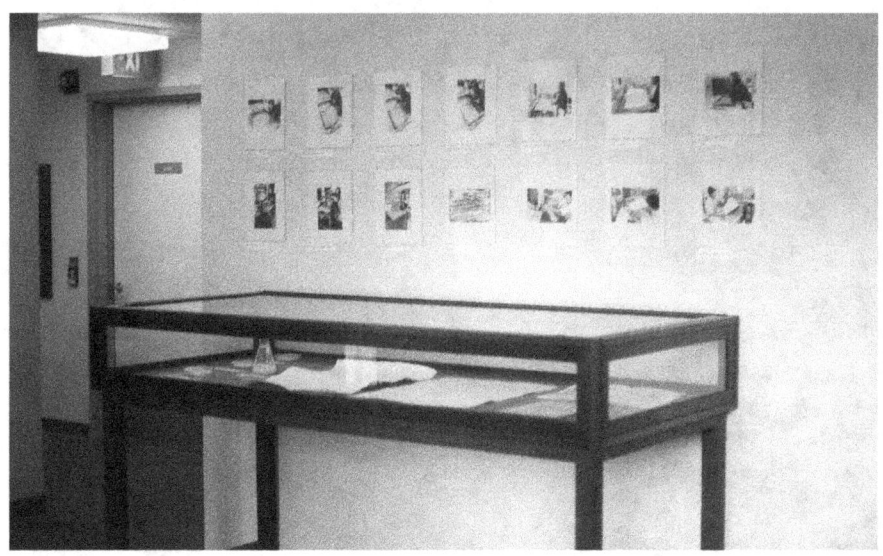

2.12   "Extension," Occidental College, Los Angeles, 1986. Materials in the vitrine and
       adjacent wall photos document how the handmade paper was produced for the
       exhibition catalogue. (Photograph courtesy the artist.)

an imitative medium, Asher's Banff Centre and Occidental College projects commented upon the early-1980s glorification of "original," expressionistic painting. Where Julian Schnabel had used broken, commercially produced crockery in his paintings to accentuate the artist's unique focalizing touch, Asher commissioned his students and artisans to fabricate individualized objects that not only replicated ordinary carpet and paper, but called into question the significance of the singular quality of artistic labor as well.

Asher's installations at the Banff Centre and Occidental College juxtaposed the socially and historically specific discourses of craft, originality, and individual authorship with the experiential practice of viewing—and mode of subjectivity—that Benjamin associated with the historical dominance of mechanical reproduction. The Banff viewers were addressed as potential producers, specifically rug-hookers, when the installation's sound component instructed them to "unwind a good length of yarn from the ball and let this lie freely on the top of your work." This direct mode of address alternated with extracts from Benjamin's text on the cultural effects of reproduction, asking viewers, for example, to consider "what . . . a human being actually gain[s] by this training in mimetic attitudes." In this fashion, Asher allegorically linked the mimicry implicit in the reproduction of the carpet squares to the social conditioning of producers and receivers alike. The principle of imitation that informed the material production of the carpet squares was comparable to the socially informed mimicry that human subjects performed—and reproduced—in their approach to viewing art.

The questions regarding the social and experiential dimension of spectatorship that Asher posed to the Art Institute's A. James Speyer in his 1980 letter lingered in the 1981 "Vocation/Vacation" and the 1986 "Extension" projects. Both exhibitions raised questions about whether an audience can truly arrive any closer to an original, or unmediated, experience of an artwork while viewing these authentic, handmade products of human labor. Did Asher's installations position the viewer as a privileged, direct recipient whose experience was affected by the presence of the original—the handmade carpet pieces or handpressed paper? If Benjamin's "aura" was not (following Crimp's distinction) "an ontological category . . . but rather a historical one,"[81] then any mode of viewing, even when directed toward an original, handmade object, was now irrevocably mediated by the extensive history of reproductive manufacturing technologies.

Through his 1980s projects at the Banff Centre, the Art Institute of Chicago, and Occidental College, Asher indicated that the reproduction of spectatorship in a museum or gallery remains a social practice that is typically mediated by institutional codes of knowledge, whether the objects of viewing are original or reproduced. In his letter to Speyer, he noted that "the subjects around a work of art . . . might inadvertently empty the work of its authenticity" and maintained that historical and technological mediation were always attended by social mediation.[82] The labor of reception by contracted museum viewers in the "74th American Exhibition" and the replicating labor by the artists in "Vocation/Vacation" and by the students in "Extension" were both fundamentally social practices. In each work, contracted labor by hired participants contributed to the production and reproduction of materials that provided concrete support for conventional art and exhibition projects—whether that was the painting on the wall, the carpet on the floor, or the paper on which the exhibition catalogue was printed. The process of this labor along with its results were subsequently presented to museum or gallery viewers, indeed making "the *reception* of Benjamin's text rather than the *text* . . . one of the focal points of Asher's investigation," as Buchloh would argue in his "Vocation/Vacation" catalogue essay.[83]

Nonetheless, these "didactic and ironic aspects" of demonstrating the material production of art—terms that Charlotte Townsend-Gault ascribed to Asher's Banff Centre installation—did not cancel out or contradict the affective experiential potential of his work. On the contrary, Townsend-Gault maintained that Asher's arguably "instructional" agenda "cannot obliterate a source of strong satisfaction [derived from viewing the work] . . . that cannot be accounted for entirely in terms of the theory it embodies." [84] The experiential work of reception that Townsend-Gault associated with the Banff Centre installation exceeded a mere conceptual decoding of the relations of production, recalling the affective economy of Asher's individuated, experiential modes of labor in his earlier Claire Copley and Morgan Thomas installations. Indeed, the close connection between an exhibition's material production and the intimately experiential affective surplus of its viewing practices would return to the center of Asher's practice when he resumed his participatory work in 2000.

Concern for the Other: Social Relations in the Twenty-First-Century Museum ————

Alongside his participatory projects of the 1970s and 1980s, Asher's oeuvre included numerous projects that examined entire institutional structures and systems of knowledge. In these projects, a viewer's attention was directed not so much toward accentuated locations of subjectivity as toward the broader discursive apparatus. Yet when Asher returned to participatory work in the 2000 Los Angeles County Museum of Art (LACMA) exhibition "Made in California: NOW," his entry point still involved the themes that had been emblematic of his 1970s and 1980s participatory approach—the social relations of the production and reception of art—but now the works set out to use the nexus of social relations as a basis to critique the context of representational politics within the contemporary art museum.

On a curatorial and institutional level, "Made in California: NOW" fulfilled multiple functions in LACMA's exhibition program. On the one hand, it was organized to complement the museum's three-part series, "Made in California: Art, Image, and Identity, 1900–2000"—a large-scale survey of Californian visual arts and culture during the twentieth century. More importantly, however, the "NOW" exhibition served the needs of LACMA's educational mission through the museum's experimental LACMALab division. According to the museum, LACMALab was founded in order to "test . . . innovative ways for visitors to access, interact with, and respond to art."[85] As LACMALab's inaugural exhibition, "Made in California: NOW" was explicitly geared toward attracting "children with their families"[86] to the exhibition, a task that LACMALab's director Robert L. Sain tackled by commissioning "participatory environments" from eleven contemporary Californian artists.[87] Including works from artists such as Allan Kaprow and Eleanor Antin—in addition to Michael Asher—these "environments" spilled over from the main exhibition hub in the Boone Children's Gallery to other parts of the museum, featuring works that harnessed site-specific, often participatory strategies to activate their target audience: young people.[88]

This patently educational use of participatory, site-specific art was consistent with the ways in which art museums have broadened their mandates from their modernist charge of providing sites for contemplative artistic practice to creating a nexus for generating educational activity. Asher's contribution to "Made in California: NOW" was certainly faithful to these institutional imperatives. Yet, rather than echoing the museum's desire to heighten the educational impact of a museum visit by addressing the exhibition's target audience of children from the authorial vantage point of curator-producer, Asher chose to redraw the intersubjective boundary between the production and reception of a museum exhibition by arranging for a group of Los Angeles teenagers to take over the production of the work. "I had a particular interest," the artist later explained, "in how the students became motivated to teach themselves."[89] To these ends, he invited a group of students from nearby Fairfax Senior High School, a culturally and ethnically diverse public school with a magnet program in visual arts, to reinstall one of LACMA's permanent collection galleries.

The contract Asher negotiated between himself, the museum, and the participating students included a list of specific rules. First, LACMA staff members were directed not to interfere with the students' efforts, apart from apprising them of professional procedures regarding safety, conservation, and budgeting. These rules were instituted, Asher said, to ensure that reinstallation "results could not simply be written off as unknowing."[90] The students' operational autonomy at the museum was to be safeguarded by an outside facilitator, who was assigned to coordinate the reinstallation team and moderate meetings with LACMA's senior staff and exhibitions committee.[91] Beyond this broad organizational structure, the students were given a few other conditions: they were to use all the works of painting and sculpture that were already on display in the gallery; they were not to endanger the security of either the artworks or the audience in their installation; and, finally, they were not to exceed their allocated budget of five thousand dollars, the LACMA standard for reinstalling a gallery in the permanent collection.[92]

The first group of eleventh-graders, who reinstalled a display of nineteenth-century European art in LACMA's Leona Palmer Gallery in the fall of 2000, was followed two years later by a second group of Fairfax High School students, who reorganized LACMA's Modern and Contemporary Council Gallery in 2002. This time, the museum engaged Asher and the students in an individual exhibition based on the first group's success. Both reinstallations departed conceptually and visually from modernist art historical and museological conventions, in which individual paintings and sculptures are typically given visual autonomy within a "white cube," or an ostensibly neutral aesthetic environment. The students did not take for granted that the gallery walls had to be white; they felt free to paint or light them in other colors. Gallery lighting in the reinstallations thus did not simply exist to provide ease of contemplation; instead, the lighting heightened affective viewing experiences. The students did not necessarily see the most important painting in the gallery as the one attributed to a highly canonized painter. For example, the first group chose to relegate Eugène Delacroix's *Henry IV Conferring the Regency upon Marie de Medici (after Rubens)* (before 1835) to a stairwell, while assigning prominence in display to a painting with a particular subject matter. Thus, they chose to place Sir Edwin Henry Landseer's *A Group of Animals* (ca. 1851), a generously sized painting depicting donkeys, cows, a dog, and a pony, on the most conspicuous wall in the gallery. Finally, paintings were not always exhibited against a wall or around the perimeter of the gallery; the second group of students brought them forward as three-dimensional elements in space (figure 2.13).

These departures from established museological conventions were not accidental; they could be traced to Asher's premise that the students be treated on equal footing with museum professionals. Such functional egalitarianism recalls Rancière's notion that equality is a precondition for practice, an operational paradigm that is already in the process of implementation, instead of being a principle that is projected to the future as an end result to be achieved through authoritative political or educational projects.[93] By mandating that the "kids" have independent authority from the outset, Asher did not assume the students' inequality in the museum hierarchy and thus did not seek to rectify any inequality by "educating" the students to make choices informed by the "correct" professional models, and then judging the students according to how well they had absorbed the "proper" museological methods and values.[94] Assigning the students operational equality from the beginning meant that the students were not treated as innocent outsiders whose reinstallation of the LACMA permanent collection galleries could have been bracketed as a "kids say the darndest things" comic (but ultimately trivial) digression from serious or professional museum practice.

Asher's insistence on the students' equality within his LACMA project thus ensured that the participating teenagers were treated as professionals rather than patronized as subordinate learners. Moreover, his persistent emphasis on practices of labor aligned his approach with Rancière's tenet that equality is "a condition that only functions when it is put into action."[95] The equality of the students at LACMA, accordingly, was practiced as labor rather than declared as a statement. In this regard, Asher's approach to involving young people in the museum departed radically from most museum education programs, which make it their business to present existing museum material in a form easily digestible by children and young adults. Not only did the operational equality that he secured for the high school students entrust them with the role of producers—as opposed to that of hapless recipients of the museum's educational mandate—but it also

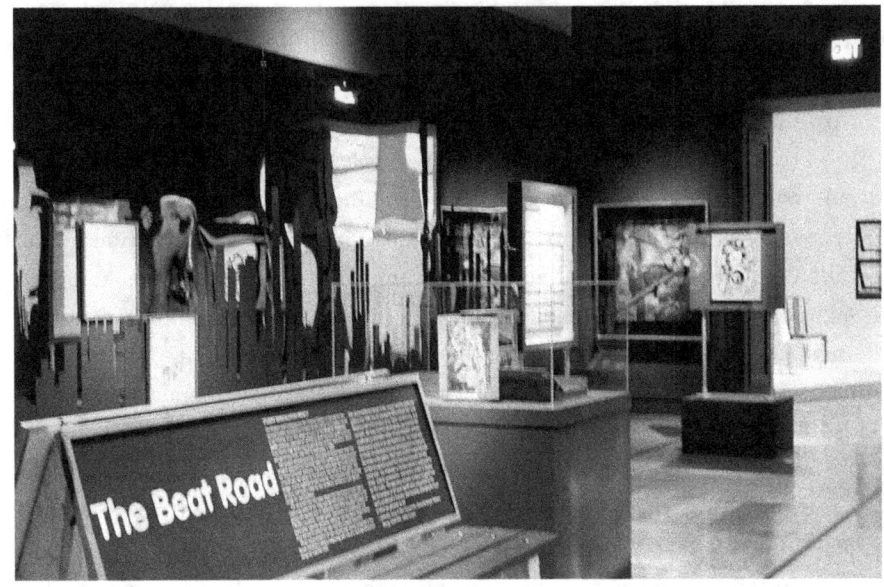

2.13   Los Angeles County Museum of Art, 2002. Second rotation of the reinstallation of the
permanent collection in the Modern and Contemporary Art Council Gallery by
students from Fairfax High School. Viewing southwest. Two bus benches: the back of
the bench facing the wall contains exhibition credits; the bench facing the camera has
a statement by students on the left and Asher's project description on the right.
(Photograph courtesy the artist.)

meant that the student reinstallations were presented as authored and situated viewpoints within the museum. The first group of students, for example, labeled paintings and sculptures with first-person, signed narratives that explained the student writer's individual interest in a particular work. Further, the students' acknowledgment of the situatedness of their own enterprise was by no means apologetic, nor did it seek to diminish the authority of their installation.

That the LACMA students—so unlike Asher's 1977 LAICA contractees—were comfortable with their authority within an artistically designated museum site became evident in the way in which they related to museum visitors. The second student group addressed their viewers directly in their visually distinctive reinstallation, titled "The Beat Road." In this reinstallation, the team of students transformed LACMA's Modern and Contemporary Council Gallery into a dimly lit urban environment bordered by reflective, indigo-tinted walls and shadowed by a cityscape in silhouette (figure 2.14). The gallery space was then punctuated by bus benches (acquired from city storage), a purchased replica of a street light, and pedestals designed by students and constructed out of metal pipes by museum staff (figure 2.15). The pedestals were used to support works of modernist painting and sculpture by artists ranging from Marcel Duchamp and Piet Mondrian to Isamu Noguchi and Lucas Samaras. Background music by John Coltrane, among others, connected the early-twentieth-century era of experimentation in art with similar developments in music, supporting the students' determination to situate the artwork within the social and historical context of urban culture and the jazz era. The Plexiglas-mirrored wall panels on the two facing long walls of the gallery reflected artworks and museum visitors in a distorted manner, twisting the images and bending the museum's physical parameters. A hermetically sealed white cube this was not.

In their curatorial statement, affixed to the back support of a relocated bus bench, the participating students identified themselves by name and extended a direct invitation for spectators to experience their installation: "We hope that our efforts please you and that the unorthodox presentation of the art and utilization of three-dimensional space in no way frightens you."[96] This unconditional appeal for viewers to be "pleased" and not "frightened" is a powerful model of anticipating the projected museum visitors' response to a museum experience. The fact that the students' exhibition statement addressed the well-being of the visitors and the quality of their experience points to the students' relational concern for their audience. The notion that a museum exhibition might either

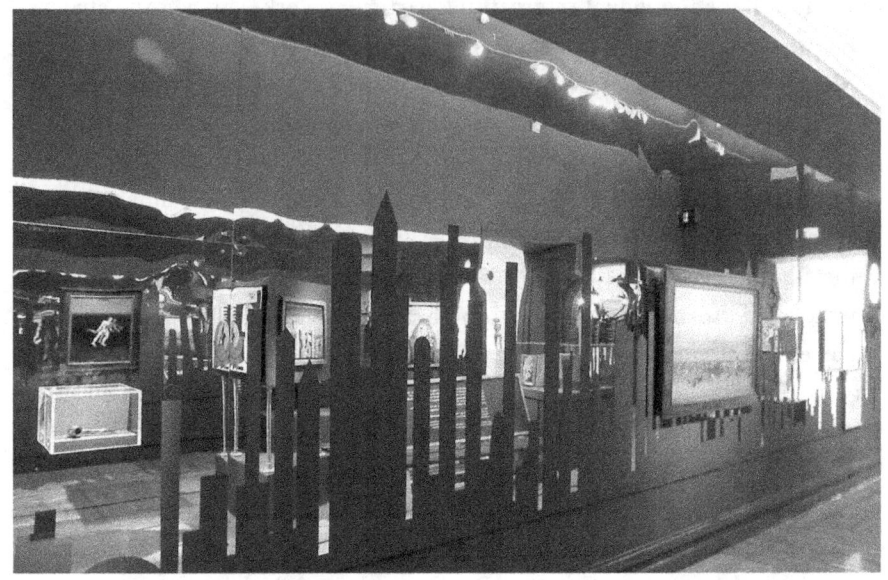

2.14   Los Angeles County Museum of Art, Los Angeles, 2002. Second rotation of student
reinstallation. Viewing southwest. Detail of wall designed by students with cityscape
on mirrored Plexiglas. (Photograph courtesy the artist.)

2.15   Los Angeles County Museum of Art, Los Angeles, 2002. Second rotation of student
reinstallation. Viewing west. Lamppost with wall label information adapted from
signage system used at bus stops in Los Angeles. (Photograph courtesy the artist.)

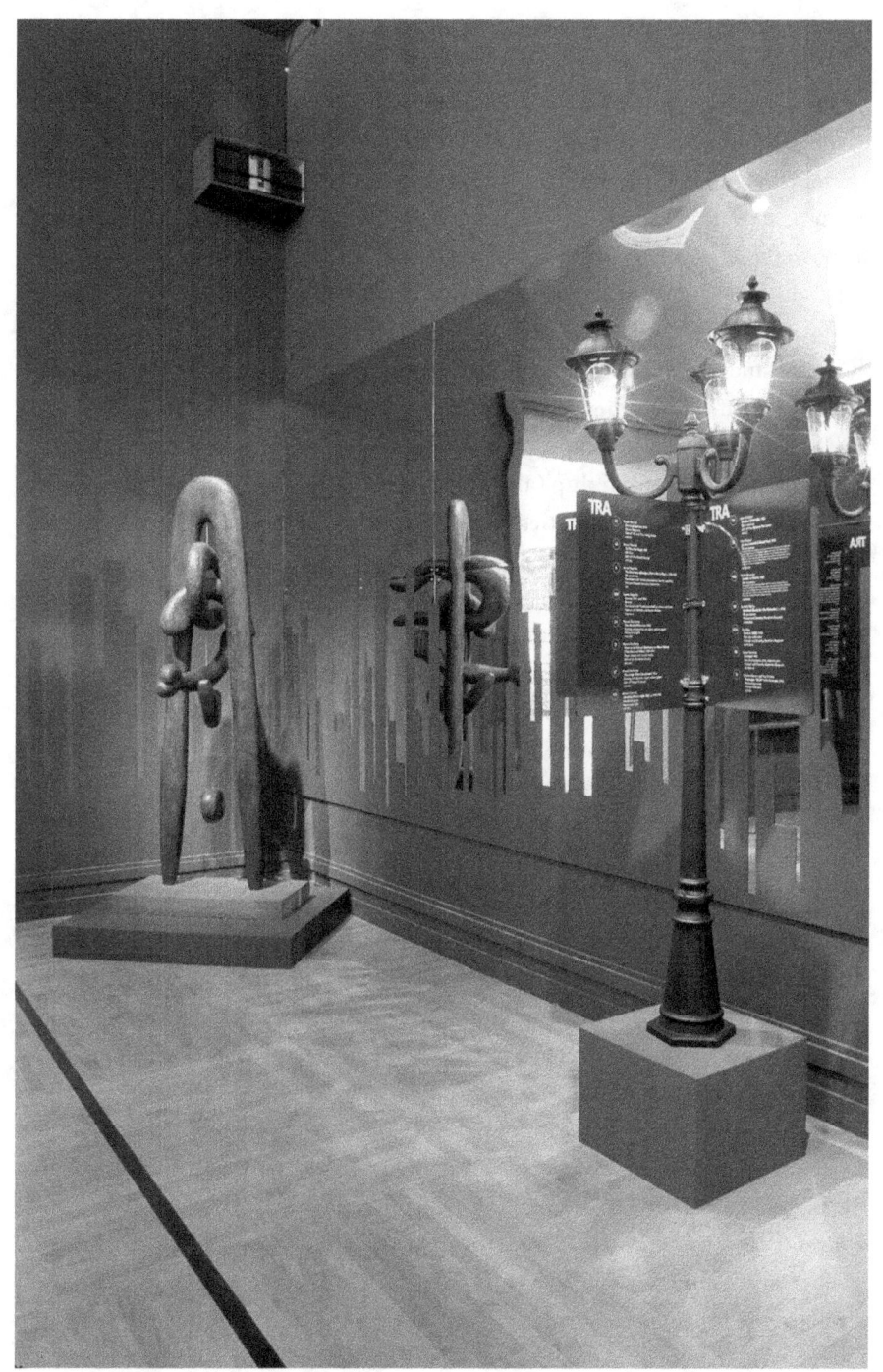

please or frighten a visitor is strikingly atypical in its interest in the emotional aspects of museum experience. A more common curatorial exhibition statement might focus on the artwork's formal or historical significance, the theme of the exhibition—anything but concern for the visitor's affective response. The students' statement also departed from the legal register of warning signs, so often posted in museums, about explicit or disturbing content, which tend to be posted on the advice of the museum's legal counsel (out of concern for scandal and litigation) in order to conditionally abdicate the institution's authorial responsibility. Rather than distance themselves from a projected liability, however, the students espoused authorial responsibility for the effects their installation produced. They believed that what they produced—the situation of viewing art in a museum—was an experiential event within the affective economy of the museum, and that authorship (and responsibility) for their choices was located in their own situation aesthetics rather than generic institutional conventions. The statement hinged upon the experiential labor of social relations that the students took upon themselves, as producers, as much as they assigned that affective labor to their recipients, the museum visitors.

As in Asher's earlier participatory projects, the structural limits the artist had set in place at LACMA allowed the students a considerable amount of freedom. This participatory independence of conduct was nevertheless coupled with an imperative to take responsibility for one's behavior within the work. Asher's contract with LACMA and the Fairfax High School students allowed the participating students to reckon with their responsibilities at LACMA in an egalitarian manner that bypassed museum hierarchies and discarded museological, pedagogical assumptions about appropriate outcomes. Robert Sain, LACMALab's director during "Made in California: NOW," attested to the magnitude of Asher's authoritative shift within the museum when he stated that "[f]or anyone outside the culture of [LACMA], it is hard to appreciate how alternative or radical it was, having an infiltration of the system through kids."[97]

Just as he had bestowed on Copley the task of independently responding to visitors in her gallery for the duration of his piece, Asher at LACMA entrusted the high school students with making decisions about how to reinstall the gallery and address museum visitors in their "Beat Road" experience. The emphasis on such relational modes of labor—an emphasis facilitated by Asher's egalitarian structure—connected the students' reinstallation with Asher's overall participatory oeuvre, in which the labor of establishing and maintaining social relations complements a more tangibly material labor process of production, reproduction, and reception. Unlike the 1977 LAICA participants, whose labor within the gallery was ultimately directed at reinforcing existing social boundaries between gallery insiders and outsiders, the participatory labor of the 2000 and 2002 high school students at LACMA sought to open the museum for affective relational experiences while undoing the habitual social and psychological constraints that mark the hierarchical social relations of the art museum. By leveling the epistemological playing field in an adjuration for autodidacticism that insists *anyone* can play a more nuanced viewing game, Asher again highlighted the opaque edge between viewing art and administering the way art is viewed. Rather than endorse the museum's existing educational mission, he underscored the constraints placed on viewers by the museum's self-ascribed explicatory function. Through emancipating the students' labor, by letting them dictate the ground rules, Asher turned the tables to examine the very linchpin of institutional praxis—the act of directing and explaining the viewer's gaze.

Conclusion: Experiential Subjects within Contractual Limits

In the evolution from a liberatory Fluxus style of viewer empowerment to works that tackle complex issues of phenomenological presence and social control, the concept of participation in recent art history has come to mean the process by which an artist activates spectators positioned as passive into taking up concrete involvement in a given installation or event. The 1970s participatory art of Acconci, Bruce Nauman, Dan Graham, and Hans Haacke, for example, engaged the spectator through a series of visually commanding and sometimes exploitative artist-issued directives, subjecting the viewer to physically and psychologically restrictive environments (in the case of Acconci, Nauman, and Graham)—or pieces that summoned the viewer to situate themselves within collective social relations (Haacke).[98] When one considers these often didactic and in some cases blatantly aggressive forms of viewer engagement, it is no wonder that Asher sometimes hesitated to designate his projects as "participatory." One specific instance of this hesitation can be found in his comments about his 1977 contribution for the exhibition "Los Angeles in the Seventies" at the Fort Worth Art Museum. In this work, Asher had asked employees of three adjoining museums—

the Fort Worth Art Museum, Kimbell Art Museum, and the Amon Carter Museum of Western Art—to share a common parking lot for one week. The artist speculated that closer contact generated by random staff encounters in the shared parking lot would generate more varied social interaction.[99] Asher's request for staff involvement in this project was typically unobtrusive, since the employees were not directed to use a specific parking slot, arrive at a mandated time, or interact with one another on any prescribed basis. His parking lot project once again built upon the elements that characterize the artist's overall approach to the emancipatory effect of participation: museum employees were asked to perform an aspect of their daily labor within the artist's broad guidelines, which left ample room for individual interpretation regarding their activity.

Because Asher's contracted participants at Fort Worth were not explicitly separated from their institutional surroundings or drawn into patently extraordinary behavior, questions were raised about whether these museum staff members had actually "participated" in the typical sense of the word. The Fort Worth project thus constitutes a limit case within Asher's participatory trajectory. Strictly speaking, parking one's vehicle is an activity that takes place outside working hours, and thus falls on the margins of professional conduct. It may even be argued that a museum staff member's act of parking has only limited value in exploring the institutional dynamics of a given set of museums. In many ways, parking is a habitual act, often idiosyncratic (but by no means inconsequential), and is informed by one's personal preferences regarding safety, shade, ease of access—even certain aesthetic considerations such as having a good view. Moreover, whereas the private quality of parking one's car imbues the act with a distinct intimacy, in many professional spheres the division of parking spaces serves to connote a corresponding schema of hierarchy, with the most desirable slots in close proximity to main entrances, architectural promenades, and other significant structural features. At the very least, Asher's request for museum staff members to modify their parking patterns sought to extend the art institution's reach into semiprivate aspects of staffers' lives (or to underscore the collective framing that informs the social act of parking, greeting one's workmates, noting the make and model of cars driven by one's colleagues, and so on). In other words, his parking lot project reframed the affective economy of the space in which art professionals transition to and from their private and professional worlds, and gave this transitional territory heightened ideological significance.

Had he considered his Fort Worth project "participatory," Asher concluded, it "would have meant that [the museum workers'] daily work activities be transformed into a 'performance' or become part of an exhibition spectacle."[100] Although arguably the mere presence of the artist's request already drew these "daily work activities" into a publicly mapped framework, Asher's concern is understandable when read against his broader regard for the significance of professional labor.[101] While "performances" or "spectacles" were exactly what many of his contemporaries in the 1970s sought to achieve with their participatory work, Asher's participatory agenda throughout his career has been based on preserving the professionally appropriate context of the "daily work activities" he requests from his contracted participants.

Unlike most artists whose work elicits participation by activating general museum or gallery audiences, Asher's participatory projects, including the Fort Worth piece, rely on contracting the labor of specific arts professionals. In Asher's oeuvre, participation does not hinge on involving or implicating museum or gallery visitors in order to underscore a premeditated meaning or prearranged set of artistic or political objectives, and thus giving priority to the artist's cognitive intentions. Instead, the specificity of roles and activities in his participatory projects aligns the participant's preexisting institutional role with the material aspects of the artist's situations. This focalizing emphasis on professional modes of labor distinguishes Asher's mode of participation from the phenomenological or rationalized agenda of 1960s and 1970s minimalist and conceptual installations. Being contracted to perform one's familiar "daily work activities" in front of museum or gallery visitors significantly differs from minimalist or conceptual strategies of exposing viewers to an artist's schema during the course of a museum or gallery visit. Although Sol LeWitt's participatory wall drawings also relied on a type of contracted labor, his project differed from Asher's activities in that the drawings were completed behind the scenes before the exhibition, rather than in full view of museum visitors.[102] The participatory activities that Asher calls for, on the other hand, remain within the already-sensible elements of one's everyday professional realm. These modes of participatory labor are not absolutely unrestrained; nor would it be appropriate to describe them as volunteer labor because the participants are compensated for their involvement in Asher's work through money, the gaining of professional prestige, or an increment of educational credit.[103] Instead of engaging in a collective, anonymous experience in the manner of museum or gallery visitors, Asher's participants contribute their names, demeanor, and professional reputations to the artist's work when they agree to be involved. Such explicit professional commitment means that all labor within his work remains individuated for the participants. Claire Copley was not an anonymous actor nor just anybody impersonating a generic gallerist; she was the owner of the gallery in which Asher's work took place, and had a personal and professional stake in the exhibition's success.

Asher's participatory activities are further individuated by the artist's resistance to providing an overabundance of instructions to participants. His measured reserve regarding authorial didacticism leaves any ensuing participatory activity experientially open to a number of analytical and affective responses. Accordingly, gallerists, museum workers, and students have imparted their roles with a sense of individuation by making specific selections regarding their conduct within Asher's situations—as well as by interpreting their engagement in the process and how this engagement affected them. Participation in his work thereby provides an opening for contracted individuals to dissociate themselves from their everyday collective social relations in order to confront the question of how their own identity is formed in relation to the social and ideological forces within the art institution.

This individuation of participatory experiences is further supported by Asher's practice of providing all participants with a professionally egalitarian standing within the gallery or museum. The administrative equality that he negotiated for the students involved in the LACMA reinstallation project, in particular, produced an experiential transformation that recalls Rancière's "political event." Rather than casting light upon an existing state of (ossified) institutional order, political events shift the boundaries of visibility in a manner that enables individual subjects to perceive new possibilities in the social world, according to Rancière. Kristin Ross explains that "[n]othing 'real' seems to happen" within Rancière's political event,

and yet the new language, the new configuration, permits us to see a real event in place of the mere atmospheric swamp of earlier descriptions. Gone is the misery that is supposed to awaken our political outrage but which instead merely underlines what was already there, our sense of unchanging conditions and a naturalized identity of the victim—that whole massive appearance of permanence that restricts not only the emergence of individual subjectivities and political energies but even the mobility of ideas and the spontaneity and provocation of artistic invention.[104]

By unraveling the affective and analytical certainties of social relations within art institutions rather than thrusting one's attention upon the already well-traveled terrain of power relations, Asher's participatory works produce nuanced political events. Instead of reinforcing the "appearance of permanence" within normal institutional practices, his arrangements redistribute the boundary between what is visible or invisible, thinkable or unthinkable within the art institution—such as the previously unthinkable model of high school students independently reinstalling the collection of a venerated museum, and perhaps even having better luck at it. The freedom of conduct that is inscribed within Asher's contracted labor of production and reception requires participating subjects to claim responsibility for their behavior and actions within the work. The resulting social relations between and among Asher's viewers and participants attest to the kind of "individual subjectivities and political energies" that Ross ascribes to Rancière's scenario. There was a change that took place in Copley's relation to both her social practice and her gallery visitors, just as visitors to the student reinstallation at LACMA were addressed with an unprecedented concern for the emotional quality of their viewing experience.

In Asher's work, transformative effects extend from contracted participants to regular museum or gallery visitors. Although he does not visibly strive to morph ordinary viewers into participants toiling for a prearranged goal, spectatorship within his participatory works is never passive.[105] In fact, his participatory situations continue to foreground the experiential labor of spectatorship that was already evident in his earlier sensory installations, such as the sound-absorbing room in the 1969 exhibition at the La Jolla Museum of Art. At the Anna Leonowens Gallery, the centrality of the viewer was communicated by Asher's decision to leave the space empty and largely unmodified, rather than embellish or dynamically call attention to his artistic gesture. Specifically, he argued that "[t]he absence of objects . . . shifted the viewers' attention to their own preconceptions of what an exhibition should look like."[106] Through both sensory and cognitive modes of perception, his viewers become engaged in an experiential, individuated process of producing meaning, without the tautological set-up of explicit participatory directives or activation.

Asher's refusal to provide a set of detailed instructions for his participants, combined with his physical absence from the exhibition site, makes it tempting to downplay the influence of the artist's authorial agency in these participatory works. Yet, whether they take place within materially empty galleries (Claire Copley and Anna Leonowens) or socially occupied spaces (LAICA, the "74th American Exhibition," and LACMA), these sophisticated interstices would not be complete—or possible—without the artist. Responses by Copley and by Asher's LAICA participants vouch that his physical absence from the scene only accentuated his structural presence in the situation. At both the Claire Copley Gallery and LAICA, participants responded (and perhaps addressed their conduct) to the artist as much as to the gallery visitors, with whom they interacted on a more visible basis. That Asher understood the artist's influence within his own situation aesthetics became clear in a set of projects, completed alongside his participatory trajectory of the 1970s and 1980s, in which he framed the artist within contractual structures at least as binding as those his participants entered into.

3

In the Name of the Artist

In January 1971, Robert Morris published an article in *Artforum* describing his encounters with work by three young artists active in the field of "existence art."[1] Entitled "The Art of Existence—Three Extra-Visual Artists: Works in Process," the article described works by Marvin Blaine, Jason Taub, and Robert Dayton, fictional figures whose practice Morris contextualized through recourse to veterans of the "existence" scene.[2] These seasoned artists included "[s]everal artists on the West Coast, such as Michael Asher, Larry Bell, Robert Irwin, and recently, Bruce Nauman."[3] In his overview of this oeuvre, Morris described the work of Asher, Bell, Irwin, and Nauman as "presenting situations that elicit strong experiences of 'being' rather than the implied actions of the 'having done' common to much 'thing' art now available."[4] Here, Morris refers to a shift from object-based art that reflects the process of its making (and implicitly the subjectivity of its author) to art that was geared toward facilitating subjective experience. The California artists he mentions at the outset of "The Art of Existence" served to exemplify this shift in artistic sensibility.

Asher's established status within Morris's "existence art" movement, however, is complicated by the fact that Asher had been exhibiting outside California for less than two years when Morris's article was published.[5] Furthermore, what does the fact that Morris's three younger artists were fictional entities convey about the "real" artists he mentioned, whose work was illustrated along with diagrams and constructions by "Blaine," "Taub," and "Dayton"? Morris quotes Taub, for example, as "admir[ing] Asher's work but find[ing] it too 'estheticized, like all California art.'"[6] Through this description, Morris evoked Asher as a recognizable artist who is emblematic of a stylistic and geographically recognizable brand of art.[7] Citing the names of Asher, Irwin, and Nauman served to bolster the credibility of Morris's parody of the prioritization of the artist's private experience.

In art criticism and history, names of artists stand in for historical and geographical moments, trends, and ideologies. For Morris, the name "Asher" was a recognizable sign in the same classificatory fashion in which names like "Daniel Buren" and "Hans Haacke" are fixed under the banner of "institutional critique." Within such nominal moves, the names of these artists ostensibly serve to explain general tendencies or trends in art, condensing and reconciling particular histories under common denominators.[8] We extrapolate from the specific to the general, and vice versa, associating names with assumptions and knowledge learnt in other, related contexts.[9]

The focus on Asher's name could seem out of place in the context of his practice, which is commonly identified with making institutions visible at the expense of centering upon the figure of the artist. Indeed, Asher is never physically or photographically present in his work. Many of his installations do not include any human presence or image apart from the work's beholder. And when his work does include people, the individuals on display are contracted participants rather than the artist. In this manner, Asher departed from the far more common conceptual lineage of Vito Acconci, Douglas Huebler, and Eleanor Antin, among others, whose work was dependent on the artist's direct participation in performance, film, video, or photographic representation.

But "Asher" has nevertheless featured pivotally in a number of Asher's own projects that have investigated the artist's role in the institutional field of art. The name of the artist as an ideological device was particularly central to Asher from the mid-1970s to the early 1980s. During this period, Asher drew up name-based proposals and completed projects for institutions ranging from the Van Abbemuseum in Eindhoven, the Netherlands, to Los Angeles Contemporary Exhibitions (LACE) and the brand-new Museum of Contemporary Art in Los Angeles (MOCA). These projects were interspersed with the artist's participatory approaches in the Claire Copley exhibition in 1974, the 1977 Copley/Morgan Thomas gallery exchange, "Vocation/Vacation" in 1981, and the "74th American Exhibition" in 1982. They expanded Asher's interest in participatory social relations between individuals in the context of art institutions: viewers, participants, and museum or gallery staff members.

Although these name-based projects are executed under Asher's name, and thus retain a citational reference to this particular artist, they do not reveal much information about the artist's personality or the intricacies of his private life. Instead, his mobilization of the artist has investigated administrative power within institutional situations: the financial, legal, and managerial arrangements that depend on standardized institutional procedures. The figure of the artist in Asher's work becomes a sign, an indexical marker for a distinctive subject position, much like the "Asher" that Morris evoked in his 1971 *Artforum* article to authenticate his parody of "existence art." Ultimately, such works probe the limits of artistic agency by asking what can be done in the name of the artist. Even though Asher flirts with the objectification of the artist by appropriating administrative modes of operation and then subjecting himself to them, he does not ultimately treat the artist as a passive receptacle of institutional signification. Within Asher's situation aesthetics, the signifying and executive power of the artist could well be described as a situation agency that implicates both the institution and the artist in stratified systems of power and knowledge.

The Linguistic Replacement

Asher's first explicit engagement of the figure of the artist took place in his 1975 show at the Otis Art Institute in Los Angeles. The Otis project chronologically followed on the heels of his Claire Copley and Anna Leonowens exhibitions, two participatory projects that Asher completed the previous fall.[10] At Otis, however, Asher focused upon the artist's role within the artwork instead of specifically contracted participants. His preliminary notes for the Otis project questioned whether artists could in fact be "separat[ed]" from their artworks.[11] To investigate the artist-artwork continuum, Asher first proposed to make himself available to gallery visitors, albeit by request rather than by his constant presence in the Otis gallery space.[12] Within this model, the artist would have been freely accessible to visitors without the mediation of artwork.[13]

The work Asher eventually executed at the Otis Art Institute took a decidedly different turn. In advance of the exhibition, he closed the gallery space, making it inaccessible to the public. Then he affixed a statement to the announcement board in the foyer of the gallery immediately to the left of the gallery's double doors (figure 3.1). Made with standard white plastic quick-change letters, Asher's declaration read: "IN THE PRESENT EXHIBITION I AM THE ART." The statement was spelled entirely in capital letters without punctuation, and was placed below a copy of the announcement card Otis had distributed to advertise the event, turning the exhibition into a linguistically intimate embrace of the artist's public role.[14]

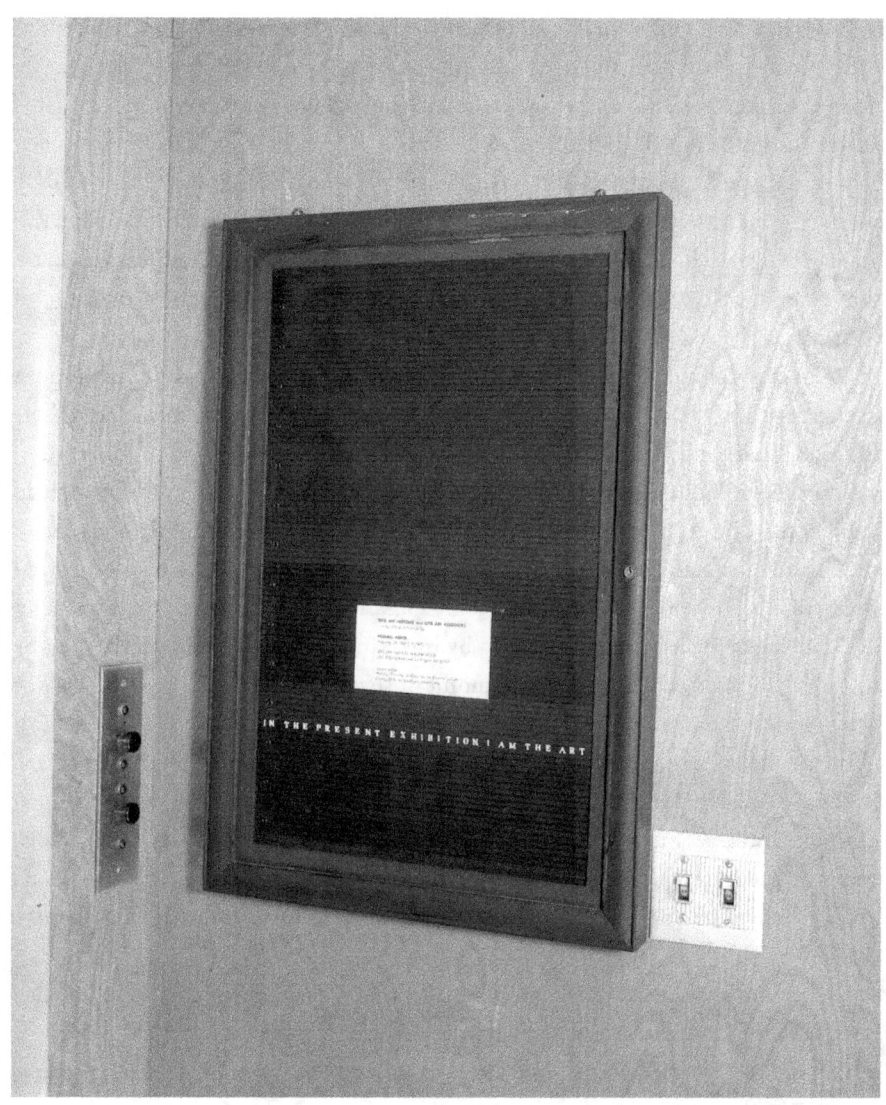

3.1   The gallery of Otis Art Institute, Los Angeles, 1975. The announcement board in the lobby. (Photograph by Frank J. Thomas; courtesy of the Frank J. Thomas Archives.)

Asher thus coded his presence in the artwork at Otis through a series of semiotic and symbolic substitutions. Although he had initially considered individualized personal contact with viewers, in the realized work Asher opted to substitute language for his own physical presence. A similar substitution took place in the message board statement, which normally signified artwork that would be inside the gallery but here indicated that the exhibition would be located in the gallery's foyer. The content of Asher's statement comprised the third displacement, as the "I" in the statement stood in as a replacement for the artwork (and the artist): "I am the art."

As a personal pronoun, "I" is a relational trope. Linguistic philosopher Emile Benveniste points out that "I" and "you" acquire their meaning from their use, in which each "instance of discourse," or the spatiotemporal production in which the subject claims the position of the "I," makes the pronoun (and the subject position represented through it) tangible and concrete.[15] In that sense, the "I" also acts as a referent for the physical body, which may or may not be present to signify for itself. Thus, a subject gains instant and automatic discursive authority for his or her position by invoking the "I." When it is claimed by the speaking subject in the present moment (even when referring to the past or future), such an utterance of the "I" differs from others, drawing a distinction between the speaker and others.[16] Asserting the facticity of a subject's existence in the world, speaking in the first person claims one's right to have a voice, an outlook, and a definitive subject position with discursive authority.[17] Yet it does not produce independently verifiable information, because personal pronouns are, in Benveniste's words, "'empty' signs that are nonreferential with respect to 'reality.'"[18]

In Asher's work at Otis, however, the artist's recourse to the "I" took place within a situation that was clearly marked by institutional as well as discursive authority. As an artist invited to exhibit in the art school's gallery, Asher's statement—"in the present exhibition I am the art"—evoked artistic and individual license. Bolstered by the printed exhibition announcement card, which secured an administrative guarantee for his statement on the message board, he had laid a convincing claim for his right to make such a statement. Thus, he conjoined the individual discursive agency Benveniste ascribes to personal pronouns with the overarching institutional support invested in Asher's work by the gallery at Otis—not merely in its own name, but in the name of the artist. The linguistic signifier "I" was mobilized within an already defined discursive context of the collective cultural characteristics of the artist.

Asher's a priori right to signify in the Otis situation was affected by the artist's choice to put himself—even if through language only—on display. As he subsequently pointed out, the work could be understood to communicate "an objectification of the producer as subject."[19] Suggesting the artist stands in for the object on display, such objectification does not completely hew to the unfettered agency inferred by Benveniste's analysis of personal pronouns, nor does it dovetail with the traditional power invested in the artist's activities. Instead, Asher's "I" at Otis functioned as a linguistic and visual sign that was open to viewer interpretation.

The inherent availability of the pronoun "I" also meant that Asher's claim to it was by no means exclusive. When released into circulation on the Otis message board, the "I" of the statement was placed at the disposal of gallery visitors, who could elect to identify with the subject of the sentence, to put themselves in the position of the artist. Asher acknowledged this possibility of viewer identification in the Otis work, remarking that those visitors "chose their own subjectivity over a confrontation with the artist's statement."[20] On the one hand, his reference to a "confrontation" might pertain to the viewer's reaction to the artist's perceived audacity. On the other hand, the confrontation he had in mind could actually be a comment on the general instability of the pronoun "I," as well as the intersubjective situation that Benveniste might see as "an instance of discourse," in which viewers oscillate between receiving the artist's address (as the subjects reading Asher's statement) and inserting themselves into the work by identifying with the speaker. In this sense, Asher's use of the "I" also mobilized an ambiguous zone between artist and visitor, where a viewer might occupy the position of the artist, thus opening the work for multiple subjects to declare themselves "the art."

In Asher's subsequent projects there was no such ambiguity regarding the identity of the speaking subject. Although he would later observe that "[the Otis] work is the only one to date that I have defined in the medium of language,"[21] he has continued to evoke the artist's presence within the artwork as a linguistic, signifying, and authorial element. In these projects, the artist's proper name is summoned to designate the artist as simultaneous subject and object: as an author operating within the exhibition and as an object on display for the gallery or museum visitor. "Audio by Artists," curated by Ian Murray, was one venue that served as a platform for Asher's investigation of the instrumental value of the artist's name. Murray's series involved ten half-hour programs consisting of audio works by conceptual artists. In his notes for the project, Asher considered the ways in which media brings the artist-speaker closer to the audience, bridging the gap between artist and listener.[22] The ultimately realized form of Asher's contribution to "Audio by Artists," included in the second showing of Murray's series at the Banff Centre's Walter Phillips Gallery in 1983, featured the artist reading his name and postal address on tape in a brief audio segment.[23] By revealing his contact information to project listeners, Asher made a gesture at his own objectification. His tactic of addressing the listener with a recitation of his literal, traceable location investigated the boundary between the public and private facets of the artist's name.

Asher also placed his name (but not his address) on display in his exhibition in the "Matrix" series at the University Art Museum in Berkeley, California, in 1983. Unlike his "Audio by Artists" recitation, in this case Asher used his name to call attention to the figure of the artist as a producer in the institutional field of art. In this installation, which was among his first archival projects, he used information from the production credits of a number of documentary films from the Pacific Film Archive, which is part of the university's art museum. He chose the films based on their titles, combing the archives for film titles whose first letters spelled out each consecutive letter of his own first and last name.

The exhibition at the University Art Museum presented viewers with a series of posters designed by Asher that listed the credits for the people involved in the production of the selected films (figure 3.2).[24] The initial letter of each film's title was emphasized by the typeface used in the posters, in that the initial letter of the name of the chosen typeface matched the initial letter of the film title. For example, Asher's poster listing the production credits for the documentary *Children in Peril* was set in Century Bold. Each poster represented one letter of the artist's first name and surname. Thus, M-I-C-H-A-E-L was spelled out in seven individual posters that included the production credits for *Minimata*; *India*; *Children in Peril*; *House Un-American Activities Committee*; *America's Crisis: Education: Semester of Discontent*; *Eighty Million Women Want?* and *Living North*. A-S-H-E-R consisted of posters for *America Lost and Found*; *Small Victories*; *Harvest*; *Eyes on Russia: From the Caucasus to Moscow*; and *Riotmakers: The Technology of Social Demolition*. The posters were uniform in appearance: each was printed

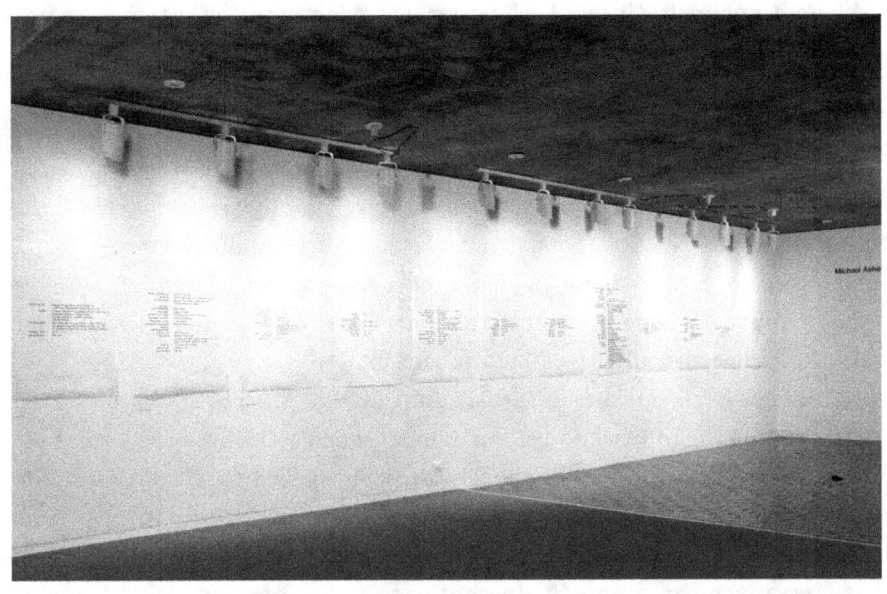

3.2   "Matrix," University Art Museum, Berkeley, 1983. Asher's film posters installed on
       the museum wall, followed by the artist's name. (Photograph by Photo Department,
       UC Berkeley; courtesy the artist.)

on white paper, slightly curling at the top and bottom edge, identical in shape and size.[25] In black type, the text of the posters was centered on the page with ragged left and right margins, although the character count varied according to the number of credits listed. Each poster included two vertical columns of text. The left column listed production activities (such as writer, producer, director, narrator, and composer) along with entries for the "release date" and "running time" of the film. The column on the right displayed the proper names corresponding with the job titles listed on the left. These posters were attached to the wall with pushpins in a uniform line. Labels below the posters included the title of each film. The same typeface was also used on the wall label for the poster in question, because Asher considered the labels and posters part of the same entity.[26] Following the posters, the artist's name was inscribed in large black letters on an adjacent wall.

Asher's deployment of the artist's name in the "Matrix" exhibition served to foreground the intersection of the individual and collective functions of the artist within the field of art. Although the name spelled out through the film titles was unmistakably his own, the system of producers outlined in the posters underscored the collective approach to creative production within the cinema, in which crew members are credited according to professional function. In keeping with the tradition of promotional posters, the proper names of these individuals also designated the personal agency of each member of the production team, who joined forces to produce the documentary.[27] The proper names contained in the film credits, along with the systems of production they represent, were, on the one hand, subordinated to the name of the artist when the film credits were condensed under the letters of the artist's own proper name. Asher did, after all, direct the project of creation, classification, and display of the posters, thereby reflecting his authorial agenda. Yet the association of the film crew members with the production of his own name within the exhibition space also implied that Michael Asher, both as an individual with a proper name and an authorial position within the institution, was in fact a composite of group tasks. This position would not have been possible without the assistance and agency of a variety of systems of representation, each bolstered by an interface of professionals or experts. Viewed together, then, the exhibit invited the viewer to consider the interpersonal construction and support of the artist's authorial position.

The "Matrix" exhibition marked the third time that Asher deployed the name of the artist as a linguistic signifier within the work of art. The first instance, the notice board statement at Otis in 1975, engaged the first-person pronoun, allowing the possibility for intersubjective exchanges if the gallery visitor elected to identify with the author of the "I" in question. On the surface, the use of the generic "I" as opposed to the proper name "Michael Asher" makes the Otis work seem more oblique, although a more thorough examination of the "I" would reveal the proper name "Michael Asher" in that situation as well. The subsequent projects for "Audio by Artists" and "Matrix" eliminated any ambiguity by placing the artist's proper name on display, objectifying the name—his own name—as the location of and property of the artist as well as the museum, the viewer, and the entire systemic chain of representational and interpersonal connections that make the artist-subject possible. All three projects mobilized chains of substitutions between art and artist, material object and linguistic signifier. Yet, although these works relied on the general cultural condition of authorship that allows the artist's name to stand in for, or signify, cultural products, the display of the artist's proper name was ultimately facilitated by a preexisting contract between the artist and institution. This contract granted Asher, the artist, a considerable amount of agency in the form of authorial power over what could be exhibited. At the same time, "Michael Asher" was instrumentalized within the artwork as a conceptual motif available to viewer contemplation. In that sense, both the artist's proper name and his "I" were situated in the crux of objectification and agency, condensing authorial power and the conditions of its exposure into the figure of the artist.

Administrative Relations: Value, Property, and Management Power

In a subsequent set of projects from the late 1970s and early 1980s, Asher extended his formal inquiry of the artist's proper name into institutional authority. These works would evaluate the ways in which authorial power intersects with managerial power within the administrative structures of art institutions. Asher first began exploring the artist's managerial power in 1978, with a set of related proposals intended for two different institutions: Los Angeles Contemporary Exhibitions (LACE), and the Van Abbemuseum in Eindhoven, The Netherlands. At the time, LACE was an alternative space that had just been founded by artists; in contrast, the Van Abbemuseum was an established museum with an ambitious exhibition program and an extensive modern art collection. Nevertheless, in both proposals, Asher sought to insert himself into the administrative and financial structure of the host institution by positioning his proper name within the executive discourse of the institution.

For LACE, Asher's project proposal was conceived in response to a letter he received from LACE Gallery Artists in February 1978.[28] The nonprofit organization requested that members of the Friends of LACE Gallery write letters in support of the gallery to the City of Los Angeles, whose Department of Building and Safety had threatened to close the exhibition space because of fire code violations. Asher had a series of discussions with Jill Giegerich, one of the artists who ran LACE, who had asked him to submit an exhibition proposal for the gallery that she would then curate. Asher submitted a proposal that addressed the relations among artists exhibiting at this cooperative gallery.[29] This proposal was laid out in the form of a legal contract, in which Asher proposed to take on the administrative position of LACE's "landlord" for a period of four months.[30] During this time, Asher would assume LACE's lease of the space and would sublease it back in exchange for monetary compensation and symbolic recognition. His portion of the rent would have matched the rent LACE already paid for their space at 240 South Broadway in downtown Los Angeles—in effect, doubling the rent and dividing it equally between Asher and the owner of the space.

Asher's LACE proposal contained a number of conditions clarifying the nature of his involvement. Although daily management of the exhibition space would be performed by LACE officials, Asher would retain the right to be informed of exhibitions held in the space as well as any modifications to the exhibition area that took place during his lease period.[31] Other artists exhibiting at LACE would be informed of Asher's project one month before the date of their opening. Visitors to LACE would have found a notice in the lobby outlining Asher's work, along with information about all other exhibitions held at LACE during his landlord period.

Contextualizing his LACE proposal within the power relations among artists, Asher's project notes considered the ways in which artists support—or do not support—one another's work.[32] The landlord arrangement, Asher argued, was a way of enforcing support between him and other LACE artists. This reordering of administrative oversight pointed at the psychological underpinnings of artist-subject relations at LACE, centralizing Asher's own subjectivity along with the involvement of other artists. Asher made this argument in his proposal when he suggested that artwork on display was inescapably linked to, and carried a reminder of, the artist behind the work:

This work . . . hopes to question the function of self within it and the works [by other artists on view at LACE] it envelopes. If we are to assume that some degree of self is necessarily attached and inseparable (by ego, responsibility, ideology) to each work presented in the space of L.A.C.E. then we see that not only do these works physically come in contact [with] or touch the work in which I have title to, but further overlap it creating a psychological space by virtue of the separate identities of the makers in conjunction with my contribution, to share a common ground with each others' work. . . . The impact of the work so far described may be experienced as tapping the contextual nerve of its participants' identity and also intentions enclosed within their works.[33]

The relations between self and others that formed within and between the artists at LACE provided Asher with a conduit for considering the ways in which the exhibiting artists practiced their identities within this institutional setting. Rather than segregate himself from the other artists, Asher counted himself among their ranks, acknowledging that his own LACE work would also be "open to manipulation by others." Instead of "rendering helpless the function of the gallery and artist," he acknowledged the agency of other artists with whom he would have shared the LACE exhibition space.

But Asher's proposed involvement at LACE would have been distinguishable from the work of other artists because the name-switch gesture brought a new set of power relations into play. By attempting to insert himself into the operational structure of the organization and "tak[e] administrative control of the support of that property," Asher combined his investigation of the psychological relations between artists with an intervention in the material and economic relations that governed LACE's daily operations. The meaning of the work was predicated upon the artist's participating in the operative set of institutional procedures in addition to commenting upon them on a symbolic level. Asher addressed the importance of this functionality in his proposal when he wrote, "I wish to create a situation using that which is given as part of the system (rent) and which makes the structure available and functional from day to day for differing presentations." The conditions of the proposal sought to materialize the socioeconomic structures of support for the artist, too. Asher referred to this fact in his proposal by stating that, as compensation for his duties as landlord and benefactor, "L.A.C.E. will be supporting, specifically, my work for the duration of the lease."

The LACE proposal came directly on the heels of another series of Asher exhibitions, all completed during 1977, which explored the interplay of participation and agency through forms of social labor and discourse within the institutional space, as discussed in chapter 2. His LAICA project was held in January and February of 1977, for example, and overlapped for three days in February with his concurrent participatory project at the Claire Copley and Morgan Thomas galleries. At the Van Abbemuseum in August of that year, Asher's installation involved the replacement of ceiling panels in one half of the museum's galleries, with some of the installation workers' labor taking place during the museum's hours of operation. Then, from October through November 1977, he requested employees of three adjacent Fort Worth museums to switch their parking lots in his work at the "Los Angeles in the Seventies" exhibition.[34]

All of these exhibitions explored managerial arrangements within art institutions. Asher's LACE proposal of April 1978 further implicated the artist in the administrative functions of art institutions. Instead of excavating the managerial functions of gallerists and the social behavior of museum staffers, Asher now began to investigate the artist's potential to trace managerial circuits of power and their administrative distribution within art institutions. The conduit for this investigation was not the artist's physical presence, but the authority vested in his name as an artist. The LACE proposal was not accepted for realization (technical reasons were cited), but Asher carried its conceptual structure over to another, almost simultaneous proposal that also implicated the artist in the administrative circuit of the art institution.

Along with his proposal for LACE, Asher was working on an idea he had had in response to a request from Rudi Fuchs, the director of the Van Abbemuseum. Shortly after the artist's August 1977 exhibition at the Van Abbemuseum, Fuchs had asked Asher to submit a proposal for the museum's permanent collection. Between 1978 and 1985, Asher submitted two different proposals to the Van Abbemuseum. Although both were officially "received" by the museum and considered for purchase, neither proposal was ultimately admitted to the permanent collection.

Asher submitted his first fully developed proposal to the Van Abbemuseum around May 1978.[35] In addition to close chronological proximity, it shared many operational strategies with the LACE proposal that he had formulated in April 1978.[36] Like the proposal for LACE, Asher's Van Abbemuseum concept involved the creation of "a landlord / tenant relationship" between the artist and museum.[37] At the Van Abbemuseum, however, Asher proposed to purchase the title to two separate rooms within the museum's exhibition space for the period of two and a half years. He would then sublease the rooms back to the museum, which, in turn, would continue using them for its everyday purposes of exhibition. Once more, as in the LACE proposal, the artists showing work in these rooms would have been notified in advance of Asher's involvement. The project would also be announced to visitors to the Van Abbemuseum by "a card or note at the front desk" that explained the administrative and financial arrangement between Asher and the Van Abbemuseum.[38] Like the LACE proposal, Asher's 1978 Van Abbemuseum proposal sought to insert the artist into the administrative structures of the art institution. If his proposal had been accepted, Asher would have inserted his name between his fellow artists and the institution, placing him in a position to provide nominal oversight for the institution and the artworks displayed in the exhibition rooms covered by the arrangement.

Within this reconstructed set of administrative arrangements, Asher proposed to direct attention to contractual transactions between himself and the museum. As in the proposal for LACE, his act of purchasing "the title" to rooms Three and Eight in the Van Abbemuseum, then subleasing these rooms back to the museum, would reorient the artist's involvement with the management of institutional facilities.[39] Within this new situation, the artist would exert—in name, at least—a considerable amount of managerial authority over the institution as well as accumulate a monetary surplus from the sublease arrangement.

Asher's notes on the Van Abbemuseum proposal identified a relation between the economic implications of his proposed arrangement and the question of how artists in general were compensated for their work. Within this socioeconomic frame, the proposal's structure of remuneration would become "a subsidy or funding for [Asher]."[40] After all, Asher noted, "any sale of a work funds or subsidizes an artist's existence and his artmaking."[41] The wording of his proposal further linked the artist's financial compensation to the museum structure. "By establishing both title and economic influence," he wrote, "the work can be created and incorporated into part of the museum system."[42] But Asher's proposal was further designed to actively address the entire institutional framework, rather than to reside passively in one of the galleries. Instead of taking on "the production of an artifact or physical alteration of the existing space," he sought to have his project "understood through the way in which the given space is then dealt with and used."[43] In this case, the signifier for this project—the visible stand-in for the cumulative administrative and economic structure of the museum—was the artist's name.

Once Asher formally submitted his proposal to the Van Abbemuseum, it entered a system in which acquisitions for the permanent collection were considered, processed, and adjudicated.[44] At first blush, there was reason to believe Asher's proposal was headed for realization. Fuchs wrote letters to this effect in 1979 and 1980, informing him on at least two occasions that his proposal had been accepted by the appropriate museum committee.[45] According to Fuchs, the sticking point for the committee concerned the precise duration for which Asher would be compensated by the museum. Specifically, the committee wanted to know whether they could halt the compensation process at a predetermined point.[46] Asher's proposal was even initially approved for purchase by the municipality of Eindhoven—yet the proposal failed to move forward to its implementation phase.[47] In a letter to Eindhoven city officials dated in March 1981, Fuchs cited technical reasons for abandoning Asher's project.[48]

Even as his Eindhoven project ground to a halt, Asher expanded his investigation of the institutional limits of the artist's name. Shortly after his negotiations with the Van Abbemuseum came to a standstill, Asher received an invitation to exhibit at the newly established Los Angeles Museum of Contemporary Art in 1983. This exhibition would provide him the perfect opportunity to further seize the performative powers at play in the name of the artist.

Performing Dedication: Resituating the Power to Name

Founded in 1979 by a group of local collectors and other arts patrons, the Los Angeles Museum of Contemporary Art (MOCA) was created to establish Los Angeles as a major contemporary art destination. While the museum's flagship building at Bunker Hill was under construction, MOCA's board of trustees arranged for a temporary exhibition space. The board secured two adjacent warehouses from the City of Los Angeles in the Little Tokyo district, and commissioned architect Frank Gehry to renovate the buildings for exhibition use.[49] The new facility, which was named the Temporary Contemporary, was inaugurated by two exhibitions in November 1983.[50]

During the grand opening of the Temporary Contemporary, the museum's galleries housed a group exhibition entitled "The First Show: Paintings and Sculpture from Eight Collections, 1940–1980." This show had been compiled from the private holdings of eight American and European art collectors, four of whom were trustees of the new museum.[51] The show's lenders included local figures such as Fred and Marcia Weisman, along with international collectors Charles and Doris Saatchi, Peter and Irene Ludwig, and Giuseppe and Giovanna Panza di Biumo. Running concurrently with "The First Show," MOCA initiated a series of one-person shows called "In Context"; Asher's exhibition was first in this series.[52] In addition to showcasing new work by Asher, MOCA launched Asher's *Writings 1973–1983 on Works 1969–1979*, which it copublished with the Press of the Nova Scotia College of Art and Design, where the book had been under development since the early 1970s.

Asher's proposal for the MOCA exhibition rekindled the artist's investigation of the stratified administrative order of art institutions. Asking that MOCA enter into a lease agreement with him, Asher proposed to purchase the title to the museum's lobby space for a one-time payment of one hundred dollars, then sublease the lobby back to the museum.[53] Asher's proposal specified that the "rental fee" he charged for this sublease would be "commensurate with [fees for] warehouse space in the adjoining area of downtown Los Angeles."[54] His pricing of the sublease suggested that warehouse real estate, even when used for museum purposes, still belonged to an overall economy of goods and commerce. In his proposal, Asher sought to secure a term of four years for his rental arrangement. His ownership of the lobby would be communicated via a sign that carried his name, along with "an information sheet or a card" that would be placed in the lobby explaining the arrangement to museum visitors.[55]

The operative concepts of Asher's MOCA proposal were, to some extent, carried over from the previous 1978 LACE and Van Abbemuseum proposals, both in terms of the artist's controlling the museum space and leasing it back to the host institution. The difference was that while the LACE and Van Abbemuseum proposals had sought to contain exhibition rooms, the MOCA proposal targeted the museum's lobby, a space dedicated to social interaction and administrative procedures such as purchasing tickets and displaying information about current exhibitions. Asher's MOCA proposal also implicated the artist more deeply in the museum's administrative order. At LACE and Van Abbemuseum, Asher had proposed that he would become a "tenant/titleholder"[56] whose participation would affect other artists' activities in the space. In the MOCA proposal, Asher sought to dedicate a specific area in the museum to an artist—namely, himself. The former was a claiming of privilege, while the latter was a bestowing of an honor usually granted in recognition of some type of outstanding or meritorious service by museum benefactors—most typically a large financial donation. The LACE proposal simply called for "a description of the work [to] be placed in the entrance hall with descriptions of the exhibitions held during the sublease period."[57] At MOCA, however, Asher requested a sign that would contain "[his] name attached to the lounge area in the same display order that functions for donors."[58] In this manner, Asher's proposals expanded from seeking to place the artist as administrator of museum activities to naming the artist as the recipient of an honor associated with museum donors.[59]

In contrast to LACE and the Van Abbemuseum, MOCA accepted and implemented Asher's project, with only minor modifications. These concerned specific aspects of legal terminology and duration. Because MOCA's lease with the City of Los Angeles, which carried only a nominal rent, prohibited a sublease without the city's written consent, Asher's contract with MOCA was renegotiated as a "license" instead of a lease.[60] Henceforth, MOCA licensed the lobby area to Asher, who sublicensed the area back to MOCA while retaining "aesthetic control" of the area.[61] The only other aspect of Asher's proposal that was modified in the process was the duration of the arrangement, which was set from November 1983, when the museum opened to the public, to July 1985, instead of the four years originally proposed by Asher.

And so, during the first twenty months after MOCA's grand opening in the Temporary Contemporary, the Los Angeles Museum of Contemporary Art honored Michael Asher in its lobby, the one space every museum visitor was guaranteed to pass through. This dedication was commemorated by a square orange plaque securely fastened onto a structural pillar between a set of stairs and a ramp, which were the two entryways leading to the museum's exhibition galleries (figure 3.3). The size, shape, color scheme, and typeface of the plaque adhered to MOCA's visual identity guidelines for signage commemorating donors in the museum.[62] Measuring eighteen by eighteen inches, the silkscreened plaque contained the inscription "The Michael Asher Lobby" in white lettering. More extensive information on Asher's project was on hand at the admissions desk in the

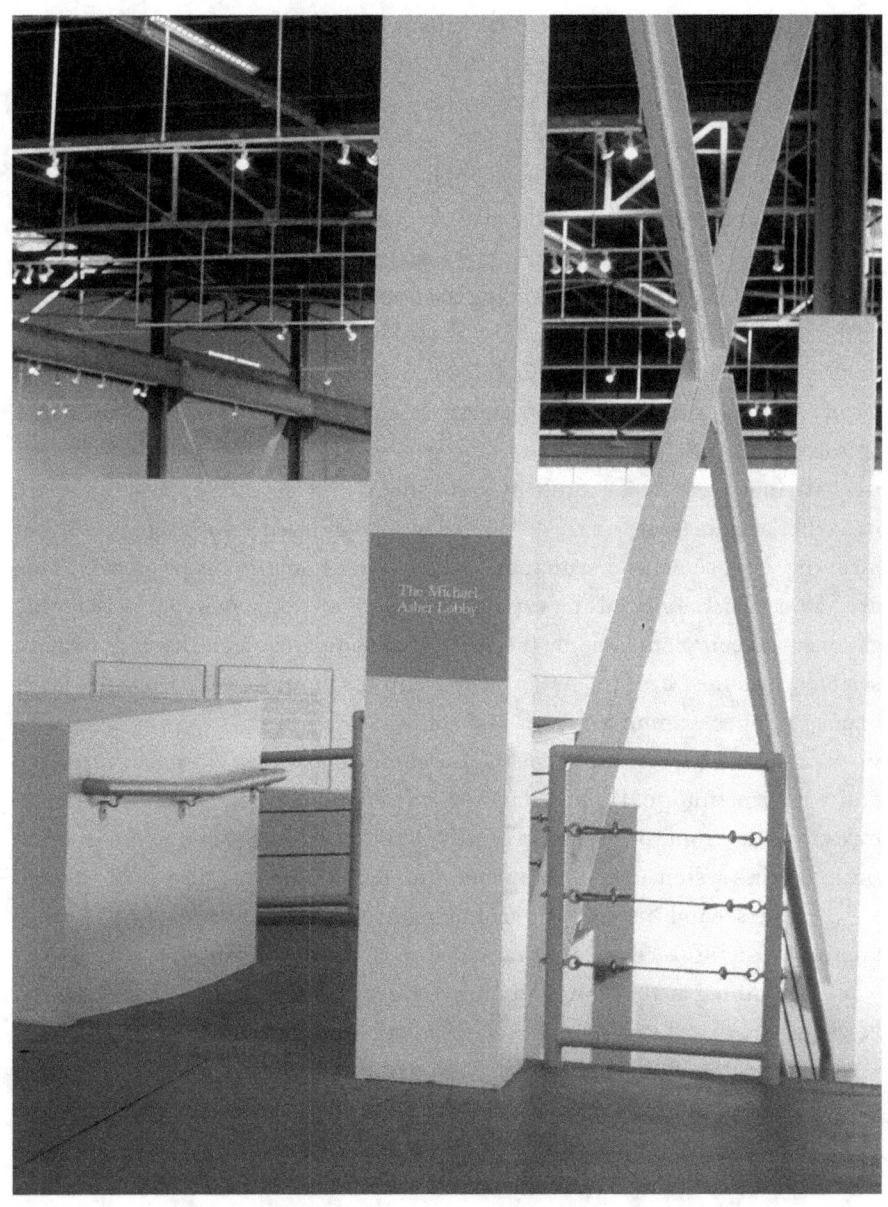

3.3   "In Context," Temporary Contemporary, Los Angeles Museum of Contemporary Art,
       Los Angeles, 1983. The sign with inscription "The Michael Asher Lobby" installed in
       the lobby of the museum. (Photograph courtesy the artist.)

lobby, where Asher had requested the museum place a stack of folded "business cards" whose color and typeface matched the dedication plaque. Inside the card, a text described the connection between the commemorative plaque and Asher's exhibition, identified the naming of the lobby as an artist's project, and outlined the contractual arrangement between Asher and the museum (figure 3.4).[63]

In this piece, the name of the artist became a location for Asher to mobilize within MOCA's administrative structures, recontextualizing the name along two primary lines. First, Asher's licensing contract with MOCA established the name of the artist as licensor (or titleholder) of the lobby space. His role as license holder was explained in both the folded card at the admissions desk and the legally binding contract between the artist and MOCA that made him—in name, at least—a functional participant in the museum bureaucracy. Because the contract attributed capitalist authority and control over the lobby space to the artist, Asher's name took on a fresh "use value" that allowed for a "repositioning of meaning, both social and economic," as the artist stated in his proposal.[64] This use value, which engaged the artist in a system of rents and contractual obligations, was complemented by the emotional and psychological empowerment scripted into the "license" Asher claimed in his contract with MOCA. To have license implies exemption from restrictions. Accordingly, Asher's license at MOCA extended beyond the scope of an individual artwork, circumscribing the entire host institution. It allowed the artist to take control of the economic structure of the museum (purchasing the title to the lobby space) and to incorporate the museum's system of donorship and commemoration into his work.

In the second instance of recontextualizing the name of the artist, Asher appropriated the recognition granted to a museum benefactor or donor at MOCA. He hinted at this commemorative interpretation in his proposal when he requested that the lobby placard include the name of the artist in a manner reserved for donors.[65] The visible marker of this dedication, a bright orange plaque bearing the inscription "The Michael Asher Lobby," was positioned so that visitors encountered it on their way to view the Temporary Contemporary exhibitions. Asher's carefully folded business card remained on the MOCA admissions desk without being discarded by museum employees. The plaque was not removed by museum security guards. Overall, MOCA's representational order seemed to smoothly integrate Asher's work of homage, a fact that MOCA reinforced by adhering to their obligation to pay what they called "rent" to the artist (albeit with some initial delay).[66]

3.4 "In Context," Temporary Contemporary, Los Angeles Museum of Contemporary
Art, Los Angeles, 1983. Folded business cards with Asher's statement inside, placed
on the admissions desk. (Photograph courtesy the artist.)

The act of naming is a linguistic convention that, when executed under the proper circumstances, does what it says. Such conventional acts of speech are termed "performatives" by linguistic philosopher J. L. Austin, who differentiates them from ordinary statements.[67] Austin is specifically concerned with the cultural conditions under which utterances function as acts and produce concrete events. Arguing that performative speech acts need to take place within a framework of shared conventions, he cites a number of legitimized institutional or cultural procedures that involve authorized individuals, including the marriage ceremony, naming a ship, making a bet, and bequeathing something in a will.[68] These procedures bestow a particular kind of agency upon specific individuals, such as ministers, ship captains, and wedding ceremony participants, whose words constitute or result in actions. Austin further maintains that these visible formalities must be accompanied by the appropriate set of intentions, inner motives, and subsequent behavior to validate the speech act.[69] When all of these conditions are met—external propriety and internal sincerity—Austin asserts that the resulting performative speech acts yield tangible effects in the material world.

The museum practice of naming spaces and events draws from this performatively conferred legitimacy. The distribution of architectural space in accordance with a stratification of names is a conventional and well-established part of donor relations, in which the museum names structural spaces in honor of its benefactors. Potential areas include exhibition halls, museum wings, lobbies, entrances, and auditoriums, as well as events and gestures such as prizes, commissions, lecture series, and fellowships—all of which honor specific individuals or corporations in compensation for a donation or service. In that sense, the commemoration of spaces is both a system of compensation (paying tribute to) and privilege (the honoree claims a rarefied status within the museum). Even the most casual museum visitor can attest to the fact that this "accepted conventional procedure having a certain conventional effect"[70] (to quote Austin) transforms a museum's spaces into dedicated topographies of commemorative plaques or inscriptions that confer personalized honor upon the named dignitary. Within this architectural and administrative inscription of names, the highest honors are conferred in direct relation to the size or prominence of the architectural feature; a single bench or back terrace clearly do not have the same status as a highly visible exhibition space, gallery stroll—or lobby.

It is precisely this functional economy of dedication that The Michael Asher Lobby foregrounded at MOCA. Asher's identity as an artist, however, complicates the institutional status of The Michael Asher Lobby. If, as Austin claims, performative speech acts are ultimately validated by the speaker's authority to perform a particular act, such as naming,[71] what authority did Asher have at MOCA? Although MOCA certainly invited him to contribute to the museum's physical and discursive premises, conferring the artist with a considerable degree of institutional legitimacy, Asher's situation differed from conventional donor recognition in several ways. First, the act of commemoration did not benefit the museum in the usual manner, as the institution did not receive a monetary donation from Asher. Nor was the honor of naming the result of exceptional service to the institution. In fact, the dedication served to highlight both Asher's contribution and status as an artist at MOCA. Although museums conventionally treat the artist's labor as a donation (because museums seldom remunerate artists for the work they perform, instead directing possible compensation toward the acquisition of art objects), the artist's labor is rarely, if ever, recognized with an official or commemorative institutional dedication.[72] In other words, artists are not interchangeable with donors within the administrative hierarchies of art institutions. By accepting the terms of Asher's proposal, the museum committed to eschewing its customary practice of paying tribute to providers of financial and political resources in favor of dedicating a portion of its physical space to a provider of content.

The legitimacy of Asher's position at MOCA becomes critical if we hold with Austin's call for the appropriate consequences of the speech act. Although Austin concedes that certain performatives merely require appropriate intentions (expressed through thoughts and feelings), he maintains that others necessitate follow-up action.[73] Austin exhaustively outlines the improprieties that might render any given act "void" (which occurs when the externally marked conventions, such as a specific procedure or authority, are not obeyed) or "hollow" (when internal motives, intentions, and subsequent conduct do not conform to the established meaning of the particular speech act).[74] According to this formula, the external performances of speech acts must be ratified by the subject's attitude, the internal response on the part of all participants: those who author the utterances as well as those who are affected by them.[75]

The peculiar self-referentiality of Asher's naming procedure at MOCA—the fact that the artistic content provider and the object of institutional dedication were identical—foregrounded this chasm between what Austin calls "ordinary" and "parasitic" language uses. The latter, which occurs in the context of a theatrical performance, for example, demonstrates "hollow or void" attitudes on the part of the subjects who participated in the speech act, in contrast to "ordinary" language use that, in Austin's view, is imbued with sincerity.[76] Was the MOCA lobby truly dedicated to Asher, or did the self-referentiality within Asher's naming render his act hollow and—following Austin—ultimately ineffectual? Austin's division between forms and intents, or external and internal truthfulness, is challenged in Judith Butler's argument for the constitutive effects of speech acts. For Butler, the conventional modes of address such as naming result in tangible effects regardless of internal motives and conflicts. Acts of speech, among other discursive formations, constitute subjects, securing them in the representational order that makes social existence possible in the first place.[77] This constitutive role of performativity separates Butler from Austin. While Austin's theory juxtaposes external performance with internal sincerity, Butler attributes credibility to the appropriation of culturally intelligible acts—not because all acts would be sincere in Austin's sense, but because the iterative forms themselves possess the potential for an ingrained legitimacy.[78]

Read through Butler, Asher's act of naming the MOCA lobby executed a "performative contradiction," or the purposeful embrace of authority conventionally invested in names. Butler argues that "subjects who have been excluded from enfranchisement" sometimes gain the power to "seize the language of enfranchisement . . . claiming to be covered by that universal, thereby exposing the contradictory character of previous conventional formulations of the universal."[79] Asher's naming of the MOCA lobby identified the power invested in conventional museum dedication and seized the collectively endorsed identity of museum honorees. Yet his dedication did not attempt to obscure its source. Rather than blurring the boundaries of institutional authority, Asher's detailed explanation of his procedure and authorization worked to dispel ambiguity from the situation. It was quite obvious to MOCA visitors—at least those who read the explanatory materials on the admissions desk—that Asher was an artist who had been invited by the museum to make a project for a temporary exhibition. But Asher's naming of the lobby also seized hold of the psychological and emotional credibility museums invest in donors. In museums, names pledge the naming subject's allegiance to the object of dedication to the same extent that they pledge the museum's dedication to those named. The visible sign of the museum's recognition—whether a sign on the wall, title in the program, or brick in the commemorative wall—is a condensation of such institutional interest and affect. Perhaps because the name-bearing plaque usually does not contain any supplemental information about why this particular individual or corporation was honored by the museum, institutional recognition conveys a unity and cohesiveness that at once solidifies the dedication in institutional history and deflects any ethically compromised associations: corruption, greed, oppression, undue influence, or outright legal complications that may tarnish the relation between the subject and object of dedication. Indeed, the museum invests the act of dedication with modes of affect that seem singularly uncomplicated: an expression of appreciation, gratitude, honor, subservience. When the museum honors its benefactors and donors—even those who receive significant monetary compensation for the transaction, for example in the form of tax breaks—it retrospectively verifies that those collectors, trustees, supporters, and various council, committee, and advisory members share the mission of supporting the museum.

By inserting the artist into the subject position of the donor, The Michael Asher Lobby participated in this "affective economy" of museum dedication,[80] while questioning the inevitability of the authority conventionally invested in donor names. In so doing, Asher identified a fault line between individual and institutional subjectivity, asking who speaks in the name of the museum and whose interests are represented by the acts of naming that bind donors and artists to museums. The two registers under which Asher deployed the name of the artist at MOCA—licensor and donor—connected the socioeconomic structure of museum administration with the affective economy of dedication, demonstrating the impossibility of separating the two. In turn, MOCA's acceptance of Asher's proposal opened up a rare critical space for the artist and the museum to ask questions about the interests that museums serve—and the interests that artists serve when they exhibit in museums.

In 1985, as The Michael Asher Lobby approached the end of its run, Asher returned to thinking about a proposal for the Van Abbemuseum's permanent collection. In the spring of 1985, Asher had received a postcard from museum director Rudi Fuchs asking him to resume work on his proposal.[81] Fuchs also invited the artist to visit the Van Abbemuseum when in Europe that summer, and Asher subsequently met with the museum's representative in Arnhem, where

Asher was in the process of preparing his work for the 1986 Sonsbeek exhibition.[82] Shortly thereafter, Asher finalized and submitted a new proposal for the museum's permanent collection. This proposal, "Working Title: 'The Michael Asher Trust Fund,'" which was written on Van Abbemuseum stationery, expanded the conceptual project Asher had initiated in his LACE and MOCA undertakings, along with that of his earlier 1978 Van Abbemuseum proposal. Yet this new proposal entailed a thematic shift away from the landlord-tenant arrangement to the management of museum collections.

In his 1985 Van Abbemuseum proposal, Asher envisioned the creation of a trust fund that would benefit Asher and the museum alike through periodic withdrawals of interest.[83] This interest would be split between the payment of a regular stipend to Asher and the provision of dedicated funds to the Van Abbemuseum for acquiring works by other artists (selected by the museum) for the museum's permanent collection.[84] This compensation structure implied a complex set of conceptual moves. Asher's proposal for the trust fund embraced the standard museum procedure of compensating artists through the purchase of artworks for the museum's permanent collection, although it directed this opportunity to artists other than Asher. The method of remunerating Asher for this work, however, was distinctly unconventional, as the proposal might have given the impression that the Van Abbemuseum was subsidizing an artist rather than purchasing a tangible art object from him. By casting the artist as a direct recipient of financial support, Asher's proposal made the socioeconomic relations between artists and art buyers exceedingly visible.

Asher's new Van Abbemuseum proposal appropriated and expanded the artistic strategy from his 1983 MOCA lobby project, particularly as this concerned the position of a donor in his work. Although the Van Abbemuseum would have been responsible for raising the initial capital for his trust fund, the actual title of the fund would have appeared under Asher's name, as would the deployment of funds for other artworks purchased for the permanent collection. The Michael Asher Trust Fund was envisioned by the artist as a continuous project that would join other works of art in the museum's collection. "Can the trust [fund] be held together infinitely, just as a work in the permanent collection[?]" Asher asked.[85] As a matter of public record, the museum would commit to "publish[ing] the bookkeeping and acquisition of the trust," thereby documenting the funds, transactions, and purchased works by artists other than Asher.[86] The resulting cluster of works at the Van Abbemuseum would thereby be officially donated by

The Michael Asher Trust Fund. On the one hand, this fact would stand out as the ultimate act of generosity on the part of the artist.[87] In effect, Asher's trust fund would be donating works by other artists to the museum, where they would be located permanently. On the other hand, Asher's act of official sponsorship would be inextricably linked to the artist's institutional recognition of himself. The museum records would reference The Michael Asher Trust Fund as the donor of the each new work, and Asher's name would be evoked anew with each purchase or exhibition of work acquired with funds from his trust. Asher would be positioned as a perpetual donor, as well as a perpetual artist, at the Van Abbemuseum.

The critical impact of The Michael Asher Trust Fund proposal relied on a chain of substitutions: that of the artist's name for a material art object, the artist's name in place of a donor's name, the function of official administrator for the artist's conventional function. Herein, the figure of the artist, so often positioned as the self-serving recipient of institutional support handed out by unselfishly dedicated administrators, now walked both sides of the line. By positioning the name of the artist as the name of the administration, the figure of the artist could be equal parts benefactor and recipient, captain and crew.

Given that Asher's Van Abbemuseum proposal drew into complicity the museum's entire network of curators, donor base, administrators, and future artists (whose work would have been purchased by the monetary interest generated from The Michael Asher Trust Fund), it is not entirely surprising that the proposal was not accepted. But this was not due to any lack of effort on the artist's part. Asher's correspondence addressed to Jan Debbaut (director of the Van Abbemuseum after Fuchs from 1988 to 2003) and Piet de Jonge (curator at the museum from 1982 to 1989) indicates the artist was developing the proposal actively, providing new information, and asking the museum to check the implications of his proposal in terms of legality and taxation.[88] These letters, however, were met with muted response until de Jonge informed Asher in 1987 that the Van Abbemuseum would not realize his proposal.[89] The curator did not provide reasons for the museum's decision.

The Van Abbemuseum proposal took its place as the last in a series of Asher's projects, from 1975 to 1987, that directly engaged the administrative, institutional, and museological limits of the artist's name. Taken together, these projects and proposals expanded artistic agency within its own institutional framework. Their transformative potential is amply reflected by the difficulties their prospective host institutions, such as the Van Abbemuseum, expressed in processing the proposals. In a quintessentially performative contradiction, Asher's repositioning of artistic agency in relation to institutional practices of naming-for and naming-after reversed the artist's objectification through linguistic means: an act of naming that renames the namer, the one who instantiates the institutional meaning of the name. In Asher's exhibitions at the Otis Art Institute (1975) and "Matrix" (1983), as well as his project for "Audio by Artists" (exhibited in 1983), the name of the artist literally replaced the art object. In the LACE-Van Abbemuseum-MOCA-Van Abbemuseum sequence, the artist's relations to the art institution gained further momentum by claiming access to greater administrative agency: the power to name, commemorate, designate, collect tribute—to recognize and wield authority. In so doing, the performative figure of the artist functioned as a tool for fleshing out administrative systems of support in art institutions, while also inviting artists, institutions, and museum visitors to more closely evaluate their emotional, spatial, economic, and psychological relations to the artist or the art institution.

Because they actively intervened in the administrative order of art museums, Asher's situations could surely be designated as events; they disrupted institutional routines, and, in general, followed Foucault's designation of "show[ing] the heterogeneity of what was imagined consistent with itself."[90] Yet to qualify Asher's situations as events would ignore the ways in which they remain legible within their institutional framework. Although his use of the name deployed the tactic Foucault describes as "the appropriation of a vocabulary turned against those who had once used it,"[91] the intersubjective encounters this nominal repositioning engendered were emphatically not singular—nor did they institute discontinuity in institutional power relations. Rather, the institutional framework of the museum became the condition of possibility for a new take on the artist's agency and objectification in museum situations. For The Michael Asher Lobby required the context of MOCA, just as The Michael Asher Trust Fund could have functioned only within an established art museum, such as the Van Abbemuseum, which had both a permanent art collection and an active acquisitions program. Instead of claiming unfettered freedom to act within the museum, Asher used his name—which signified the name of the artist and, by extension, the name of all artists—to rekindle the viewer's awareness of institutional power and control.

When the Van Abbemuseum project ground to a halt in 1987, the name of the artist receded to the background in Asher's artistic practice. Twenty years later, in 2007, however, Asher's name was again posted at MOCA, not as an exhibiting artist but as a bona fide donor in conjunction with an exhibition that featured works Asher had donated to MOCA.[92] His gift consisted of thirty-seven works of art by artists including Larry Bell, Judy Chicago, Joe Goode, and Donald Judd. MOCA called Asher's donation, made in 2006, "one of the largest artist's gifts in the museum's history."[93] The museum's contextualization of Asher's donation as an "artist's gift" conferred the dual mantle of artist and donor upon Asher in a manner that was similar to what the artist himself had assumed in his 1983 exhibition in the same institution. In 1983, MOCA had paid "rent" to the artist. Now MOCA, rather than Asher, was at the receiving end: it acquired a collection of artworks without any monetary transactions required to close the deal. Although the museum did not reciprocate Asher's gift by naming a space (a lobby, for example) after the artist, it nevertheless celebrated the event by organizing an exhibition of the artworks Asher had donated. "Artists' Gifts: Michael Asher" was on display at MOCA's Grand Avenue facility from September 2007 to January 2008. Such an event was the institutionally appropriate method of honoring the donor; in this case, the donor also happened to be an artist.

Even though the exhibition "Artists' Gifts" was not an artwork by Asher, its institutional framing offers an opportunity to reexamine the themes that the artist had investigated in his proposals for LACE and the Van Abbemuseum as well as in his realized exhibition at MOCA in 1983. Viewed against the history of these projects, Asher's MOCA donation calls attention to the hierarchical social relations in art institutions such as museums and nonprofit spaces. For why did MOCA single out the fact that Asher's donation was given by an artist? What distinguishes an artist from other donors? Surely the museum would not qualify an exhibition of donated works as "philanthropists' gifts," or "corporate chairmen's gifts." The specificity of the artist's subject position, emphasized by the exhibition title "Artists' Gifts," excluded the artist from the universality that the museum otherwise might grant its donors. Just as in the 1983 Michael Asher Lobby, the name of the artist was not interchangeable with a donor's name, even though Asher's donation bore all the hallmarks of a successful Austinian speech act: its motives, actions, and subsequent results were appropriate and authorized.

At the same time, the wall text that accompanied "Artists' Gifts: Michael Asher" at MOCA recognized artists' contributions to the museum in a broader sense. In the statement, the museum described the importance of contemporary artists to its activities, and outlined some of the ways in which artists had contributed to the museum's direction. Asher's donation was identified as "highlighting one of the numerous and meaningful ways in which the local, national, and international artists' community has honored MOCA with its support since its inception."[94] MOCA was "honored" as a recipient of "support" by artists. The emotional and psychological register of this rhetorical gesture granted agency to the artist as the one who gives. This emphasis on agency contrasts with a conventional exhibition situation in which the museum is more likely to control the presentation of the artist and artwork materially and rhetorically. In this regard, MOCA's act of recognizing artistic agency through Asher's donation continued the reciprocity of power and control that the museum had initiated with Asher in 1983 when it agreed to grant control of its lobby space to the artist.

Asher's situations that incorporate the name of the artist are particularly appropriate examples of how the artist's name translates into power and control, and of the limits of the artist's appropriation of naming. Though an artist's name accompanies most works of art, it is usually placed on a label separate from the artwork. Asher, on the other hand, has on occasion integrated his name into his very artwork in a way that both objectifies the artist and entrusts the name with uncontestable agency. At first glance, the name of the artist, when placed on display in these works, was relegated to the status of an object that was subject to exposure beyond the artist's control. At the same time, Asher used the name of the artist to seize hold of functional areas of art institutions, controlling financial transactions, and administrative procedures. The name "Michael Asher" in these works possessed agency that allowed the artist to investigate the terms and conditions of how institutions support artists by commissioning proposals, purchasing works for their permanent collection, and organizing exhibitions.

Asher's seizing of administrative power in the museum recalls a tendency within 1960s conceptual art that Benjamin H. D. Buchloh has described as an "aesthetic of administration."[95] Having negated art's traditional aesthetic (or even visual) values, along with the competencies to produce and appreciate them, Buchloh argues, conceptual art "subject[ed] the last residues of artistic aspiration towards transcendence . . . to the rigorous and relentless order of the vernacular of administration."[96] Buchloh questions the ideological consequences of this approach (which he associates with the "positivist instrumentality" of "late capitalism"[97]), contrasting it with the institutional critique performed by artists such as Daniel Buren and Hans Haacke, whose work called attention to the pervasive influence of these institutions.[98] One might wonder, however, whether Asher's comprehensive instrumentalization of the artist merely replicated or reinforced the administrative order of museums, or whether it advanced the task of institutional critique, which Buchloh identifies with "analyz[ing] and expos[ing] the social institutions from which the laws of positivist instrumentality and the logic of administration emanate in the first place."[99] By inserting the artist into the administrative circle along with salaried staff and influential donors, Asher's naming situations foregrounded the collective, if unspoken, rules that determine the socioeconomic place of the artist in the hierarchy of art institutions. Under these circumstances, the artist's good name vouched for the legitimacy of his proposal. For the inviting museum, the artist's name translated to cultural capital, facilitating an exchange of material and symbolic power between the artist and institution. Asher further investigated the emotional edge of such power exchange in a number of projects in the 1980s and 1990s where instead of asking the museum to support the artist, he offered his emphatic support to the hosting institution by building walls, advertising the exhibition, and compiling archival data.

4

Institutional Support

In 1984, the Stuart Collection commissioned a permanent public sculpture from Asher for its collection on the University of California, San Diego campus. Asher visited the campus and considered several options, but he did not decide on a project immediately.[1] While he was deliberating over his sculptural proposal, he asked to redesign the Stuart Collection's stationery, an idea the foundation gladly accepted. Completed in 1985, Asher's stationery comprised a set of letterhead and matching business envelopes that are still used by the foundation for its general correspondence (figure 4.1). Asher did not call the stationery a work of art, a "project" by Michael Asher, but intended it to be used as a functional element of everyday institutional procedures.

Asher has contributed to institutional self-presentation in a number of his works by engaging in promotional practices, augmenting exhibition architecture, and contributing to the compilation of institutional histories. These projects expand his investigation of institutional rules and norms into his own functional participation, in that the artist seemingly discards his own authorial position in favor of speaking in the name of the institution—and for its benefit. Rather than letting himself be contained by the presentational strategies of institutions, Asher has in these cases provided direct support to museums, foundations, and exhibitions.

In Asher's paradigm, institutional support has material and psychological dimensions. The material meaning of the term "support" is familiar from late modernist discourse, where the artwork's support is the material background, or even the architectural frame of the work of art. In addition to the painting's underlying canvas, broader material elements such as walls, heating systems, windows, and doors have functional roles in most art institutions. Yet these elements usually receive scant attention compared to the artwork. Asher has consistently investigated these elements of material support, as Anne Rorimer points out in her discussion of Asher's 1976 work for the "Ambiente Arte" exhibition at the Venice Biennale. Rorimer observes that this project "makes clear

University of California, San Diego B-027 La Jolla, California 92093 619-452-2117

4.1   Stationery for the general correspondence of the Stuart Collection, San Diego, 1985. (Courtesy the artist.)

how Asher's work seeks to uncover and express its *support* or context, rather than being placed within or being dependent upon it."[2] In the Venice Biennale project, Asher procured folding stools for the use of visitors to the Italian Pavilion, where "Ambiente" was located. He has also removed a gallery wall (Claire Copley Gallery in 1974), removed windows and doors (Clocktower, 1976), and reinstalled exterior wall paneling in a museum's interior (Museum of Contemporary Art in Chicago, 1979). In other projects, he has rerouted a museum's heating system (including the radiators and the water pipes that connected them) into the front lobby (Kunsthalle Bern, 1992), and lowered an entire mezzanine floor to the main gallery level (Kunstraum Wien, 1996).

But the notion of institutional support covers more than the museum's material components. Rorimer points at such expansive interpretation of support in Asher's work when she equates "support" with "context." Consider the psychological relations that form when institutions support artists—Asher included—by commissioning works and including them in exhibitions. In these situations, the museum operates with the assumed stability of a provider of resources, endorsement, and cultural capital. For the museum, the practice of supporting an artist means entering into a psychologically complex contract in which institutional support implies almost unconditional endorsement of the artist whose work the museum displays.

Asher examined the psychological undercurrents of institutional support by doubling the institutional support that he received and returning it to the institution in three projects executed in the 1980s and 1990s. These three exhibitions were Documenta 7 (Kassel, Germany, 1982), "l'art conceptuel, une perspective" (Musée d'art moderne de la Ville de Paris, 1989), and "The Museum as Muse: Artists Reflect" (Museum of Modern Art, New York, 1999). In each case, Asher provided functional services to the exhibition in which he participated or to the museum that was hosting his work. He addressed specific institutional conditions (exhibition contexts, contemporary art world perspectives, or historical conditions) that contributed to institutional self-presentation. In these situations, the artist's engagement with the official agenda of the host exhibition or museum foregrounded institutional subjectivity, articulating values and ideologies that informed institutional forms of self-presentation. In particular, these projects investigated how individual curators and museum directors shape collective institutional policies and practices.

Asher's three support projects were prefigured by his contribution to the "Heute" section of the exhibition "Westkunst" (Cologne, Germany, 1981), in which he responded to the exhibition's unconventional curatorial structure. He had been invited to participate by German curator Kasper Koenig, the coordinator of "Westkunst," a large-scale survey of Western art since 1939. Koenig had supported Asher's work in the early 1970s during his tenure as editor at the Press of the Nova Scotia College of Art and Design.[3] In the "Heute" section, which was originally meant to feature commissioned projects, Koenig sought to showcase emerging artists.[4] The historical portion of the "Westkunst" exhibition, however, had consumed the city-allocated budget of approximately $1.6 million, leaving "Heute" essentially without funding.[5] To salvage the contemporary section of the exhibition, the city of Cologne entrusted local art dealer Rudolf Zwirner with $50,000. In turn, Zwirner solicited a number of European and American art dealers to send to the exhibition works by designated artists. The dealers were required to cover the expenses associated with the participation of their artists if these costs exceeded $1,500.[6]

The curatorial responsibility for "Heute" was assigned to dealers using a two-tiered structure: Zwirner determined the artists he wanted, and the sponsoring dealers arranged the rooms with work from artists in their stables. Although Zwirner's own gallery was not explicitly included in the exhibition, he did ask the Holly Solomon Gallery to include two artists whom his gallery also represented.[7] For critic Grace Glueck of the *New York Times*, "The result is essentially a trade show, with each dealer offering his hottest item."[8] Indeed, the selection of the artists in "Heute" reflected the early 1980s art market: artist-delegates were associated with the two faces of nascent postmodernism, neo-expressionist figurative painting (represented by Anselm Kiefer, Francesco Clemente, and Sandro Chia, among others) and appropriation art (including works by Jenny Holzer, Barbara Bloom, Troy Brauntuch, and Jack Goldstein), much of it photographic.[9] Asher, whose invitation survived the Koenig-Zwirner transition, was the only artist in "Heute" without commercial gallery representation. His conceptual approach, which he shared with some of the artists in the main "Westkunst" exhibition (such as Bruce Nauman and Marcel Broodthaers), further set him apart from the other "Heute" artists.[10]

Asher's separate status within "Heute" was reinforced through the placement of his work in the entry hallway to this part of exhibition. This display contrasted with that of the other artists, whose work was shown in enclosed rooms clustered around the hallway. The work itself consisted of eight mass-produced chairs on four low, carpeted display platforms flanking the walls between doorways (figure 4.2). Contributed by galleries represented in "Heute," the chairs faced viewers frontally, and their designs ranged from streamlined metal tubular seats to folding chairs made of wood, plastic, or canvas (figure 4.3). Some of the platforms housed three chairs, while others held only one or two, with gaps in between. Each gallery participating in "Heute" was allocated a space on the platforms, regardless of whether they contributed chairs to Asher's project. Whether or not it contained a chair, each space was labeled with the name of one of the galleries represented.

The chair display was accompanied by a wall statement that contained the text of a letter that Koenig had sent to the dealers sponsoring "Heute." In this letter, Koenig asked, on Asher's behalf, to borrow an office chair from each gallery.[11] The dealers were asked to send this chair along with the artwork in a mutual shipment (the irony of pairing office furniture with valuable artworks seems both conceptually intentional and practical on Asher's part).[12] Eight dealers obliged, while six dealers declined the request.[13] The chairs that Asher had in mind were those intended for visitors to the gallery's office, the type that are typically placed "next to or across from the [gallery] director's chair."[14] They were clearly not the chairs the dealers used themselves: their flimsy construction made it obvious they did not offer enough physical support for long-term comfort. But neither were these chairs meant for casual gallery visitors. Supplied by the dealer for the seating of clients, these were the chairs that held prospective buyers, critics, and artists—visible elements of the mundane yet absolutely indispensable material support structures that enable the gallery to operate as a business.

In the context of "Heute," the visitors' chairs formed an allegorical relation to how participating galleries materially supported and financially underwrote the exhibition. They foregrounded the ideological influence the commercial dealers were given by Zwirner in representing the art of "today."[15] Asher advanced this line of interpretation in his exhibition statement, describing "Heute" as "a hybridization of art fair and museum setting" and "compromised by the contributions of 'private interests' to its support."[16] In the midst of a heated art market centered on figurative painting, Asher's chair arrangement in "Heute"

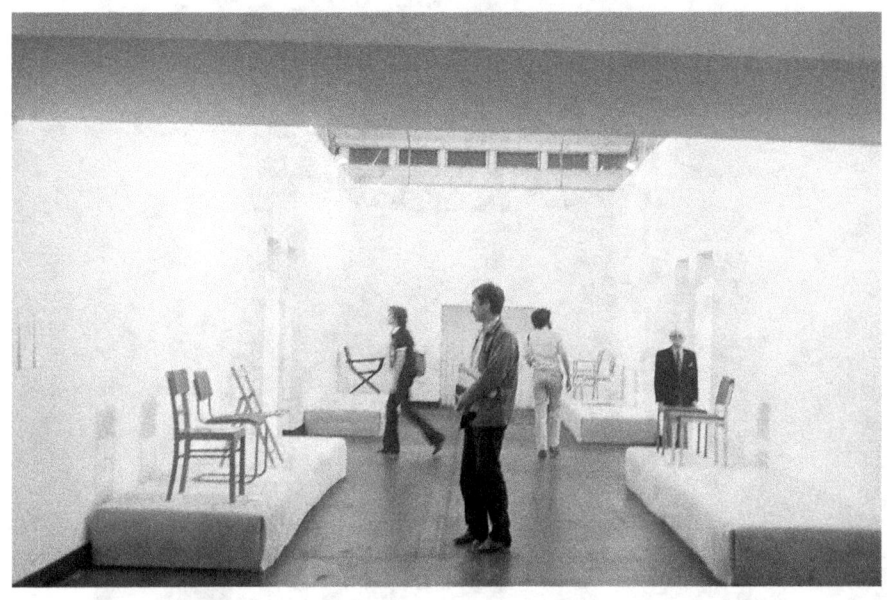

4.2 "Westkunst 'Heute,'" Cologne, 1981. Installation of visitor's chairs. (Photograph
courtesy the artist.)

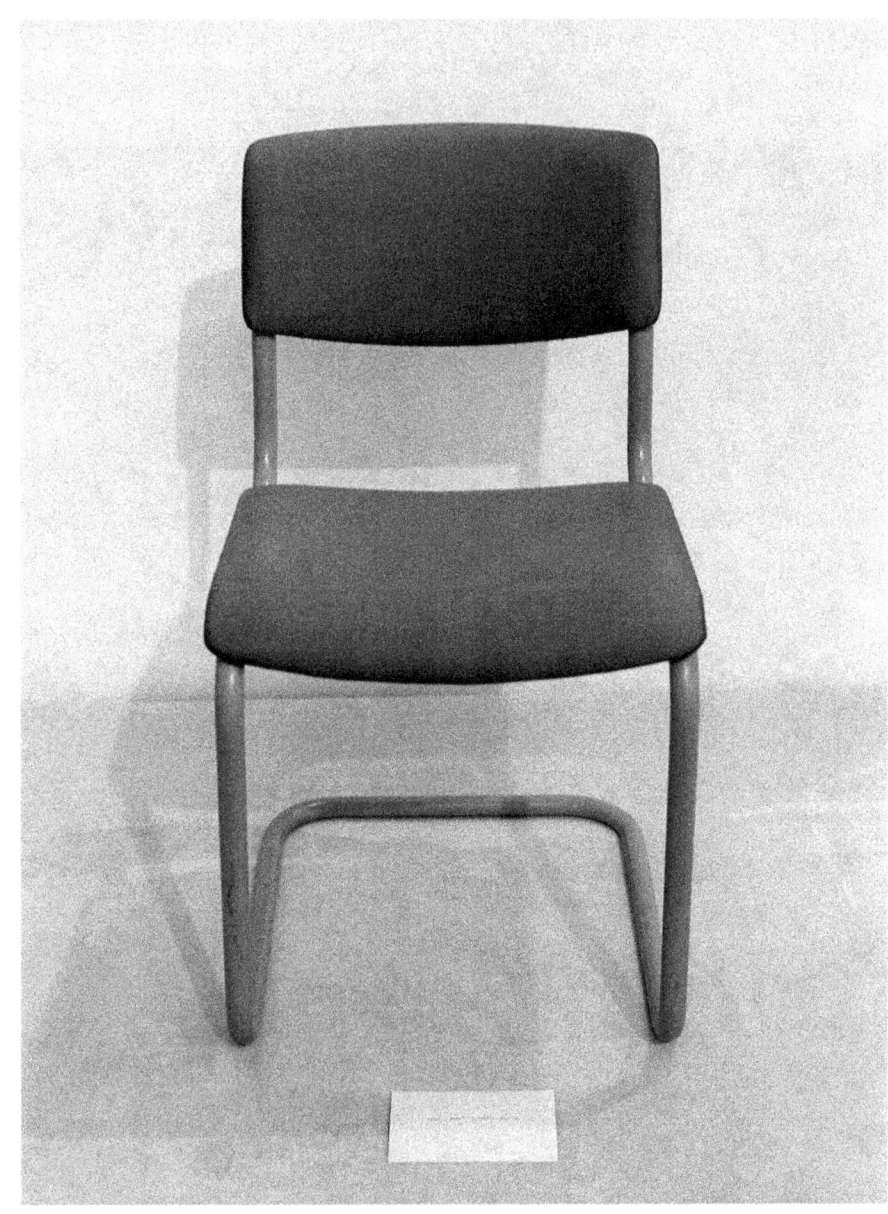

4.3 "Westkunst 'Heute,'" Cologne, 1981. Installation of visitor's chairs. Detail view, chair from Rüdiger Schöttle Gallery. (Photograph courtesy the artist.)

functioned as a reminder of the conceptual moment in Western art that was now chronologically bracketed on both sides by expressionist painting.

Asher's conceptual strategy in "Heute" was further distinguished by the artist's insistence on the presence of specific material objects. The dealers' chairs on display in "Heute" were specified in a manner that differed drastically from a more generic use of objects in conceptual art (exemplified by Joseph Kosuth's folding chair, placed on display along with its photograph and textual dictionary definition in *One and Three Chairs* of 1965). In "Heute," the material presence of Asher's chairs signified specific lines of institutional influence: economic, ideological, and social. Institutional support flowed from the City of Cologne to Zwirner to the dealers and finally to the artists. The multiplicity of the chairs, along with the absences among them, fractured the faceless totality of the exhibition's economic arrangement into individuated relations between Zwirner (or Koenig) and Metro Pictures (which did not send a chair), for example, and Paula Cooper (which did). The materiality of these seating arrangements conveyed traces of the experiential, phenomenological relations that formed between the dealers and visitors to their offices. Each piece stood in for the interpersonal dimension of the gallery business as a set of socioeconomic, but also psychological, relationships between individual artists, dealers, and clients. In Asher's treatment, all these individuals adhered to ideological mandates, but they were also subject to tangible physical limits. By focusing on the social situations that form between the dealer and client sitting in the dealer's office, Asher's "Heute" work investigated the individuation of social relationships and situations within institutional support structures—a theme he continued to examine the following year (1982) with his contribution to Documenta 7.

Documenta 7: Restaging Curatorial Influence

Like his project for "Heute," Asher's work in Documenta 7 responded to the organizing principles behind the exhibition. In Documenta's case, those principles were first articulated by artistic director Rudi Fuchs in a letter to his invited artists in the fall of 1981.[17] In the letter, Fuchs mused on the "gentle and discreet" nature of art as a realm removed from the clutter of everyday life.[18] Such romantic insights dovetailed well with the mainstream art world at the time, which was dominated by a neo-expressionist return to painting as an emotionally charged, individualist practice.

But Fuchs's letter also discussed more practical matters. He sought to renovate the Museum Fridericianum, the main exhibition venue of Documenta 7, which he described as providing an inadequate amount of wall space. In his letter, Fuchs informed his artists that he would oversee the construction of additional permanent brick walls in the Museum Fridericianum.[19] Given that, by the early 1980s, international exhibition venues were more than accustomed to displaying the three-dimensional art forms of installation, video, and performance, Fuchs's point about the lack of available white wall space might have seemed anachronistic. If conceptualist interventions and site-specific installations were increasingly accompanying (or even substituting for) paintings and photographs in contemporary art exhibitions, why did Fuchs suddenly need additional wall space?

Fuchs's letter became the basis for Asher's Documenta project. In this work, Asher addressed Fuchs's request for increased display space by importing a set of walls to the Orangerie, another exhibition venue.[20] Asher further instructed that his walls were to be used for displaying wall-based work (primarily paintings and photographs) by other artists. This project extended a recent project Asher had just completed at Haus Lange, part of the Krefeld Kunstmuseen 128 miles away from Kassel.[21] For his exhibition at the Museum Haus Lange, he duplicated the walls inside the building that were used for displaying two-dimensional art (figure 4.4). The additional set of walls was rotated ninety degrees from their original position and placed inside the same building. Some of these walls fit inside the elegant Haus Lange alongside the fixed set, while other wall segments either pressed against the exterior boundaries of the exhibition rooms or extended into the grounds outside the villa.

Haus Lange was one of two modernist villas designed by Ludwig Mies van der Rohe for residential use in the late 1920s, and later converted into contemporary art exhibition spaces.[22] In his Documenta project, Asher appropriated the interior wall structure of the other villa, Haus Esters, creating a duplicate set of the walls used for exhibition purposes there. These duplicate walls were then installed in the Orangerie in Kassel for the duration of Documenta 7 (figure 4.5).[23] The reproduced walls had the same dimensions as those of the original Haus Esters walls and replicated their distinctive material features, such as the tall natural wood molding that lined the horizontal and vertical edges.[24] A label

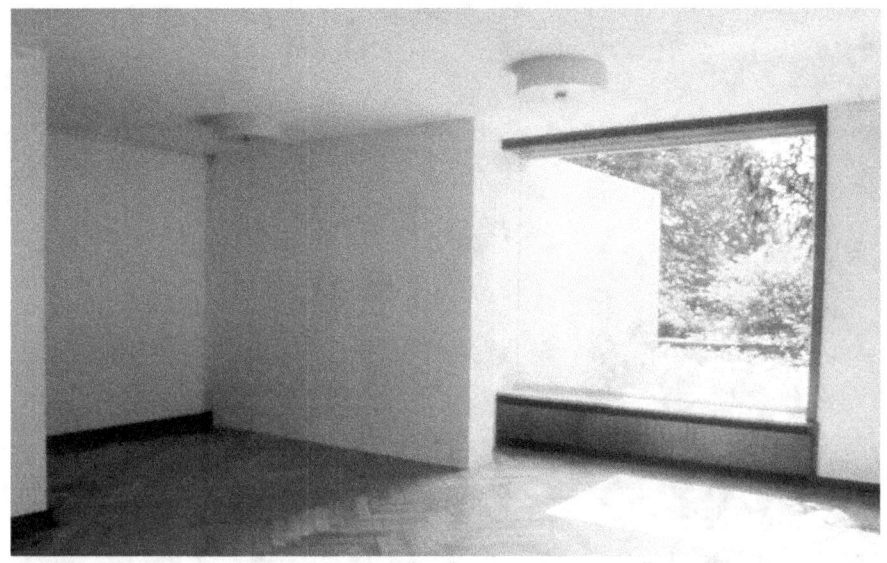

4.4   Museum Haus Lange, Krefelder Kunstmuseen, Krefeld, 1982. Detail view of installation. (Photograph courtesy the artist.)

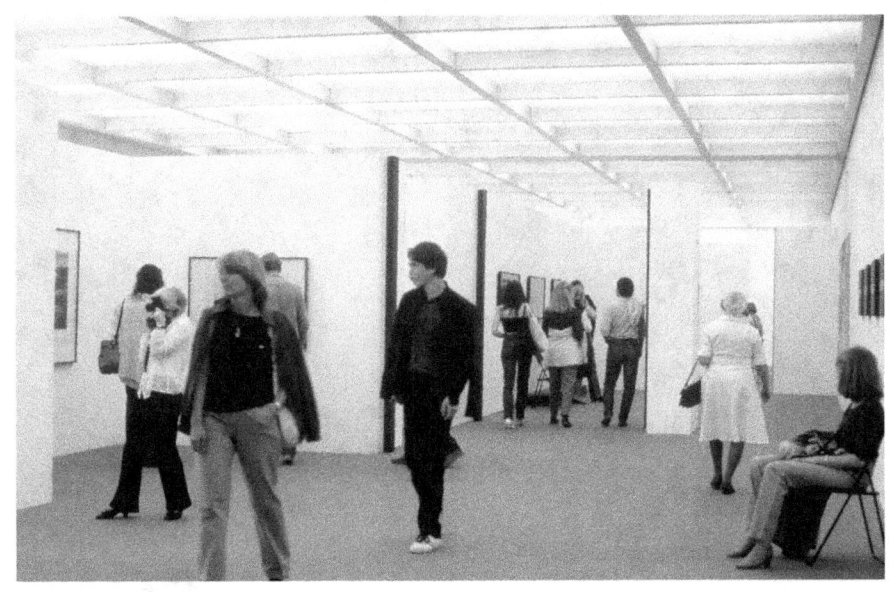

4.5 Documenta 7, Kassel, 1982. Reconstruction of interior walls used for exhibitions at the Museum Haus Esters in Krefeld, installed for the duration of Documenta 7 in the Orangerie. (Photograph taken prior to attaching Nussbaum floor molding.) (Photograph by Anne Rorimer; courtesy the artist.)

attached to one of the walls identified them as a work by Michael Asher. In a brief artist's statement posted next to the wall label, Asher outlined the references to Haus Esters, explaining that the original walls were used "as the existing exhibition display system" in that building.[25]

On one level, Asher's replication of Krefeld's Haus Esters walls in Kassel's Orangerie referenced the fetishization of bare modernist aesthetics in exhibition architecture. This was a particularly appropriate reference in the context of Documenta 7, considering Fuchs's evocation of modernist values in his exhibition program. But on another level, Asher's contribution addressed the reciprocity of institutional relations between artists and curators, and the question of how the power to receive is transformed by the power to give. By providing functional exhibition walls to a Documenta exhibition venue, Asher did respond to, and thereby support, Fuchs's complaint about the lack of wall space.[26] At the time of Documenta 7, Fuchs was the director of the Van Abbemuseum and, like Koenig, had a track record of supporting Asher's work. Fuchs had organized Asher's 1977 exhibition in the Van Abbemuseum, spearheaded the publication of an accompanying catalogue that documented his works in Europe from 1972 to 1977,[27] and subsequently asked him to submit a proposal for the permanent collection of the Van Abbemuseum, as discussed in chapter 3. For a curator with a history of supporting institutional critique and dematerialized conceptual art (he had also presented solo exhibitions by Buren and Haacke in the Van Abbemuseum in the late 1970s), Fuchs demonstrated unusual attachment to institutional stability in his Documenta 7. In his writings before Documenta, Fuchs contrasted the permanency of museum structures against changing art. "In showing advanced, unconventional art, advocating its cause," Fuchs wrote in 1980, "the museum is part of an enlightened system; it will play a role in the advancement of cultural change but that doesn't alter its conservative nature as an idealistic institution."[28]

Fuchs's description of the museum as "conservative" is reflected in his call for additional permanent walls for the Museum Fridericianum in advance of Documenta 7. By privileging the exhibition machinery over the art contained therein, Fuchs implicitly prioritized the lasting institutional structure over the specific, temporary needs of any given exhibiting artist. Douglas Crimp notes Fuchs's centralization of the exhibition's material framework in the director's presentation of Documenta 7 at a press conference before the exhibition.[29] This emphasis on the allocation of institutional resources to bricks and mortar continued in Fuchs's catalogue foreword, in which he states that "we construct an exhibition after first having made the rooms for this exhibition. In the mean-time the artists attempt to do their best, as it should be."[30] Fuchs's insistence on building permanent walls reflects a view in which the institution is cast as primary, conservative, and permanent vis-à-vis secondary, ostensibly radical, and temporary artworks.[31]

The support that Asher provided Fuchs responded to this ideological position. Fuchs initially called his exhibition "Documenta 7: A Story." In the exhibition catalogue, however, Fuchs replaced his original subtitle with a much longer, perhaps more descriptive phrase: "*In which our heroes after a long and strenuous voyage through sinister valleys and dark forests finally arrive in the English Garden, and at the gate of a splendid palace.*"[32] He followed this description with the explanation that "[a]t least such a subtitle reflects our desire for a clear order and a quiet atmosphere."[33]

On the surface, Asher's work fit Fuchs's agenda perfectly. His crisp, white walls were orderly as well as quiet, and perhaps even "heroic" in scale. And they were certainly clear when compared to the emotional energy communicated by the new figurative work prominently featured in Fuchs's Documenta. What kind of artwork needs ample white wall space if not paintings by Salomé or David Salle, or Cindy Sherman's large-scale photographs, all of which were installed on Asher's walls?[34] Lawrence Weiner's inscription on the facade of the Museum Fridericianum, "Many colored objects placed side by side to form a row of many colored objects," seemed to accurately describe much of the art Fuchs included in his Documenta.[35]

Asher's move of providing institutional support to Fuchs's vision could be described as extremely generous, even self-effacing. Asher supplied the replica of Haus Esters's walls for the Orangerie instead of making a proposal that would have placed even more objects on the existing walls, which ostensibly would have further complicated the logistics of Documenta. By choosing to assist the artistic director, Asher, the artist, thus designated Fuchs, the artistic director, as the subject in need of support: Fuchs lacked walls, Asher furnished them for him. This practical move reversed the conventional institutional power relations, in which curators are endowed with the power to provide support to artists, who are willing to receive it. In Asher's affective gift economy at Documenta, the artist took over the power to provide, designating the institutional representative (Fuchs) as the recipient of the artist's gift.

Although Asher's gesture of giving appeared to subordinate his own authorial subject position to Fuchs's agenda, the practical use of his gift of wall space can be seen to have challenged any subordination of Asher. Rather than effacing his own authorship from Documenta, Asher's gesture enclosed the paintings and photographs by Salle, Sherman, Salomé, and others displayed on his walls (figure 4.6). The placement of other artists' works within Asher's wall structure visibly bracketed the autonomy of these artists and challenged Fuchs's promotion of such autonomy. Instead of heeding Fuchs's advice to "disentangle art from the diverse pressures and social perversions it has to bear,"[36] Asher's contribution dissolved the boundaries between works of art and their material support, demonstrating how inextricable art was from the institutional pressures and social context that Fuchs himself installed and supported as the artistic director of Documenta 7.

Asher's work continued the artist's investigation in "Heute" of socioeconomic relations within art institutions. Both the exhibition walls in Documenta 7 and the visitors' chairs in "Heute" were the types of everyday material supports commonly used in art institutions. Gallery offices need chairs for conducting business with clients as much as exhibition venues need walls to display two-dimensional works of art. Appropriated by Asher, these material support structures evoked the socioeconomic ties that bind individual subjects—such as artists and curators—to organizational procedures. Asher's "Heute" contribution foregrounded the exhibition's funding and organizational structure, while his Documenta 7 project responded to Fuchs's need for walls by structurally supporting works by other participating artists. In both exhibitions, Asher connected these material support structures with social relations within art institutions. In particular, by reversing and returning the institutional support that he had received from Fuchs, Asher acknowledged the social and psychological ties that bind artists, curators, and museum directors to each other within art institutions. Rather than exempting himself from this affective economy of support, Asher participated in the circulation of generosity by making use of the social contracts between artists and exhibition organizers in order to reiterate what anthropologist Marcel Mauss found in his study of the gift economy: that the dual obligations to give and receive are accompanied by the imperative to reciprocate.[37]

Orangerie 1. Obergeschoß / *1st Upper Story*

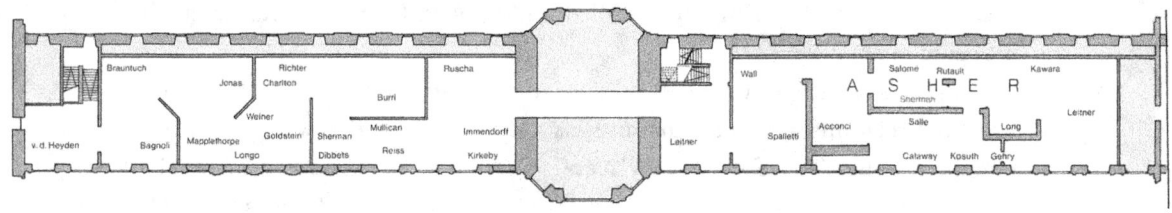

4.6   Documenta 7, Kassel, 1982. Floor plan of the first upper story of the Orangerie. Asher's installation was in the east half of the floor, delineated with thicker lines.

Asher returned to the question of institutional support in 1989 with his work for the exhibition "l'art conceptuel, une perspective." This historical survey, held at the Musée d'art moderne de la Ville de Paris, was among the first large-scale retrospective exhibitions to focus on 1960s conceptual art—a project that several American and European group exhibitions extended in the 1990s.[38] In preparation for the exhibition, curator Claude Gintz asked invited artists to contribute works dating from the historical era of conceptual art, defined for this exhibition as the time period between 1962 and 1972.[39] Gintz was particularly interested in having Asher restage his 1972 work at Documenta 5, in which Asher had reconfigured the spatial parameters of an enclosed space by painting it half black and half white.[40] Asher declined this invitation, citing his reluctance to duplicate works for any exhibition that differed historically and discursively from the site of the original. His response to Gintz constitutes perhaps the most direct explanation of what Asher sees as site specificity:

> Certainly, contemporary modernist practice would welcome me to the fold and possibly be quite thrilled if I would reconstruct an older artwork. I originally asserted that I did the work you request specifically for Documenta v and the conditions I saw pertinent to [Documenta 5's artistic director Harold] Szeemann's thesis of his exhibition. I also attempted to problematize some modernist thought that seemed mainstream in 1972. To reconstruct this work would be possible if we could reconstruct the site of modernism 16 years ago and the actual context of Documenta 5. But if we were even able to do this, why and for what purpose would we be doing it?[41]

The question Asher raised about "reconstruct[ing]" a historical moment became the linchpin of his contribution for "l'art conceptuel." The artist's refusal to reexhibit a "historical" work in the planned exhibition prompted Gintz, in his reply to Asher, to extend the definition of historical context by suggesting Asher might consider the retrospective mission of "l'art conceptuel" in his work.[42] In the end, Asher did exactly that: he considered the reception of conceptual art as a historical art movement in the late 1980s, and, specifically, how "l'art conceptuel" would play into that reception.

Asher developed three initial proposals for "l'art conceptuel." His first proposal addressed the generational understanding (or lack of understanding) of conceptual art by viewers who were old enough to have had the opportunity to experience the 1960s art movement firsthand. Asher proposed that the museum invite senior citizens to visit and obtain a poster from one of the original conceptual art exhibitions (for example, the 1969 "When Attitudes Become Form"). He speculated that seniors in 1989 were of a generation that might have accepted pop art and minimalism but rejected conceptualism. Asher's work would then present these seniors with an opportunity to continue the reception of the original conceptual art at the point in the art historical narrative where they had left off.[43] Practical difficulties kept this initial proposal from realization, however, since the original posters of the early conceptual art exhibitions had by the late 1980s become rare—and valuable—historical documents.[44]

Asher's second proposal featured many of the thematic elements that were to define his final work for "l'art conceptuel." In this proposal, he extended his consideration of the place of conceptual art in the life history of senior citizens. This work would have consisted of advertisements for "l'art conceptuel" in academic journals, magazines, and newsletters aimed at an older readership, such as the journal *Ageing and Society* or the newsletter *Gray Panther Network*.[45] This version of the proposal continued to address a generationally defined viewership, while directing its focus to the retrospective mission of "l'art conceptuel." Shortly after sending this proposal to Gintz, though, Asher submitted a third proposal that changed the focus of the work from senior citizens to academic art historians.[46]

Asher's third, and ultimately realized, proposal for "l'art conceptuel" retained the idea of placing advertisements for the exhibition in a select group of publications. Yet this third proposal replaced senior journals and magazines with seven European art historical journals: *Apollo*, *Art History*, *Daidalos: Berlin Architectural Journal*, *The Journal of Aesthetics and Art Criticism*, *La revue du Louvre et des musées de France*, *Romagna arte e storia*, and *Simiolus*. The addressed reader shifted from a generationally defined senior citizen to a professionally defined art historian (and in the case of *Apollo*, art collector), whose attention was now called to the historicization of 1960s conceptual art. In a letter to Gintz, Asher noted his interest in what conceptual art meant for its viewers in the 1960s, and in the factors that might inspire that original audience to promote retrospective revisitations of conceptual art.[47] But Asher called into question the ideological effects of fitting conceptual art into a preservationist retrospective format, because that very art had historically challenged institutional structures such as traditional exhibition formats. He further asked how "l'art conceptuel" could advance critical discourse: "will this retrospective be experienced and even used as a tool to problematize aesthetic practice just as the practice it represents managed to do?"[48]

Asher's work for "l'art conceptuel" might be interpreted as a response to the issues he raised in his letter to Gintz about canonizing historical conceptual art into an object of art historical discourse. A retrospective approach involves judgments made by art historians, critics, curators, and collectors; and Asher's advertisements were a targeted contribution to this discourse of valuation. In his correspondence with Gintz, Asher further reflected on the individual emotional and psychological motives that might inform the retrospective invocation of an art movement such as conceptual art, noting that "a retrospective can represent a sense of nostalgia or a long missed rendering of the past, so often used to substantiate what we feel is missing as well as confirming what we have chosen to believe."[49] In Asher's description, the retrospective urge on the part of curators, exhibition visitors, and art historians consisted of complex, individually motivated affective investments in recreating a past in order to address the needs of the present. Yet Asher also felt that the retrospective evaluation of an art movement was a process capable of producing new knowledge. In a statement that was posted in the exhibition and reproduced in the catalogue, he promoted the productive dimension of this "historical objectification" of conceptual art, commenting that the exhibition presented an opportunity to involve multiple voices in the process of writing art history.[50]

Asher's own role in "l'art conceptuel" was complex. By participating in a retrospective exhibition of conceptual art, he accepted his inclusion (and his own "historical objectification") in the history of that movement. At the same time, he did not conform to the exhibition's curatorial agenda by recreating a work of his from the original heyday of conceptual art. This move set him apart from the other artists in the exhibition, and instead aligned him with the curators, critics, and art historians who debated the historicization of conceptual art.

The visibility of Asher's own authorial position was downplayed in his work for "l'art conceptuel." This was true at least for those readers who came across Asher's advertisement in the art historical journals (figure 4.7). These art historians and collectors were probably unaware of his role in the production of the advertisements, for these ads did not mention that involvement. Instead, the announcements were placed in the journals as promotional advertising for the exhibition "l'art conceptuel." On the other hand, exhibition visitors (or those who read the catalogue) encountered the advertisements in the context of Asher's work. Although the journals were not on display in the exhibition, a wall label informed the viewer of Asher's project and listed the journals that carried his "announcements."[51] The label also informed museum visitors that these art historical journals were available for purchase in the museum's bookstore.[52]

Asher's decision to use his own authorial position to produce advertisements that supported the exhibition "l'art conceptuel" by promoting it to academic art historians expanded the artist's commentary on institutional self-presentation begun in "Heute" and Documenta 7. In these exhibitions, Asher challenged the objectification of his work (and, perhaps not coincidentally, the discursive subordination of his work to the curator's plan for the exhibition) by addressing the entire discursive framework of the exhibition. In "Heute," his gallery chairs called attention to the funding structure of the exhibition. For Documenta 7, Asher seemingly embraced Fuchs's curatorial agenda by producing supplementary display walls for the exhibition. For "l'art conceptuel," Asher's emphatic support of the exhibition's retrospective mission through advertising promoted the exhibition to art historians.

These situations—"l'art conceptuel" perhaps most explicitly—connected the host exhibition's retrospective mission with the practice of art history and criticism, where the historicizing of recent art took place. Asher's advertisement for "l'art conceptuel," for example, was an invitation for art historians to participate in the discourse of conceptual art, and a challenge to the idea that any one event or institution has the exclusive right to claim history. This call for openness in art's discourses and institutions returned in his 1999 project for "The Museum as Muse: Artists Reflect."

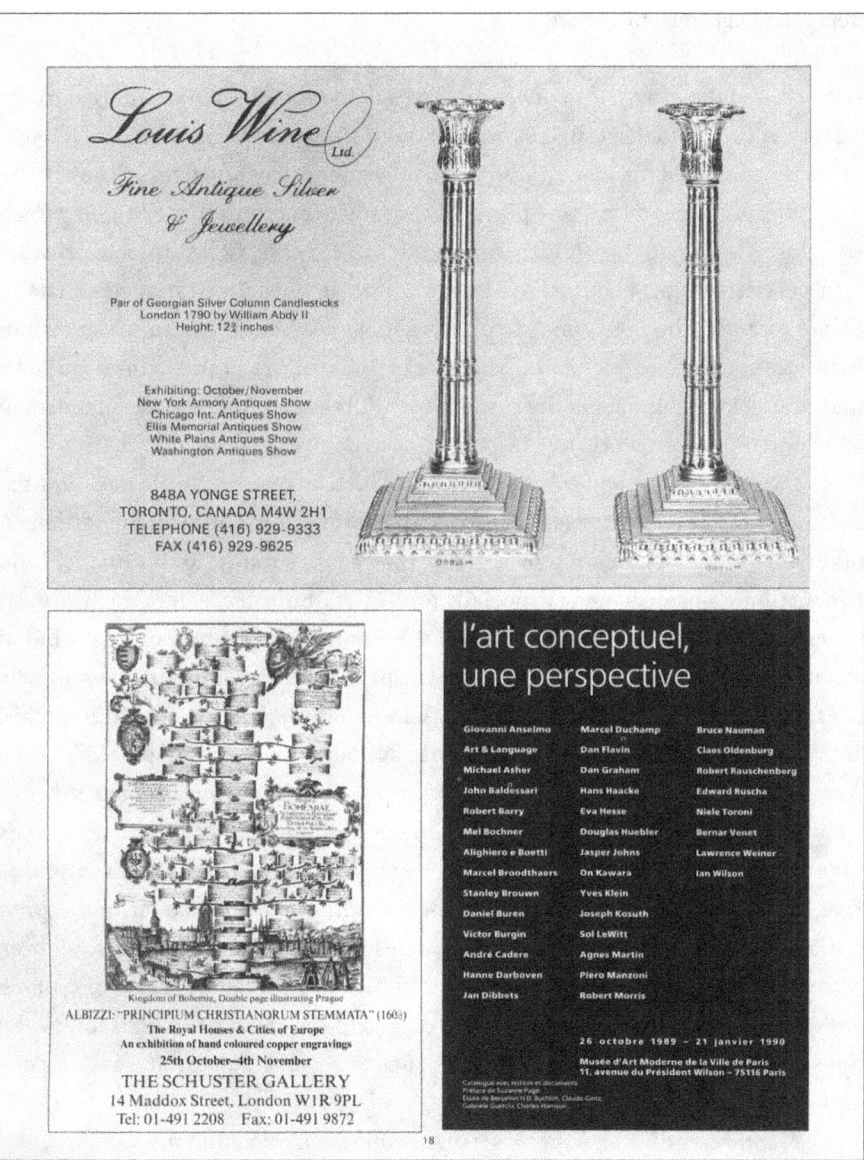

4.7 Advertisement for "l'art conceptuel, une perspective," in *Apollo: The International Magazine of the Arts* (October 1989).

The decade following "l'art conceptuel" was marked by a flood of interest in the history of conceptual art. Retrospective exhibitions, anthologies, and academic histories solidified the place of the materially ephemeral practices in the artistic mainstream. During the same period, a version of institutional critique, which was closely associated with historical modes of conceptual art, further trickled into mainstream art institutions in the 1990s as museums engaged artists to comment upon the museums' display practices. Although not an exhibition of institutional critique per se, the Museum of Modern Art's 1999 exhibition "The Museum as Muse: Artists Reflect" sought to address this intersection of museum and contemporary art practice by providing a historical context for it.

For Asher, "The Museum as Muse" provided an opportunity to consider the writing of history within institutional self-presentation. In contrast with most of the invited artists, Asher was asked by the show's curator, Kynaston McShine, to contribute a project made especially for the exhibition.[53] Asher's early project notes for "The Museum as Muse" revolved around the question of what kind of attention museums, in particular MoMA, paid to their public image and self-presentation.[54] The first proposal that Asher sent to McShine sought to obtain from museum collections artworks whose authenticity was in dispute. McShine turned down this idea, arguing that the physical handling of such artwork would be difficult and problematic.[55] Addressing McShine's concern, Asher's second proposal suggested assembling a catalogue of paintings and sculptures that MoMA had deaccessioned from the founding of the museum to the present. Asher envisioned this catalogue as "a descriptive list in chronological order" that would comprise basic identificatory information about each artwork, along with a corresponding photograph. The design of the catalogue would follow the appearance of the museum's own catalogues of recently acquired works (accession catalogues).[56]

McShine's reply to Asher's second proposal arrived one month later, and expressed tentative support for the project. McShine did not object to Asher's concept in itself, nor did he object to the labor of assembling the information— although he referred to the labor required as considerable—but he was concerned about the cost of printing the deaccession catalogue. In an effort to reduce this cost, McShine suggested electronic and possibly Internet-based presentation of Asher's publication.[57] Asher insisted on, and ultimately won support for, the inclusion of a printed catalogue. Explaining that the printed format would more directly relate to the museum's accession catalogue, he proposed that funds raised by selling his catalogue might be used to offset the cost of printing it.[58] Asher argued that the printed catalogue would also enable "a discrete relation to the reader," a relation that brought into play two specific institutional sites: the MoMA exhibition space housing "The Museum as Muse" and the museum's bookstore, where copies of the catalogue would be available to museum visitors.[59]

This second proposal, cataloguing the museum's deaccession history, was realized for "The Museum as Muse." The work consisted of a slim red catalogue that mimicked the latest edition of MoMA's accession catalogue in both design and content, from paper stock to typeface and organization of listings. The work's design made only two departures from the official MoMA accession catalogue. The first was the inclusion of the words "Catalog of Deaccessions 1929 through 1998 by Michael Asher" printed in gold on the cover, overlaying the MoMA accession catalogue title *Painting and Sculpture from The Museum of Modern Art*, printed in white. The only other difference was that Asher's name was printed on the bottom of each interior page of the catalogue; otherwise, the format of the catalogue duplicated that of the accession catalogue. Following a series of publication credits, an introduction, and acknowledgments, the pages of the catalogue contained a list of each artwork removed from MoMA's Department of Painting and Sculpture during the museum's seventy-year history (figure 4.8). The list had been compiled by a MoMA intern without Asher's direct involvement (though the artist had offered to cull the titles from the museum's records himself). The entries were arranged alphabetically according to the deaccessioned artist's last name. Although the entries included information about the year the museum had acquired the work in question—which was coded into its accession number— there was no corresponding information about the year the work exited MoMA.

Visitors to "The Museum as Muse" encountered Asher's work at the conclusion of the exhibition. A thin stack of catalogues was placed in a vertical wooden display at the end of one of the museum's courtesy benches for exhibition visitors (figure 4.9). An adjoining label on the wall identified the project as a work by Michael Asher, and informed museum visitors that they could claim a copy of the catalogue at the bookstore by showing their entrance ticket. In the bookstore, however, Asher's catalogues were stored behind the cash register desks, where they were kept out of sight. If asked, clerks would furnish a copy to visitors. This mode of distribution, instituted by the museum and not the artist, drew attention

CÉZANNE

CÉZANNE, Paul.

CHOCQUET IN AN ARMCHAIR. (1877?). Oil on canvas, 17¾ x 14¼". 20.34

L'ESTAQUE. 1883–1885. Oil on canvas, 23⅞ x 27¾". 264.54

FRUIT AND WINE. (c. 1885–88). Oil on canvas, 20⅞ x 25⅜". 11.34

MAN IN BLUE CAP (UNCLE DOMINIC). 1865–66. Oil on canvas, 32¼ x 6⅛". 17.34

THE ROAD. 1871–72. Oil on canvas, 23½ x 28¾". 14.34

PEARS AND KNIFE. (c. 1878). Oil on canvas, 8⅛ x 12¼". 10.34

THE WATER CAN. (c. 1880–1882). Oil on canvas, 10⅝ x 13¾". 7.34

PORTRAIT OF MME. CÉZANNE. c. 1885–87. Oil on canvas, 18⅛ x 15⅛". 19.34

CHADWICK, Lynn.

THE JEWEL. Metal, glass, and plastic, 9⅜ x 10½ x 13⅝". 771.69

CHAGALL, Marc.

FLOWERS. 1925. Oil on canvas, 37¼ x 29⅝". 620.73

CHAMBERLAIN, John.

MAZ. 1960. Painted scrap metal, 44¼"h., at base 8⅛ x 9⅞". 1.61

NORMA JEAN RISING. 1967. Galvanized steel, 66 x 38 x 38". 627.73

CHARLOT, Jean.

BUILDER CARRYING STONE. 1930. Oil, 27½ x 27½". 178.35

THE DANCE (LA JARANA). (n.d.). Oil. 179.35

THE DRINKER. (n.d.). Oil. 180.35

DE CHIRICO, Giorgio.

DELIGHTERS OF THE POET. 1913. Oil on canvas, 27⅜ x 34". 525.41

EVANGELICAL STILL LIFE. 1916. Oil on canvas, (irreg.) 31¾ x 28⅛". 583.67

CONVERSATION. 1926 (?). Oil on wood, 13¼ x 10¼". 1.35

HORSES AND TEMPLE. (n.d.). Oil on canvas. 68.61

CIKOVSKY, Nicolai.

GIRL IN GREEN. 1937. Oil on canvas, 36 x 30". 295.38

COHEN, George.

IMAGO. 1955. Construction of varnished and painted wood, metal, string, sponge and cloth, 34¼ x 12⅜ x 2⅜". 16.61

COSGROVE, Stanley.

MEXICAN LANDSCAPE. 1942. Oil on composition board, 10⅛ x 18". 581.42

CROSS, Henri-Edmond.

WOODLAND IN PROVENCE. 1906–07. Oil on paper mounted on canvas, 21¾ x 17¼". 182.35

DALI, Salvador.

IMPERIAL VIOLETS. 1938. Oil on canvas, 39¼ x 56⅛". 527.41

DAUMIER, Honoré.

BUST OF GUIZOT. 1832, this cast 1930. Bronze. 6½" h., at base 3¾ x 5" (irreg.). 621.39

THE LAUNDRESS 1861(?). Oil on wood, 19⅝ x 13⅛". 27.34

THE REFUGEES. (n.d.). Oil on canvas, 15¼ x 27". 613.43

DAVIE, Alan.

STEPPING STONES OF THE DRAGON. 1962. Oil and gold paint on canvas, 18 x 22". 500.65

DAVIES, Arthur B.

ENERGIA. Oil on canvas, 42½ x 20½". 1.67

DAVIS, Stuart.

CARREFOUR. Oil. 837.63

PLACE DES VOSGES. 1929. Oil on canvas, 21 x 28". 183.35

SUMMER LANDSCAPE. 1930. Oil on canvas, 29 x 42". 30.40

DEGAS, Hilaire-Germain-Edgar.

ARABESQUE OVER RIGHT LEG, LEFT ARM IN LINE. (n.d.). Bronze, 11¼ x 17⅛ x 4", including bronze base ¼ x 4⅞ x 3¾". Separate marble base, ⅞ x 4¾ x 6½". 503.70

RACE HORSES 1884. Oil on canvas. 18¼ x 21⅝". 38.34

DELAUNAY-TERK, Sonia.

MARKET IN MINHO (STUDY 7). 1916. Distemper and encaustic on canvas, 12¼ x 17⅜". 151.55

DELVAUX, Paul.

THE ENCOUNTER (LA RENCONTRE). 1938. Oil on canvas, 35⅝ x 47½". 326.63

DERAIN, André.

MADAME DERAIN. 1920. Oil on canvas, 14¾ x 9¼". 44.34

THE FARM. 1922–24. Oil on canvas, 19¾ x 24". 46.34

LANDSCAPE SOUTHERN FRANCE. 1927–28. Oil on canvas, 31½ x 38". 45.34

GUITAR PLAYER. 1928. Oil on canvas, 32½ x 38⅜". 417.41

NIGHT PIECE WITH MUSICAL INSTRUMENTS. After 1930. Oil on canvas, 9⅛ x 15⅜". 679.54

DESPIAU, Charles.

LITTLE PEASANT GIRL. 1904. Original plaster. 15¾" h., including plaster base 5¾ x 5¼ x 5⅛". 619.39

A. MME OTHON FRIESZ.

B. LEDA AND THE SWAN. (1924). A. Original plaster, 20⅞" h. including plaster base 6 x 6¾ x 7½" h. B. Plaster relief, 6½ x 5". 616.39. A–B

MADAME HENRY WAROQUIER. 1927. Bronze, 15¾" h., on stone base 6 x 7⅞ x 6". 616.43

SEATED YOUTH: MONUMENT TO EMIL MAYRISCH. 1932. Bronze, 6' 5 15/16" x 3' 5/16" x 4' 7⅛". 623.39

ANNE MORROW LINDBERGH. 1939. Bronze, 15½" h., on wood base, 4½ x 8⅛ x 6¾". 657.39

MARIA LANI. (n.d.). Bronze, 14"h. 11.30

8

ASHER

4.8 Detail view of deaccession catalogue for "The Museum as Muse: Artists Reflect," Museum of Modern Art, New York, 1999. (Courtesy the artist.)

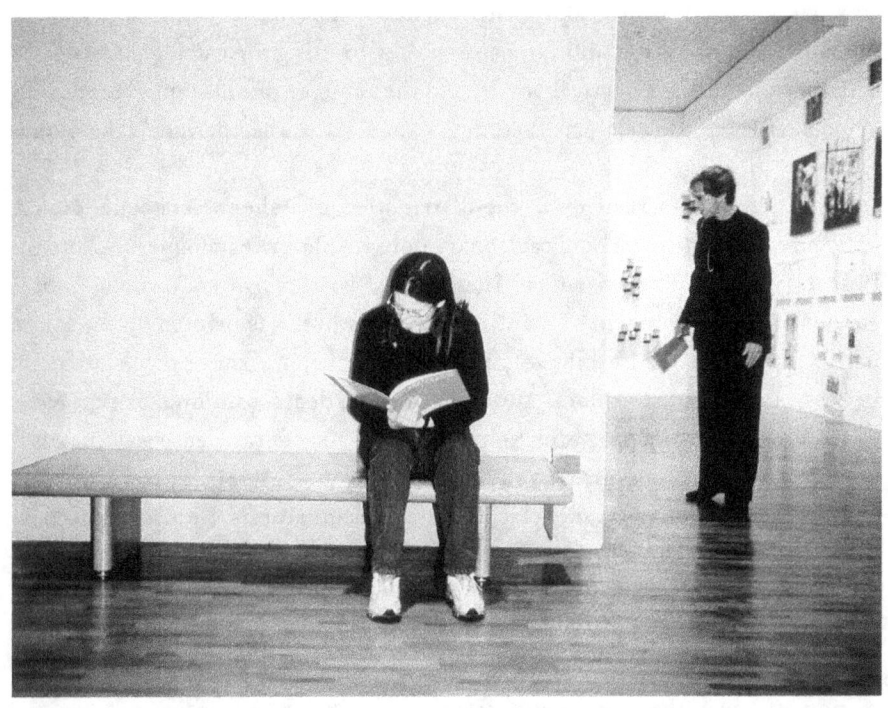

4.9 "The Museum as Muse: Artists Reflect," Museum of Modern Art, New York, 1999. Installation view, museum bench with deaccession catalogues made available within the exhibition space. Museum visitor reading the catalogue. (Photograph by Andrew Freeman; courtesy the artist.)

from Thomas Crow and Roberta Smith, each of whom separately compared this covert process to the distribution of illicit materials such as pornography.[60] In Smith's view, "One might almost expect the catalogue to come in a plain brown wrapper, not a red cover, and it seems singularly appropriate that it can be taken home for careful examination in private."[61] By limiting the catalogue's scope of distribution, MoMA effectively restricted the number of museum visitors who gained access to the catalogue's contents—at least in the "private" take-home version.

In addition to restricting the distribution of Asher's catalogue, MoMA insisted on inserting its own cautionary note inside the catalogue. "A Note on Deaccessioning at The Museum of Modern Art," written by Kirk Varnedoe, chief curator of the Department of Painting and Sculpture, was printed on the lower half of the catalogue's introductory page, directly below Asher's own statement. In the note, Varnedoe explains MoMA's policy on deaccessioning, or removing works from the museum's permanent collection. In general, deaccessioning is a practice strongly condemned by the museum world. In MoMA's case, Varnedoe emphasizes that deaccessioning facilitated new acquisitions. He also details how donors of deaccessioned works continue to be honored through the process by transferring their names from the work that was deaccessioned to a new work acquired with the proceeds.[62] In addition to describing institutional policy, however, Varnedoe's note comments on Asher's project, casting doubt on the information offered in the deaccession catalogue:

> In the present instance, we have tried to cooperate with Michael Asher's request to have a list of works of painting and sculpture sold or exchanged by the Museum over the years. Given the limitations of the project however, we have not been able to assure ourselves that the present list meets the criteria of completeness or accuracy we would require in a Museum publication. Readers are thus cautioned to be aware of possible flaws and limitations in this listing of titles.[63]

In this statement, Varnedoe presents MoMA as an institution that had done its best to support Asher's project. Psychologically, Varnedoe's statement projects an attitude of concern and disclosure on the part of MoMA; the museum is presented as an institution that cares about the epistemological quality of the visitor's experience. The affirmation of the museum's integrity is then coupled with Varnedoe's tacit disavowal of Asher's project. The disclaimer thus fractured the appearance of symbiotic unity between the artist and the hosting museum. It marked the social and discursive positions of the artist and institution as separate subject positions whose motives and intents did not coalesce, and perhaps did not even overlap. This split between the artist and institution was articulated in terms of credibility: the institution was defending its credibility against the artist while at the same time supporting the artist's contribution to an exhibition within its walls.[64]

The museum's simultaneous attitudes of acknowledgment and disavowal of Asher might be described in terms related to Sigmund Freud's characterization of the split ego.[65] "I know very well" that the catalogue information has truth value, "but all the same," the museum chose to disavow that information to maintain its investment in its control of its own institutional authority.[66] For Freud, the subject's split response of acknowledgment and disavowal allows the subject to successfully negotiate with external reality while maintaining internal coherence.[67] He describes the splitting of the ego as resulting from two coexisting but contradictory responses to reality, one of which acknowledges external reality while the other disavows it.[68] Although simultaneous recognition and disavowal certainly can spell crisis or unmanageable pressure in some cases, it usually represents a remarkably flexible mode of permanently managing, and living with, an external threat or contradictory information.

Varnedoe's statement in Asher's deaccession catalogue executed a similarly split move. On the one hand, the museum—in whose name Varnedoe was speaking—validated Asher's work by acknowledging its "cooperation" with Asher, as the artist whom the museum had invited (of its own volition) and thoroughly sanctioned to exhibit within its own institutional domain. On the other hand, MoMA repudiated the veracity of the contents in the catalogue that it had, in practice, produced itself. This repudiation disavowed both MoMA's own history and Asher. The splitting of institutional authority nevertheless remained visible within "The Museum as Muse." In contrast to some of the notorious instances of museums censoring institutional critique—such as Daniel Buren's and Hans Haacke's respective encounters with the Guggenheim Museum in 1971—Asher's work was not removed from "The Museum as Muse," nor was he barred from participating in the exhibition.[69] The visibility of the split discursive authority between the museum and artist was instead ensured by the inclusion of MoMA's disclaimer in Asher's deaccession catalogue, thus illustrating the concrete limits of institutional support for artists when the work in question reflects upon the history of the museum itself.[70]

Despite Varnedoe's cautionary note about the credibility of the entries in the deaccession catalogue, the object indeed held practical informational value. Asher had emphasized this aspect in his proposal, while negotiating with McShine before the exhibition. "I am depending upon the catalog to be received as a useful object," Asher explained, "rather than [its being regarded as] a symbolic object."[71] Critics noted both the symbolic and pragmatic dimensions of the catalogue in their reviews of the exhibition. On the one hand, the catalogue was discussed as a tactical intervention that countered the museum's own strategies of self-presentation. Another strand of criticism zeroed in on the contents of the listings. Smith, in particular, read Asher's catalogue as an authentic document of MoMA's institutional history.[72] For Smith, the precise archival data listed in the deaccession catalogue revealed previously unavailable information about the history of collecting at the Museum of Modern Art, an institution that almost single-handedly has defined the canon of twentieth-century modernism.[73]

As a survey of the relations between artists and museums, "The Museum as Muse: Artists Reflect" centralized the institution. The subtitle "Artists Reflect" described a unidirectional influence from the museum to artists. In that sense, the element of reciprocity was missing from the museum's position as presented in the exhibition: the museum did not reflect on the influence artists had on it. Instead, reflection was an activity reserved for artists invited to participate in a MoMA group exhibition. In this situation, the artists were the recipients of institutional support. Asher's project, however, reversed the museum's premise by prompting the museum to reflect on its own practices of institutional self-presentation. By contributing to MoMA's self-presentation, he inverted the support relations between museums and artists. His claim to discursive authority—the authority to speak in the name of the museum, so to say, by closely adapting the format of the museum's own accession catalogue—challenged the institution's implicit demand that the artist remain discursively, and perhaps especially emotionally and psychologically, subservient to its authority. Asher's work treated the curator as a representative of the art institution, symptomatic of the institutional attitudes and modes of address. MoMA was moved to defend its own institutional practices, spelling out the split institutional ego that simultaneously acknowledged and disavowed the artist exhibiting within the museum's own walls. The museum's insistence on inserting its own statement in Asher's deaccession catalogue indicated that MoMA, the institutional subject, was operating under pressure to repudiate its own history in defense of a self-recognized image of itself as it struggled to preserve its sense of order. MoMA's simultaneous disavowal and support of Asher in the artist's contribution to the museum's self-presentation articulated very real differences in the subject positions of artists and museums in the cultural economy of art institutions, reminding viewers of the multiple interests that go into the smooth, coherent modes of self-presentation that typically characterize the public face of art institutions.

Conclusion: The Gift of Support

It might be argued that providing institutional support is one of the subtle tactical currents that runs throughout Asher's oeuvre. In the four works discussed in this chapter, institutional support was articulated as a material and psychological interstice within the museum's paradigm of self-presentation. In "Heute," Asher foregrounded the exhibition's funding structure within the art world's socioeconomic relations by exhibiting visitors' chairs from participating galleries. In Documenta 7, he supported the curator's mission by providing more wall space for other exhibiting artists. In "l'art conceptuel, une perspective," he supported the curator's retrospective art historical mission by proactively advertising the exhibition. And in "The Museum as Muse," he advanced the institution's historical memory by compiling a list of deaccessioned paintings and sculptures.

By assuming the role of support provider alongside that of support recipient, Asher implicated himself in these "critical allegories" of the museum's ideological mission.[74] His contributions to institutional self-presentation acknowledged the complex relations that museums and exhibitions both participate in and submit to: relations of support with funding organizations, donors, lenders, critics, historians, and artists. All four projects articulated and operated through the social contracts and power relations between artists and institutional representatives. By emphasizing that individual artistic and curatorial initiatives and authorial positions influence collective modes of institutional self-presentation, these works traced specific modes of power, influence, and authority.

As an artist who carefully studies and engages the institutional conditions of his work, Asher in his artistic practice expands sites into situations that both shape and are shaped by social relations. In this manner, he individuates the institutional sphere, which often seems impersonal, structurally unreachable, even totalitarian, and reified beyond reach. In Asher's work, social relations are experiential in a Foucauldian sense precisely because they reopen the production of knowledge, rules, and subjectivity. For their viewers, participants, and institutional representatives, Asher's projects evoke knowledge, play with and against rules, and constitute subjectivity as a domain that never lacks the potential for change.

Notes

Introduction: The Experiential Matrix

1 These three-dimensional painting-objects included lusciously colored Plexiglas shapes that recalled the Los Angeles Finish Fetish movement. Others were painted wooden wedge forms designed to be so unassuming as to ideally disappear from sight. On Asher's mid-1960s object production, see Benjamin H.D. Buchloh, "Michael Asher and the Conclusion of Modernist Sculpture," *Museum Studies* 10 (1983): 285, and Ann Goldstein, "Michael Asher," in *A Minimal Future? Art as Object 1958–1968*, ed. Ann Goldstein and Diedrich Diederichsen (Los Angeles: Museum of Contemporary Art; Cambridge, Mass.: MIT Press, 2004), 150–152.

2 Asher made several versions of the checkers set in 1965 and 1966, with different pieces. In all but one set, the game pieces were identical in shape and size to common checkers pieces; the one exception (a set in Asher's collection) had pieces that were slightly taller than dime store versions. Michael Asher, telephone interview with the author, April 9, 2007; Asher, interview with the author, June 23, 2008.

3 Asher, telephone interviews with author, April 9 and May 2, 2007.

4 The checkers set, in Judd's collection, is still housed in its original white Plexiglas box. Judd also wrote a note to Asher complimenting the younger artist: "Thanks a lot for the box. It's fine." Donald Judd to Michael Asher, n.d., Michael Asher's personal papers, Los Angeles. Documents from this source will henceforth be cited "Asher papers."

5 Claude Gintz makes this point when he argues that Asher's work thus "does not yield any exchange value." Gintz, "Michael Asher and the Transformation of 'Situational Aesthetics,'" trans. Judith Aminoff, *October*, no. 66 (Fall 1993): 116.

6 Thomas Crow, "Site-Specific Art: The Strong and the Weak," in his *Modern Art in the Common Culture* (New Haven: Yale University Press, 1996), 135–143. Crow's examples include Asher's 1970 work for Pomona College and his 1979 contribution to the "73rd American Exhibition" at the Art Institute of Chicago.

7 After his 2000/2002 LACMA work, Asher was included in the 2004 LACMA survey exhibition "Beyond Geometry: Experiments in Form, 1940s–1970s," with documentation of his 1971 wall installation for the museum.

8 LACMALab was discontinued by the museum in January 2007.

9 Pierre Bourdieu, *Distinction: A Social Critique of the Judgment of Taste*, trans. Richard Nice (Cambridge, Mass.: Harvard University Press, 1984).

10 Fred Wilson's 1992–1993 *Mining the Museum* at the Maryland Historical Society is a representative example of an artist's museum intervention in the early 1990s.

11 Jacques Rancière has elaborated upon the idea of treating equality as a practical starting point rather than a goal to be reached through action. I will discuss Rancière's notion of equality in relation to the LACMA student reinstallation in more detail in chapter 2. Rancière, Solange Guénoun,

and James H. Kavanagh, "Jacques Rancière: Literature, Politics, Aesthetics: Approaches to Democratic Disagreement," *SubStance* 29, no. 2 (2000): 3–24.

12 See chapter 4 for a discussion of Asher's comments on historicity and the retrospective urge as they apply to his own work and to art historical periodicity in general.

13 Asher has participated in a number of historical survey exhibitions. For "l'art conceptuel, une perspective" at the Musée d'art moderne de la Ville de Paris in 1989, he created a new work, which I discuss in detail in chapter 4. In "Reconsidering the Object of Art, 1965–1975" at the Los Angeles Museum of Contemporary Art in 1995–1996 and "A Brief History of Invisible Art" at the cca Wattis Institute for Contemporary Art in San Francisco in 2005–2006, he exhibited works that had been adapted from a previously unrealized proposal. By 2009, Asher had exhibited early object-based works in four cases: "A Minimal Future? Art as Object, 1958–1968" at the Los Angeles Museum of Contemporary Art in 2004; "Beyond Geometry: Experiments in Form, 1940s–70s" at lacma in 2004; "Before the End (The Last Painting Show)" at the Swiss Institute in New York, also in 2004; and "Art in Los Angeles between 1960 and 1990" at the Kunstverein Braunschweig in 2006–2007. In "Los Angeles 1955–1985: Birth of an Art Capital" at the Centre Pompidou in Paris in 2006, Asher exhibited an adaptation of an early, previously unrealized proposal along with documentation of plans and installations of some of his early works.

14 By 2009 Asher had completed only three permanently installed projects. In the late 1970s, he produced a site-specific installation for a private patron in Brentwood, California, and in 1991 he completed a permanent work for the Stuart Collection on the campus of the University of California in San Diego. In 1993, he had an engraving inscribed into a rock as his contribution to "Expo '93" in Taejon, South Korea. I discuss the Stuart Collection project in chapter 1.

15 For a discussion of historical inaccessibility in relation to Matta-Clark's critical reception, see Pamela M. Lee, *Object to Be Destroyed: The Work of Gordon Matta-Clark* (Cambridge, Mass.: mit Press, 2000), xvii.

16 Buchloh, for example, commented on the unwarranted obscurity of Asher's work during a c. 2004 roundtable on the state of contemporary art, stating that "Asher [is] in many ways the most radical of the figures involved in institutional critique from the late sixties onward . . . his work is now mostly neglected; the very radicality of its contestation appears forgotten." In Hal Foster, Rosalind Krauss, Yve-Alain Bois, and Benjamin H. D. Buchloh, "The Predicament of Contemporary Art," in their *Art since 1900: Modernism, Antimodernism, Postmodernism*, vol. 2 (New York: Thames and Hudson, 2004), 674.

17 See, for example, Willoughby Sharp, "New Directions in Southern California Sculpture," *Arts Magazine* 44, no. 8 (Summer 1970): 37; Barbara Munger, "Michael Asher: An Environmental Project," *Studio International* 180, no. 926 (October 1970): 160; Fenella Crichton, "London," *Art International* 17 (November 1973): 46; Melinda Wortz, "Looking Inward," *Art News* 73, no. 10 (December 1974): 60; and Peter Frank, "Michael Asher at the Clocktower," *Art News* 75, no. 7 (September 1976): 122.

18 Germano Celant, "Art as the Experience of Experience," *Casabella*, no. 402 (1975): 46–48, and Celant, "Bonds between Art and Architecture," in *Andre, Buren, Irwin, Nordman: Space as Support*, ed. Mark Rosenthal (Berkeley: University Art Museum at the University of California, Berkeley, 1979), 10–20.

19 See, for example, Anne Rorimer, "Michael Asher: Recent Work," *Artforum* 18, no. 8 (April 1980): 46–50, and Rorimer, *New Art in the 60s and 70s: Redefining Reality* (London: Thames & Hudson, 2001). Rorimer was the co-curator of Asher's 1979 and 1982 projects for the American Art Exhibitions at the Art Institute of Chicago, and she co-curated (with Ann Goldstein) the 1995 MOCA conceptual art survey exhibition "Reconsidering the Object of Art: 1965–1975," which included Asher's work.

20 Buchloh had coauthored and edited an early sourcebook on Asher's pre-1980 works. This book, which was published in 1983, remains the most comprehensive reference on the artist's early work. See Michael Asher, *Writings 1973–1983 on Works 1969–1979*, ed. Benjamin H. D. Buchloh, Nova Scotia Series 15 (Halifax: Press of the Nova Scotia College of Art and Design; Los Angeles: Los Angeles Museum of Contemporary Art, 1983). See also Buchloh, "Michael Asher and the Conclusion of Modernist Sculpture"; Craig Owens, "From Work to Frame, or Is There Life after 'the Death of the Author'?" in Lars Nittve, Germano Celant, Kate Linker, and Craig Owens, *Implosion: Ett Postmodernt Perspektiv/A Postmodern Perspective* (Stockholm: Moderna Museet, 1987), 196–212, reprinted in Owens, *Beyond Recognition: Representation, Power, and Culture*, ed. Scott Bryson, Barbara Kruger, Lynne Tillman, and Jane Weinstock (Berkeley: University of California Press, 1992), 122–139; and Douglas Crimp, "Redefining Site Specificity," in his *On the Museum's Ruins* (Cambridge, Mass.: MIT Press, 1993), 150–186. Crimp's article was first published in *Richard Serra: Sculpture* (New York: Museum of Modern Art, 1986).

21 Hal Foster theorized the "archival turn" in "The Archive without Museums," *October*, no. 77 (Summer 1996): 97–119. The literature on artists' interest in the archive and the museum is extensive. For some examples relating to artists' projects, see Lisa G. Corrin, ed., *Mining the Museum: An Installation by Fred Wilson* (Baltimore: The Contemporary; New York: New Press, 1994); Donna De Salvo, ed., *Past Imperfect: A Museum Looks at Itself* (New York: New Press,

1994); Anne Rorimer, "Reevaluating the Object of Collecting and Display," *Art Bulletin* 77, no. 1 (March 1995): 21–24; *Els limits del museu* (Barcelona: Fundació Antoni Tàpies, 1995); Ingrid Schaffner, Matthias Winzen, Geoffrey Batchen, and Hubertus Gassner, eds., *Deep Storage: Collecting, Storing, and Archiving in Art* (Munich: Prestel, 1998); Kynaston McShine, ed., *The Museum as Muse: Artists Reflect* (New York: Museum of Modern Art, 1999); Marvin Heiferman and Carole Kismaric, eds., *To the Rescue: Eight Artists in an Archive* (New York: American Jewish Joint Distribution Committee, 1999); and Christian Kravagna, ed., *Das Museum als Arena: Institutionskritische Texte von Künstlerinnen/The Museum as Arena: Artists on Institutional Critique* (Cologne: Kunsthaus Bregenz; Verlag der Buchhandlung Walther König, 2001).

22 Buchloh, "Michael Asher and the Conclusion of Modernist Sculpture"; Owens, "From Work to Frame."

23 Crimp, "Redefining Site Specificity"; Blake Stimson, "The Promise of Conceptual Art," in *Conceptual Art: A Critical Anthology*, ed. Alexander Alberro and Blake Stimson (Cambridge, Mass.: MIT Press, 1999), xxxviii–lii.

24 Crow, "Site-Specific Art"; Kwon, "One Place after Another: Notes on Site Specificity," *October*, no. 80 (Spring 1997): 85–110.

25 Anne Rorimer, "Context as Content: Surveying the Site," in her *New Art in the 60s and 70s*, 253–258; Martha Buskirk, "Context as Subject," in her *The Contingent Object of Contemporary Art* (Cambridge, Mass.: MIT Press, 2003), 171–175, 202–208.

26 Thomas Crow is one of the few art historians who has considered the importance of viewership to Asher's practice, arguing that Asher's "minimal interventions in the space of exhibition [are attached] to a strongly figured narrative about the conditions of spectatorship in a field far wider in space and time than that provided by the gallery or museum." Thomas Crow, "The Simple Life:

Pastoralism and the Persistence of Genre in Recent Art," in *Modern Art in the Common Culture*, 190.

27 Franz Schulze, "When Is Good Art Not Art?" *Chicago Sun-Times*, July 8, 1979.

28 Kirsten Swenson makes a similar point regarding Asher's 2008 exhibition at the Santa Monica Museum of Art, commenting on his reinstallation of temporary exhibition wall studs as "too community-oriented, too much about the viewer, to be reduced to [a comment about the determining power of the institutional container]." Swenson, "If Walls Could Speak," *Art in America* 96, no. 5 (May 2008): 208.

29 That these two lineages are all too often considered separate from each other is an argument made by Frazer Ward in "Some Relations between Conceptual and Performance Art," *Art Journal* 56, no. 4 (Winter 1997): 36–40.

30 Irwin, in Lawrence Weschler and Robert Irwin, *Seeing Is Forgetting the Name of the Thing One Sees: A Life of Contemporary Artist Robert Irwin* (Berkeley: University of California Press, 1982), 75–78. For an application of such opposition to Larry Bell's work, see Peter Frank, "Larry Bell: Understanding the Percept," in *Zones of Experience: The Art of Larry Bell* (Albuquerque: Albuquerque Museum, 1997), 29–44.

31 In a 1994 *October* roundtable on the critical lineages of conceptual art, Alexander Alberro argued that in the 1960s some of the minimalist and conceptual artists advocated precisely such an elimination or severe reduction of subjectivity. For Alberro, Judd's "elimination of . . . transcendental investment from the work of art was an important step in the process toward the dismantling of subjectivity from the work itself," and Lawrence Weiner's work accomplished "the total eradication of the experience of psychic expression . . . as a radical dismantling of agency and subjectivity." Alberro, in

Benjamin H. D. Buchloh, Rosalind Krauss, Yve-Alain Bois, Martha Buskirk, Alexander Alberro, and Thierry de Duve, "Conceptual Art and the Reception of Duchamp: A Roundtable," in *The Duchamp Effect*, ed. Martha Buskirk and Mignon Nixon (Cambridge, Mass.: MIT Press, 1996), 218.

32 On Barry's poeticity, see Thierry de Duve in Buchloh et al., "Conceptual Art and the Reception of Duchamp," 208. On Barry's "progressively explicit late romanticism," see John C. Welchman, "Image and Language: Syllables and Charisma," in *Individuals: A Selected History of Contemporary Art, 1945–1986*, ed. Howard Singerman (Los Angeles: Museum of Contemporary Art; New York: Abbeville Press, 1986), 275–277.

33 Benjamin H. D. Buchloh, introduction to his *Neo-Avantgarde and Culture Industry: Essays on European and American Art from 1955 to 1975* (Cambridge, Mass.: MIT Press, 2000), xxiii.

34 Chapter 2 includes a detailed consideration of Asher's 1974 Claire Copley exhibition.

35 I discuss the critical significance of affective responses to Asher's work in "Affect and Spectatorial Agency: Viewing Institutional Critique in the 1970s," *Art Journal* 66, no. 4 (Winter 2007): 36–51.

36 On the phenomenological viewing experience, see Annette Michelson, "Robert Morris: An Aesthetics of Transgression," in *Robert Morris* (Washington, D.C.: Corcoran Gallery of Art, 1969), 7–79, and Rosalind E. Krauss, *Passages in Modern Sculpture* (New York: Viking Press, 1977), 243–287.

37 Benjamin H. D. Buchloh, "From the Aesthetic of Administration to Institutional Critique (Some Aspects of Conceptual Art 1962–1969)," in *L'art conceptuel, une perspective*, ed. Claude Gintz (Paris: Musée d'art moderne de la Ville de Paris, 1989), 50 (italics in original).

38 Victor Burgin, "Situational Aesthetics," *Studio International* 178, no. 915 (1969): 118–121. Asher has said that he read *Studio International* in the late 1960s and was most likely familiar with Burgin's "situational aesthetics." Asher, telephone interview with author, April 6, 2007.

39 For Nancy Foote, who queried artists on "situation esthetics" in 1980, the "change in attitude toward the audience" was particularly evident in the concurrent shift to impermanent art, such as installation and performance. Foote, "Situation Esthetics: Impermanent Art and the Seventies Audience," *Artforum* 18, no. 5 (January 1980): 22. Buchloh discussed the term in relation to Asher's work in "Michael Asher and the Conclusion of Modernist Sculpture," 285–289.

40 Asher in Sandy Ballatore, "Michael Asher: Less Is Enough," *Artweek* 5, no. 34 (October 12, 1974): 16.

41 Michael Asher, "June 9–August 5, 1979: 73rd American Exhibition, the Art Institute of Chicago, Chicago, Illinois," in *Writings*, 209–210. I emphasize the full definition because some critics refer only to the first part on presentational strategies and omit the reference to reception entirely. See, for example, Gintz, "Michael Asher and the Transformation of 'Situational Aesthetics,'" 128.

42 See, for example, Jacques Rancière, "The Distribution of the Sensible: Politics and Aesthetics," in his *The Politics of Aesthetics: The Distribution of the Sensible*, trans. Gabriel Rockhill (London: Continuum, 2004), 40.

43 Ibid.

44 For an extended account of the temporal, signifying reading process of Asher's work (specifically, his 1991 installation at the Bibliothèque publique d'information at the Pompidou Center in Paris), see Birgit Pelzer,

"The Insistent Detail," trans. Greg Sims, *October*, no. 66 (Fall 1993): 108–110.

45 The importance of this axis of interpretation for Foucault might be culled from the fact that he designated "experience" as the overarching concept that tied his archaeological project (as a history of thought) to his genealogical directive (as a history of events and institutions) and, ultimately, to his late work on the history of sexuality and the care of the self. On the centrality of "experience" in Foucault's work, see David Couzens Hoy, introduction to *Foucault: A Critical Reader*, ed. Hoy (Oxford, UK: Blackwell, 1986), 1–25, and Gary Gutting, "Foucault's Philosophy of Experience," *Boundary 2: An International Journal of Literature and Culture* 29, no. 2 (Summer 2002): 69–85.

46 Michel Foucault, "Preface to *The History of Sexuality*, Volume Two," in his *Ethics: Subjectivity and Truth*, ed. Paul Rabinow, trans. William Smock, vol. 1 of *The Essential Works of Foucault, 1954–1984* (New York: New Press, 1997), 199.

47 Ibid., 200.

48 "The artworld" is a term that philosopher Arthur C. Danto coined in 1964 to analyze what makes art "art." Danto argued that it was the discursivity of art (theories, debates, and histories) more than anything else that constituted art as a category. Danto, "The Artworld," in *The Philosophy of the Visual Arts*, ed. Philip Alperson (New York: Oxford University Press, 1992), 426–433; first published in *Journal of Philosophy* 61 (1964): 571–584. Danto subsequently elaborated his views in *The Transfiguration of the Commonplace: A Philosophy of Art* (Cambridge, Mass.: Harvard University Press, 1981).

49 Foucault, "Preface to *The History of Sexuality*, Volume Two," 201.

50 Brian Massumi elaborates the Deleuzian notion of affect (where affects are theorized as nondiscursive sensory intensities) in *Parables for the Virtual: Movement, Affect,*

Sensation (Durham: Duke University Press, 2002).

51 Eve Kosofsky Sedgwick theorizes affects (through psychologist Silvan Tomkins's theory) as the emotional, psychological aspects of human experience that pertain to phenomenological experience along with epistemology. See Eve Kosofsky Sedgwick, *Touching Feeling: Affect, Pedagogy, Performativity* (Durham: Duke University Press, 2003).

52 Sara Ahmed, "Affective Economies," *Social Text* 22, no. 2 (Summer 2004): 117–139, and Sara Ahmed, *The Cultural Politics of Emotion* (New York: Routledge, 2004). Ahmed maintains that emotions bind individuals to collectives at the same time that they challenge the division between the two. Although "affectivity" in her usage describes primarily feelings, it is important to note that Ahmed considers feelings within the context of social relations.

53 Asher began teaching at CalArts in 1973.

54 Emile Benveniste, "The Nature of Pronouns," in *Problems in General Linguistics*, trans. Mary Elizabeth Meek (Coral Gables: University of Miami Press, 1971), 217–222; and Emile Benveniste, "Subjectivity in Language," in *Problems in General Linguistics*, 223–230. Janet Kraynak analyzes shifters in the work of Bruce Nauman; see Kraynak, "Bruce Nauman's Words," in *Please Pay Attention Please: Bruce Nauman's Words: Writings and Interviews*, ed. Janet Kraynak (Cambridge, Mass.: MIT Press, 2003), 1–45.

55 Louis Althusser advanced an influential theory of interpellation to account for the subject's implication in sociopolitically dominant collective ideologies. Althusser speculated that those who identify with the "you" when hailed instinctively understand that they are being spoken to, identifying with the position of the recipient. Althusser, "Ideology and Ideological State Apparatuses (Notes Towards an Investigation)," in his *Lenin and Philosophy and Other Essays* (London: New Left Books, 1971), 127–186.

56 See, for example, Frazer Ward, "In Private and Public," in Frazer Ward, Mark C. Taylor, and Jennifer Bloomer, *Vito Acconci* (London: Phaidon, 2002), 34.

57 See Claire Bishop, ed., *Participation* (London: Whitechapel; Cambridge, Mass.: MIT Press, 2006), for an overview of the viewer's role in participatory art.

58 "Affective economies" is a term used by Ahmed in her article with that title.

59 Michel Foucault, "Interview with Michel Foucault," in *Power*, ed. James D. Faubion, trans. Robert Hurley, vol. 3 of *The Essential Works of Foucault, 1954–1984* (New York: New Press, 2000), 245–246.

1 Viewing Experiences

1 La Jolla Museum of Art invitation card, Asher papers.

2 For a detailed description of Asher's La Jolla installation, see Michael Asher, *Writings 1973–1983 on Works 1969–1979*, ed. Benjamin H. D. Buchloh, Nova Scotia Series 15 (Halifax: Press of the Nova Scotia College of Art and Design; Los Angeles: Los Angeles Museum of Contemporary Art, 1983), 18–23.

3 For references to Asher's projects as "environments," see Willoughby Sharp, "New Directions in Southern California Sculpture," *Arts Magazine* 44, no. 8 (Summer 1970): 35–38; Barbara Munger, "Michael Asher: An Environmental Project," *Studio International* 180, no. 926 (October 1970): 160; and Fenella Crichton, "London," *Art International* 17 (November 1973): 46. Asher, however, disagreed with the term: "I don't deal with environments. I do situational work. I'm not interested in manipulating perception." Asher, in Sandy Ballatore, "Michael Asher: Less Is Enough," *Artweek* 5, no. 34 (October 12, 1974): 16.

4 Asher, project notes for his installation in the exhibition "Spaces" at the Museum of Modern Art, n.d., Asher papers.

5 Michel Foucault, "Preface to *The History of Sexuality*, Volume Two," in his *Ethics: Subjectivity and Truth*, ed. Paul Rabinow, trans. William Smock, vol. 1 of *The Essential Works of Foucault, 1954–1984* (New York: New Press, 1997), 200, 202.

6 Ibid., 201. Peter Hallward describes Foucault's notion of thought as characterized by freedom that "demands to be interpreted . . . as something accessible exclusively as a *practice* or experience, and not as a specifiable object of knowledge." Hallward, "The Limits of Individuation, or How to Distinguish Deleuze and Foucault," *Angelaki: Journal of the Theoretical Humanities* 5, no. 2 (August 2000): 100 (italics in original).

7 Foucault, "Preface to *The History of Sexuality*, Volume Two," 201.

8 Tony Smith in interview with Samuel Wagstaff, Jr. (1966), in *Art in Theory, 1900–2000: An Anthology of Changing Ideas*, ed. Charles Harrison and Paul Wood (Malden, Mass.: Blackwell, 2003), 760. First published as "Talking with Tony Smith," *Artforum* 1, no. 4 (December 1966): 18–19.

9 Morris's articles were reprinted in Robert Morris, *Continuous Project Altered Daily: The Writings of Robert Morris*, ed. Annette Michelson, Rosalind Krauss, Yve-Alain Bois, Benjamin Buchloh, Hal Foster, Denis Hollier, and John Rajchman (Cambridge, Mass.: MIT Press; New York: Solomon R. Guggenheim Museum, 1993), 1–39.

10 Robert Morris, "Notes on Sculpture, Part 1," in Morris, *Continuous Project Altered Daily*, 1–8. This article was first published in *Artforum* 4, no. 6 (February 1966): 42–44. "Gestalt" was a term Morris borrowed from perceptual psychology, where it referred to whole forms that the human perceptive process ostensibly prioritized over their individual components.

11 Robert Morris, "Notes on Sculpture, Part 2," in Morris, *Continuous Project Altered Daily*, 15. This article was first published in *Artforum* 5, no. 2 (October 1966): 20–23.

12 Annette Michelson, "Robert Morris: An Aesthetics of Transgression," in *Robert Morris* (Washington, D.C.: Corcoran Gallery of Art, 1969), 39.

13 Michael Fried, "Art and Objecthood," first published in *Artforum* in June 1967 and reprinted the following year in Gregory Battcock, ed., *Minimal Art: A Critical Anthology* (New York: E. P. Dutton, 1968; rpt., Berkeley: University of California Press, 1995), 116–147.

14 Ibid., 125 (italics in original). James Meyer emphasizes this point in his reading of "Art and Objecthood" in his *Minimalism: Art and Polemics in the Sixties* (New Haven: Yale University Press, 2001), 231.

15 Pamela M. Lee, *Chronophobia: On Time in the Art of the 1960s* (Cambridge, Mass.: MIT Press, 2004), 43. Michael Fried later developed his theory of absorption in *Absorption and Theatricality: Painting and Beholder in the Age of Diderot* (Berkeley: University of California Press, 1980).

16 Thomas Crow, "Site-Specific Art: The Strong and the Weak," in his *Modern Art in the Common Culture* (New Haven: Yale University Press, 1996), 135.

17 Asher, *Writings*, 34, 38, 42.

18 Ibid., 76–81.

19 Ibid., 82–87. Asher's Heiner Friedrich installation acquired a social dimension when the artist included the gallery office areas within his work, continuing the ceiling paint through the back areas of the gallery and inviting viewers to visit these normally private areas as well.

20 Ibid., 89. "White cube" is a term used by Brian O'Doherty in a series of essays, first published in *Artforum* in 1976, to describe the pristine, ostensibly neutral modernist exhibition space. Brian O'Doherty, *Inside the White Cube: The Ideology of the Gallery Space,*

expanded edition (Berkeley: University of California Press, 2000).

21 Morris, in Benjamin H. D. Buchloh, "Conversation with Robert Morris," in *The Duchamp Effect*, ed. Martha Buskirk and Mignon Nixon (Cambridge, Mass.: MIT Press, 1996), 51, 52.

22 Craig E. Adcock makes a similar comparison between Morris and Turrell in *James Turrell: The Art of Light and Space* (Berkeley: University of California Press, 1990), 45.

23 For a descriptive overview of the light and space movement in the 1970s, see Jan Butterfield, *The Art of Light and Space* (New York: Abbeville Press, 1993). Asher is not among the ten California artists discussed in the book.

24 The geographically differentiated historical narrative of the emergence of minimalism in the 1960s has been reexamined by art historians who question, first, the tendency to separate the East Coast minimalists from West Coast developments and, second, the value judgments inherent in "fitting" West Coast artists into existing narratives that obfuscate the specificity of West Coast practices. See Rosalind Krauss, "Overcoming the Limits of Matter: On Revising Minimalism," in *American Art of the 1960s*, ed. John Elderfield (New York: Museum of Modern Art, 1991), 123–141; James Meyer, "Another Minimalism," in *A Minimal Future? Art as Object 1958–1968*, ed. Ann Goldstein and Diedrich Diederichsen (Los Angeles: Museum of Contemporary Art; Cambridge, Mass.: MIT Press, 2004), 33–49; and Anna C. Chave, "Revaluing Minimalism: Patronage, Aura, Place," *Art Bulletin* 90, no. 3 (September 2008): 466–486.

25 Irwin's early paintings and Bell's use of glass within his installations form exceptions to the tendency of light and space artists to eliminate the object from the installation altogether.

26 Within this brief gloss, it is not possible to elaborate the significant differences between Nordman's practice of selecting unmarked everyday "places" (her preferred term) that the artist then invites the viewer to occupy during a particular span of time and Orr's tendency to use alchemical substances such as lead and gold leaf to construct material environments that are meant to resonate within the viewer.

27 Irwin, in Lawrence Weschler and Robert Irwin, *Seeing Is Forgetting the Name of the Thing One Sees: A Life of Contemporary Artist Robert Irwin* (Berkeley: University of California Press, 1982), 75–78.

28 Ibid., 76.

29 For a description of Turrell's Mendota Hotel, his 1966–1970 studio in Ocean Park, see Adcock, *James Turrell*, 7–8.

30 LACMA's Art and Technology project is documented in Maurice Tuchman, ed., *A Report on the Art and Technology Program of the Los Angeles County Museum of Art, 1967–1971* (Los Angeles: Los Angeles County Museum of Art, 1971). See also Lee, *Chronophobia*, 9–31. The participation of Turrell and Irwin is detailed in Adcock, *James Turrell*, 61–84.

31 It should be pointed out, however, that most of the experiments conjured up by Irwin, Turrell, and Wortz during their Art and Technology collaboration were tested only by the participants themselves. The artists were not so much interested in scientific verification of any given percipient's response than they were in the experientiality derived from their own participation.

32 Turrell in Tuchman, *A Report on the Art and Technology Program*, 132.

33 Turrell and Irwin were reading, and acknowledge being influenced by, Maurice Merleau-Ponty's *Phenomenology of Perception*, Turrell in the late 1960s and Irwin in the mid-1970s. On Turrell and Merleau-Ponty, see Adcock, *James Turrell*, 34, 233 n19; on Irwin and Merleau-Ponty, see Weschler and Irwin, *Seeing Is Forgetting*, 177–181.

34 Irwin in Jan Butterfield, "Robert Irwin: 'Re-Shaping the Shape of Things,' Part 2: The Myth of the Artist," *Arts Magazine* 47, no.

1 (September–October 1972): 31 (italics in original).

35 Turrell, interviewed by Pamela Hammond in *James Turrell: Four Light Installations*, ed. Laura J. Millin (Seattle: Center on Contemporary Art and The Real Comet Press, 1982), 19; quoted in Adcock, *James Turrell*, 45.

36 Nordman's approach to the sociality of spectatorship forms an exception to the purely individuated nature of the experience sought by the light and space artists. Unlike Irwin and Turrell, for example, Nordman emphasizes that the basis of her work is a chance "encounter" between two people. She almost systematically refrains from speaking about her work or advertising it, and maintains that her ideal audience is the accidental passerby rather than a member of the informed art audience who would seek out her work.

37 Eric Orr in Janet Kutner, "Dallas/Forth Worth: Capricious Places," *Artnews* 76 (December 1977): 104; quoted in Butterfield, *The Art of Light and Space*, 156.

38 Asher in Ballatore, "Michael Asher: Less Is Enough," 16.

39 Irwin in Butterfield, "Robert Irwin: 'Re-Shaping the Shape of Things,'" 32.

40 Asher, *Writings*, 20. Irwin's La Jolla exhibition, "Recent Work by Robert Irwin," was open from August 28 to September 28, 1969.

41 Ibid., 30.

42 Asher, project notes for the La Jolla Museum of Art, n.d., Asher papers.

43 Although opticality was certainly a touchstone of light and space environments, many of the artists associated with this group considered other types of sensory experience as well. Orr, Bell, and Nordman occasionally involved auditory modes of perception in some of their works. Sound was also an important factor in many of Irwin and Turrell's (ultimately unrealized) project ideas within LACMA's Art and Technology program.

44 Carter Ratcliff, "New York Letter," *Art International* 14 (February 1970): 78.

45 Another reviewer of "Spaces," Philip Leider in *Artforum*, disputed the sensory effectivity of Asher's installation. Even while criticizing it, however, Leider lingered upon the sensory interconnectedness of the viewing experience: "The room, with its two wide open doorways is in no sense a void and never even gives the illusion of being one. The room, its space and shape, are apprehended plainly by sight. Its sounds are apprehended by ear. Its texture is apprehended by touch. The sound-proofing and sound control simply don't provide enough to make the game worth the candlepower." Leider, "'Spaces' at the Museum of Modern Art," *Artforum* 8, no. 6 (February 1970): 69–70.

46 Asher, *Writings*, 5–6.

47 Ibid., 8. Asher argued that the reduced volume of air in his work set up a conceptual contrast with other artists in "Anti-Illusion," such as Richard Serra, whose work's materiality was much more immediately pronounced than his.

48 Monte, "Anti-Illusion: Procedures/Materials," in Marcia Tucker and James Monte, *Anti-Illusion: Procedures/Materials* (New York: Whitney Museum of American Art, 1969), 11.

49 Krauss, "Overcoming the Limits of Matter," 138–139.

50 In her theorization of installation art, Claire Bishop introduces an experiential category that she terms "mimetic engulfment," which, she argues, explains how some installations are designed to embrace their viewers into their world to the degree that they lose themselves (or a sense of themselves as an entity separate from the installation) in the work. Claire Bishop, *Installation Art: A Critical History* (New York: Routledge, 2005), 82–101.

51 Asher, *Writings*, 30.

52 Germano Celant, "Art as the Experience of Experience," *Casabella*, no. 402 (1975): 47.

53   Ratcliff, "New York Letter," 78.

54   Thomas H. Garver, "Michael Asher at La Jolla Art Museum," *Artforum* 8, no. 5 (January 1970): 76.

55   Asher, *Writings*, 93.

56   Asher's Project, Inc., projection piece was recreated and staged at Orchard, a cooperative exhibition and event space in New York City, on October 30, 2005. A new print of the film was produced for the 2005 screening.

57   Asher, *Writings*, 74.

58   Ibid., 72.

59   Asher's Portland work was inspired by a 1975 work by Dan Graham, *Yesterday / Today*, and it, in turn, inspired two further television-viewing loop projects by Graham. These works by Graham were the 1976 *Production / Reception (Piece for Two Cable TV Channels)* and a collaboration with Dara Birnbaum, *Local Television News Program Analysis for Public Access Cable Television*. Although the collaboration with Birnbaum was conceptualized in 1978, it was not realized until 1980. See Dan Graham, "*Production / Reception (Piece for Two Cable TV Channels) (1976)*," in his *Video, Architecture, Television: Writings on Video and Video Works, 1970–1978*, ed. Benjamin H. D. Buchloh (Halifax: Press of the Nova Scotia College of Art and Design; New York: New York University, 1979), 55; Asher, "Excerpts of a Description from Notebook 1/11/76 Describing the First Run Through of a Television Broadcast Delivered 1/18 as a Work for the Groupshow 'Via Los Angeles' at Portland Center for the Visual Arts, Portland (Oregon) 1/9/76–2/8/76," in Graham, *Video, Architecture, Television*, 56; and Graham, "*Local Television News Program Analysis for Public Access Cable Television (1978)*," in *Video, Architecture, Television*, 57–61.

60   "Visual Art Presentation Confuses TV Viewers," *Oregonian*, January 19, 1976.

61   Asher, *Writings*, 115–116.

62   Ibid.

63   It is worth noting that Asher's Portland work left it entirely up to the concerned viewers to define what normalcy meant for them when they called the station to report technical problems.

64   Asher took several measures to contextualize his project for its viewers: it was advertised by television previews and newspaper program listings, and was announced at the outset and the conclusion of the transmission as "an artist's project"; and Asher himself manned one of the phones in the television's feedback room during the program to discuss the program with callers. All these measures were taken, Asher wrote, "so that the public would be informed and the audience would not be alienated." Asher, *Writings*, 112–113. His project notes further probe the ethics of viewer reactions and the after-the-fact publicity that the project received in mass media: "I want a work of art which constructively questions the notion of what art is without being an anti-artist or alienating the viewer. I look for participation on this level and did not expect my work to get into the front page of the paper (*Oregonian*) or on the evening news, but I feel that possibly if you address yourself to public mass media you are subject to all types of mass media controversy which does not address itself to the issues of art in dialogue." Asher, "Portland—Small Spiral Notebook M.A.—January 1976," Asher papers.

65   Asher, *Writings*, 125.

66   Pamela M. Lee, *Object to Be Destroyed: The Work of Gordon Matta-Clark* (Cambridge, Mass.: MIT Press, 2000), 116.

67   In Lee's view, the oft-mentioned "violence" in Matta-Clark's works, including *Window Blowout*, is "the *object* of critique in his work [rather than a sign of an] artist who is merely decadent." Ibid., 118 (italics in original). For a comparison of other works by Asher and Matta-Clark, see ibid., 88.

Lee considers Asher's 1973 Lisson Gallery work, in which Asher cut out a slice from the bottom of the gallery walls, in relation to Matta-Clark's installations at the 112 Greene Street Gallery in 1972.

68 Matta-Clark's intervention was promptly removed, becoming the stuff of legend rather than a viable option for a visit by critics and other viewers. Crow contends that its prompt removal "completed" the piece: "[*Window Blowout*'s] immediate object was made to act it out in a state of unreasoning panic: if this deterioration was intolerable for even a moment at the Institute for Architecture and Urban Studies, why was it tolerable day in and day out in the Bronx?" Crow, "Site-Specific Art," 134–135.

69 Nancy Foote, "Michael Asher at the Clocktower," *Artforum* 14, no. 10 (June 1976): 64.

70 Ibid.

71 Ibid.

72 I analyze the affective contents of Foote's account of her visit to Asher's Clocktower installation in "Affect and Spectatorial Agency," 45, 47.

73 Foote calls Asher "a West-Coast master of subliminal manipulation." Foote, "Michael Asher at the Clocktower," 64.

74 Asher, *Writings*, 102. Asher made this comment regarding his 1974 project at the Anna Leonowens Gallery at the Nova Scotia College of Art and Design in Halifax, Canada.

75 Foucault, "Preface to *The History of Sexuality*, Volume Two," 201.

76 Asher, *Writings*, 116.

77 This statue of George Washington is an early-twentieth-century American-made bronze cast of an eighteenth-century marble original by French neoclassical sculptor Jean-Antoine Houdon. The "73rd American Exhibition" project remains one of Asher's most widely known works. See, for example, Benjamin H. D. Buchloh, "Michael Asher and the Conclusion of Modernist Sculpture,"

Museum Studies 10 (1983): 285–289; Anne Rorimer, "Michael Asher: Recent Work," *Artforum* 18, no. 8 (April 1980): 46–50; Craig Owens, "From Work to Frame," in his *Beyond Recognition: Representation, Power, and Culture*, ed. Scott Bryson, Barbara Kruger, Lynne Tillman, and Jane Weinstock (Berkeley: University of California Press, 1992), 132–133; Crow, "Site-Specific Art," 131–150; Martha Buskirk, *The Contingent Object of Contemporary Art* (Cambridge, Mass.: MIT Press, 2003), 171–173; Whitney Moeller and Anne Rorimer, *Michael Asher: George Washington at the Art Institute of Chicago, 1979 and 2005* (Chicago: Art Institute of Chicago; New Haven: Yale University Press, 2006); and Jennifer King, "Perpetually out of Place: Michael Asher and Jean-Antoine Houdon at the Art Institute of Chicago," *October*, no. 120 (Winter 2007): 71–86.

78 My hypothetical description of a viewer's route toward Asher's work at the "73rd American Exhibition" is indebted to Asher's description of his work in *Writings*, 207–209.

79 Crow, "Site-Specific Art," 141.

80 Asher's 2005 project is documented in Moeller and Rorimer, *Michael Asher: George Washington at the Art Institute of Chicago, 1979 and 2005*. See especially Rorimer's essay "Focus: Michael Asher," in which she comments on the contextual change (31).

81 Asher wrote, "In this work I am interested in the way this sculpture functions when it is viewed in its 18th Century context instead of in its prior relationship to the facade of the building where it has been for 54 years. Once inside Gallery 219 the sculpture can be seen in connection with the ideas of other European works of the same period. By locating the sculpture within its own time frame in Gallery 219 I am placing it within the framework of a contemporary exhibition, through my participation in that exhibition." Asher, handout for the "73rd American Exhibition," the Art Institute of Chicago, 1979, reproduced in Moeller and Rorimer, *Michael*

Asher: George Washington at the Art Institute of Chicago, 1979 and 2005, 63.

82 This exhibition is documented in Michael Asher, Birgit Pelzer, and Anne Rorimer, *Michael Asher at the Renaissance Society, University of Chicago* (Chicago: Renaissance Society, 1990).

83 Michael Asher, Dirk Snauwaert, Birgit Pelzer, and Frederik Leen, *Michael Asher at the Palais des Beaux-Arts, Brussels* (Brussels: Palais des Beaux-Arts, 1995).

84 For a detailed discussion of Asher's Pompidou Center work, see Birgit Pelzer, "The Insistent Detail," trans. Greg Sims, *October*, no. 66 (Fall 1993): 93–112.

85 Ibid., 110.

86 Asher, "Description of Work Centre Pompidou," 8/4/90, "Centre Pompidou—Final Proposal," Asher papers.

87 Asher mentions the flagpole's location in the users' field of vision as they bend over to drink from the fountain, stating, "when you take a drink of water the flagpole bisects the plaque as if it were in the sight of a gun." Asher, interview by Joan Simon, in Mary Livingstone Beebe, James Stuart DeSilva, Robert Storr, and Joan Simon, *Landmarks: Sculpture Commissions for the Stuart Collection at the University of California, San Diego* (New York: Rizzoli, 2001), 180.

88 Robert Storr, "The Fine Art of Not Quite Fitting In," in *Landmarks*, 24.

89 In Storr's view, the practical use value of Asher's fountain proves that "sooner or later Conceptual art's much vaunted austerity yields to the common-sense uses of the surrounding culture, and that by that mysterious process some of its subtler lessons are subliminally learned." Ibid., 25.

90 Asher, interview by Joan Simon, in *Landmarks*, 178. The fountain is not identified as art in the immediate vicinity, but a plaque set at the curb of a nearby parking lot names the artist and includes other conventional details about the work.

91 Mary Livingstone Beebe, "Michael Asher, *Untitled*," in *Landmarks*, 173.

92 Peter Hallward has characterized the "specified" individual as one whose identity and position is preassigned to him or her. Hallward contrasts these "specified" qualities of subject positions with "specific" aspects that we actively practice to define, design, and claim. Peter Hallward, "The Singular and the Specific: Recent French Philosophy," *Radical Philosophy*, no. 99 (January/February 2000): 8–9.

93 Some members of the Campus Community Planning Committee at UCSD had originally been concerned about the project precisely because of the familiarity of the drinking fountain form. The fountain's recognizable shape was believed to prevent viewers from identifying Asher's work as a work of art. Beebe, "Michael Asher, *Untitled*," 171–172.

94 Ibid., 173, and the Stuart Colletion, University of California, San Diego, http://stuartcollection.ucsd.edu/UCSDTEST/Asher.htm.

95 Asher, "Project Proposal for Stuart Collection," in *Landmarks*, 174–175.

96 Asher's Santa Monica Museum of Art exhibition is documented in *Michael Asher*, ed. Elsa Longhauser (Santa Monica: Santa Monica Museum of Art, 2008).

97 The Santa Monica exhibition was reviewed extensively in art magazines and daily newspapers. In addition to the accounts cited below, these reviews include Christopher Knight, "Labyrinth from the Artist's Mind," *Los Angeles Times*, February 13, 2008; Roberta Smith, "How Art Is Framed: Exhibition Floor Plans as a Conceptual Medium," *New York Times*, March 8, 2008; James Rondeau, "Thinking Space," *Frieze*, no. 113 (March 2008): 164–171; and Andrea Fraser, "Procedural Matters," *Artforum* 46, no. 10 (Summer 2008): 374–381.

98 Walead Beshty, "Parallax Views: On Michael Asher at the Santa Monica Museum of Art," *Texte zur Kunst*, no. 70 (May 2008): 168.

99   Kirsten Swenson, "If Walls Could Speak," *Art in America* 96, no. 5 (May 2008): 208.
100   Mark Godfrey, "Parallax Views: On Michael Asher at the Santa Monica Museum of Art," *Texte zur Kunst*, no. 70 (May 2008): 172.

2 Contracted Participation

1   Claire Bishop, "Introduction: Viewers as Producers," in *Participation*, ed. Bishop (London: Whitechapel; Cambridge, Mass.: MIT Press, 2006), 10.
2   Although Asher's viewers might occasionally be given opportunities to "participate" in the work—in other words, to interact with the work or situation—for example, by drinking from the 1991 Stuart Collection fountain—Asher's viewer-activated works do not coerce spectators to perform particular actions. In this regard, Asher's practice differs from Bruce Nauman's use of his audience, which Janet Kraynak characterizes as "dependent participation" because of the limits, conditions, and restrictions placed on the viewers. Janet Kraynak, "Dependent Participation: Bruce Nauman's Environments," *Grey Room*, no. 10 (Winter 2003): 22–45.
3   J. L. Austin, *How to Do Things with Words*, ed. J. O. Urmson and Marina Sbisà, 2nd ed. (Cambridge, Mass.: Harvard University Press, 1975), 94–132.
4   Asher requested that his "74th American Exhibition" participants behave in the manner of "regular viewers." See "Instructions for Participating Viewers in MICHAEL ASHER work—74th American Exhibition (June 7–August 1, 1982)," n.d., Institutional Archives of the Art Institute of Chicago.
5   Michael Asher, telephone interview with author, April 6, 2007. The book project was completed under the editorship of Benjamin H. D. Buchloh, who succeeded Koenig in 1978. Buchloh's role in the project expanded to include collaboration on the writing with Asher. See Michael Asher, *Writings 1973–1983 on Works 1969–1979*, ed. Buchloh, Nova Scotia Series 15 (Halifax: Press of the Nova Scotia College of Art and Design; Los Angeles: Los Angeles Museum of Contemporary Art, 1983). On Buchloh's role in the project, see Jennifer King, "Letter of Correction," *October* 121 (Summer 2007): 114.
6   Asher, *Writings*, 101–102.
7   Ibid., 101.
8   Ibid., 155.
9   Ibid., 156.
10   Ibid.
11   Asher's notes on his Claire Copley / Morgan Thomas project hint at his valuation of social relations when he argues that the project "ultimately had to be perceived as social practice." Ibid., 157.
12   On Klein's *Le vide*, see Sidra Stich, *Yves Klein* (Ostfildern: Cantz, 1994), 132–142. On Barry's *Closed Gallery Piece* (1969), see Anne Rorimer, *New Art in the 60s and 70s: Redefining Reality* (London: Thames and Hudson, 2001), 87; John T. Paoletti, "Spaces Liberated for Thought," in *Some Places to Which We Can Come: Robert Barry, Works 1963 to 1975* (Bielefeld: Kerber Verlag, 2003), 31; and Robert C. Morgan, "Robert Barry: Language and Silence," in *Some Places*, 77. Asher executed a project formally similar to Barry's at the Otis College of Art and Design in 1975, when he closed the school's gallery and declared the artist to be the art. I discuss Asher's Otis work in chapter 3.
13   The question of how Asher-the-artist manages to impact exhibition situations without any manifest physical presence of his own is discussed in chapter 3.
14   Asher acknowledged the possibility of this nonreading of his Anna Leonowens exhibition in *Writings*, 102.
15   Ibid., 156.
16   Jacques Rancière, "The Distribution of the Sensible," in his *The Politics of Aesthetics: The Distribution of the Sensible*, trans. Gabriel Rockhill (London: Continuum, 2004), 12–16.
17   Ibid., 39.

18 Melinda Wortz, "Looking Inward," *Art News* 73, no. 10 (December 1974): 61.

19 See, for example, Sandy Ballatore, "Michael Asher: Less Is Enough," *Artweek* 5, no. 34 (October 12, 1974): 16.

20 Nancy Marmer, "Michael Asher at Claire Copley and Morgan Thomas," *Artforum* 15, no. 9 (May 1977): 74.

21 Ibid., 75.

22 The letter was mailed to Asher at the Nova Scotia School of Art and Design, where he had traveled after the Claire Copley opening to work on his book project and the exhibition at the Anna Leonowens Gallery.

23 Claire Copley to Michael Asher, October 1, 1974, Asher papers.

24 Wortz, "Looking Inward," 61.

25 Although I discuss Asher's recourse to artistic authority more extensively in the next chapter, I want to note here that Wortz indeed includes the artist's executive agency in her description of the power relations that organized the situation at the Claire Copley Gallery.

26 Copley to Asher, October 1, 1974.

27 Asher in Ballatore, "Michael Asher: Less Is Enough," 16.

28 In a discussion related to his 1973 Galleria Toselli work, Asher touched upon his relation to phenomenological modes of experience by outlining his discontent with the kinds of viewing experience that minimalist art provided. Asher, *Writings*, 92–93.

29 Rancière, "The Distribution of the Sensible," 39.

30 Asher, *Writings*, 155.

31 Jacques Rancière, "The Janus-Face of Politicized Art: Jacques Rancière in Interview with Gabriel Rockhill," in *The Politics of Aesthetics*, 49.

32 Tom Jimmerson and Helen N. Lewis, typescript exhibition proposal marked "approved 10/22/75," Asher papers.

33 Asher, *Writings*, 147. LAICA's relocation was to take place in March 1977; the Asher/Askevold/Long exhibition was the last one held in LAICA's Century City facility.

34 Asher comments on this aspect of institutional development in his early LAICA proposal, included in his unpublished notes on the LAICA project, February 7, 1977, Asher papers.

35 Asher employed approximately twelve different participants in the LAICA project. These participants were present in various combinations when the exhibition was open. Asher, telephone interview with author, December 3, 2008.

36 Asher, *Writings*, 148.

37 Ibid.

38 Asher's work had been allocated $1,300 from the NEA grant that LAICA received for the exhibition. Ibid., 147.

39 Ibid., 148–149.

40 Asher, notes on the LAICA project.

41 Asher, *Writings*, 148.

42 Robert Barry, *Marcuse Piece* (1970 to the present), as installed at the Museum of Contemporary Art, Los Angeles, in 1995. On Barry's *Marcuse Piece*, see Paoletti, "Spaces Liberated for Thought," 35, 37; and Thomas Wulffen, "A History of Disillusionment," in *Some Places*, 103.

43 Many of the LAICA participants' accounts were later published in the exhibition's catalogue, which Asher also designed. See Robert L. Smith, Tom Jimmerson, and Helen N. Lewis, *January 15–February 10, 1977, Los Angeles Institute of Contemporary Art* (Los Angeles: Los Angeles Institute of Contemporary Art, 1978).

44 Only one participant, Frederick Dolan, expressed elation rather than anxiety over his presence at LAICA, which, to him, enabled "moment[s] of liberation [that were] attain[ed through] critical distance." Dolan in *January 15–February 10, 1977*, 9. Dolan's account is also reprinted in Asher, *Writings*, 149.

45 Participant identified as Sally, letter to Asher, January 23, 1977, reprinted in Asher, *Writings*, 150.

46 Ibid.

47 Dorit Cypis in *January 15–February 10, 1977*, 8.

48 Because these notes were written simultaneously with the work, they provide different kinds of information from that in Asher's retrospective reflection on his own work. Asher, interview with author, June 25, 2008.

49 Asher, notes on the LAICA project.

50 Ibid.

51 Ibid.

52 Foucault developed his concept of the "technologies of the self" in relation to concrete modes of ethical conduct in late Greco-Roman and early Christian cultures. See Michel Foucault, "Technologies of the Self," in *Technologies of the Self: A Seminar with Michel Foucault*, ed. Luther H. Martin, Huck Gutman, and Patrick H. Hutton (Amherst: University of Massachusetts Press, 1988), 19. See also Foucault, "On the Genealogy of Ethics: An Overview of Work in Progress," in his *Ethics: Subjectivity and Truth*, ed. Paul Rabinow, trans. William Smock (New York: New Press, 1997), 253–280.

53 Foucault, "Technologies of the Self," 24–25.

54 Sally in Asher, *Writings*, 150.

55 This was written as an open letter to Asher. Sally willingly inserted her statement, "[k]nowing your [Asher's] penchant for documentation," into the LAICA work. She further writes, "I am fully cognizant of the fact that I am not *out* of this piece at this point." Ibid. (italics in original).

56 Asher, notes on the LAICA project.

57 The handout read in part: "The work for this exhibition has been conceived for the Art Institute of Chicago in relation to its existing permanent collection. It comprises two separate groups of viewers each consisting of three people who are viewing two different works of art for one half hour each day. The two works viewed are located in Gallery 226 within sight of each other." Michael Asher, exhibition handout for the "74th American Exhibition," 1982,

Institutional Archives of the Art Institute of Chicago.

58 According to Anne Rorimer, co-curator of the "74th American Exhibition," Art Institute visitors for the most part probably did not notice Asher's project. Rorimer, interview with author, December 6, 2005.

59 "Instructions for Participating Viewers in MICHAEL ASHER work—*74th American Exhibition* (June 7–August 1, 1982)."

60 Martha Buskirk, *The Contingent Object of Contemporary Art* (Cambridge, Mass.: MIT Press, 2003), 217.

61 Ibid.

62 Ibid. Buskirk also mentions two exceptions to this rule: Acconci's *Proximity Piece*, performed within the exhibition "Software" at the Jewish Museum in 1970, and his *Seedbed* at the Sonnabend Gallery in 1972. Both works allowed viewers simultaneous access to the experiential and explanatory modes of reception. Ibid., 218.

63 One critic interpreted Asher's viewers in a slightly different manner when he wrote that "[s]ix people silently staring at early 20th-Century paintings cannot help but suggest professional mourners at a much-protracted wake." Alan G. Artner, "American Exhibition Spots Trends but Misses Realism," *Chicago Tribune*, June 13, 1982.

64 Asher, exhibition handout for the "74th American Exhibition."

65 Ibid.

66 Craig Owens, "The Allegorical Impulse: Toward a Theory of Postmodernism," in his *Beyond Recognition: Representation, Power, and Culture*, ed. Scott Bryson, Barbara Kruger, Lynne Tillman, and Jane Weinstock (Berkeley: University of California Press, 1992), 53, 63–64.

67 Asher's viewing piece was initially proposed by Rorimer for the Art Institute's permanent collection. Although it was not accepted for purchase, it was subsequently realized at the "74th American Exhibition," organized by Rorimer and A. James Speyer.

Rorimer, interview with author, December 8, 2005.

68 Walter Benjamin, "The Work of Art in the Age of Mechanical Reproduction," in his *Illuminations*, ed. Hannah Arendt (New York: Schocken Books, 1969), 217–251.

69 Asher to A. James Speyer, December 12, 1980, Institutional Archives of the Art Institute of Chicago.

70 Sara Ahmed, "Affective Economies," *Social Text* 22, no. 2 (Summer 2004): 117–139.

71 Sara Ahmed, *The Cultural Politics of Emotion* (New York: Routledge, 2004), 4–8.

72 Asher, exhibition handout for the "74th American Exhibition."

73 After Asher had determined which paintings fit his criteria, Art Institute staff members compiled a list of the print sources in which the Picasso and the Duchamp paintings were reproduced. The list was included on the reverse side of Asher's exhibition handout, which was available to the Art Institute visitors during the "74th American Exhibition."

74 Asher to Speyer.

75 See Douglas Crimp, "On the Museum's Ruins" and "The Photographic Activity of Modernism" (both essays first published in 1980), in his *On the Museum's Ruins* (Cambridge, Mass.: MIT Press, 1993), 44–64 and 108–125; Owens, *Beyond Recognition*; and Benjamin H. D. Buchloh, "Allegorical Procedures: Appropriation and Montage in Contemporary Art," *Artforum* 21, no. 1 (September 1982): 43–56.

76 The illustrations of Asher's "74th American Exhibition" project in Buchloh's "Allegorical Procedures" showed three views of the Art Institute's Duchamp painting and its double set of labels. In the text, however, Buchloh sets this project aside in favor of discussing Asher's contribution to the 1981 LACMA exhibition "The Museum as Site: Sixteen Projects." Buchloh's "Allegorical Procedures" essay had further ties to Asher's work because its early version was first presented as a lecture in conjunction with

"Vocation/ Vacation" at the Banff Centre on December 2, 1981 (discussed below in text), and subsequently formed the first part of his catalogue essay for the same exhibition. See Benjamin H. D. Buchloh, "Montage and Allegorical Deconstruction," in *Vocation/ Vacation*, vol. 2 (Banff: Walter Phillips Gallery/Banff Centre, n.d. [1981]), n.p.

77 The exhibition's catalogue had originally been slated for professional printing, but problems with the press led the exhibition organizers to try running the pages through a photocopier, which was successful. Asher, telephone interview with author, January 8, 2009.

78 Five minutes of silence separated the rug-hooking instructions from the Benjamin excerpts on the audiotape. The rug-hooking manual from which the narrators read was Marion Koenig and Gill Speirs, *Making Rugs for Pleasure and Profit* (London and New York: John Gifford, 1980). Cited by Asher in *Vocation/ Vacation*, vol. 2, n.p.

79 The papermaking material samples in the vitrine included petri dishes of methyl-cellulose binder and two kinds of half-stuff (bleached and unbleached cotton rag), a beaker containing macerated cotton, and rough paper fibers. A finished sheet of paper made by Occidental College students, along with two copies of the catalogue printed on it (one open and one closed), were also displayed in the glass case.

80 In his catalogue essay for "Vocation/ Vacation," Buchloh comments on the use value of Asher's Banff project while contrasting it with Asher's critical practice: "It is one of the blatant contradictions of art educational institutions that they support simultaneously the sentimental attachment to those individual production procedures that seem to grant escape from the anonymity of the conditions of industrialization and the work of those contemporary artists who strive for a revelation of those conflicts in the conditions of contemporary production and reception of artistic constructs." Buchloh, "Montage and Allegorical Deconstruction," n.p.

81   Crimp, "The Photographic Activity of Postmodernism," 112.

82   Asher to Speyer, 2.

83   Buchloh, "Montage and Allegorical Deconstruction," n.p. (italics in original).

84   Charlotte Townsend-Gault, "Vocation/Vacation," *Vanguard* 11, no. 3 (April 1982): 23, 24.

85   lacma Communications and Marketing, "lacma Debuts Innovative and Interactive Exhibition for Children and Families" (Los Angeles: Los Angeles County Museum of Art, 2000).

86   Ibid.

87   Stephanie Barron, Sheri Bernstein, and Ilene Susan Fort, *Reading California: Art, Image, and Identity, 1900–2000* (Los Angeles: Los Angeles County Museum of Art; Berkeley: University of California Press, 2000), 322.

88   The strategy of embracing the whole museum space invites comparisons with lacma's 1981 "The Museum as Site: Sixteen Projects," which accompanied the exhibition "Art in Los Angeles: Seventeen Artists in the Sixties," although both exhibitions were clearly products of their times. Both "The Museum as Site: Sixteen Projects" and "Made in California: now" were attached to larger thematic exhibitions of regional art history, and both advanced site-specific approaches. In 1981, the younger artists featured in "The Museum as Site" accompanied seasoned veterans of the late 1950s and 1960s in "Art in Los Angeles: Seventeen Artists in the Sixties." The relationship between more established and younger artists was transposed onto museum visitors in the 2000 pairing, in which "Made in California," a comprehensive survey exhibition, was accompanied by "Made in California: now," which addressed children and families. Both "The Museum as Site: Sixteen Projects" and "Made in California" were curated by Stephanie Barron, although "Made in California: now" was organized by Robert L. Sain, the director of lacmaLab.

89   Asher in Anna Harding and Michael Asher, "Student Reinstallation of a Permanent Collection Gallery, Part Three: Conversation between Anna Harding and Michael Asher, December 2004–March 2005," in *Magic Moments: Collaboration between Artists and Young People*, ed. Anna Harding (London: Black Dog Publishing, 2005), 188.

90   Ibid., 186.

91   The first group's facilitator was a freelance museum educator, while the second group met with an artist who had teaching experience. According to lacmaLab's director, the second facilitator was selected on the basis of "ab[ility] to provide direction while not biasing any of the students' decisions." Sain in Anna Harding and Robert L. Sain, "Student Reinstallation of a Permanent Collection Gallery, Part One," in *Magic Moments*, 182. Asher describes the facilitator for this project as an artist who also possessed an understanding of art history and museum procedures. Aside from the facilitator, Asher explained his proposal to the students and attended the students' meetings with lacma's exhibition committee. He was further available to consult with the students if they requested a meeting "to show [him] their progress." Asher in Harding and Asher, "Student Reinstallation of a Permanent Collection Gallery, Part Three," 186–187.

92   Asher, "Appendix #4: A Student Reinstallation At 'Made in California: Now,' A Structure by Michael Asher," *Journal of Aesthetics and Protest* 1, no. 2 (2003). On the budget allocation, see Harding and Sain, "Student Reinstallation of a Permanent Collection Gallery, Part One," 182.

93   Rancière, "The Janus-Face of Politicized Art," 52–53.

94   On Rancière's notion of equality as a starting point in relation to Pierre Bourdieu's

and Louis Althusser's analyses of pre-
existing social inequality, see Kristin Ross,
"Rancière and the Practice of Equality," *Social
Text*, no. 29 (1991): 57–71. See also Rancière,
"The Emancipated Spectator," *Artforum* 45,
no. 7 (March 2007): 274–275.

95   Rancière, "The Janus-Face of Politicized
Art," 52.

96   Anna Kim, Dong Jin Kim, Hanna Koh,
Daniel Madrigal, Melissa Monge, Sarah Park,
and Jamie Vargas, reinstallation statement,
"The Beat Road," LACMA, 2002.

97   Sain in Harding and Sain, "Student Reinstallation of a Permanent Collection Gallery,
Part One," 183.

98   Kraynak considers the "constrained"
participation that Nauman used in the early
1970s as subordinating the viewer into the
work's structural logic in "Dependent Participation." I analyze Haacke's late 1960s and
early 1970s participatory polling pieces in
my "Affect and Spectatorial Agency," 48–50.

99   The Fort Worth project, which was
based on lateral exchanges between socially
defined human subjects, transformed
two years later into Asher's proposal that
would have sought to engage ordinary city
residents rather than museum staffers. For
the second location of the exhibition "Los
Angeles in the Seventies" at the Joslyn Museum of Art in Omaha, Nebraska, Asher first
proposed to solicit nine Omaha residents
to exchange their homes with those of Los
Angeles residents for the duration of the
exhibition. This proposal remained unrealized because of logistical difficulties. Had
it been realized, the volunteers would have
changed residences, but the project description did not specify what they would do
in their temporary lodgings (except literally
bring a little bit of Omaha to Los Angeles
and vice versa, just as the exhibition "Los
Angeles in the Seventies," of which Asher's
project was a part, ostensibly brought a little
bit of Los Angeles to Omaha). In contrast,
the work that Asher ultimately realized at the
Joslyn Museum of Art dealt with the placement of decorative objects in the museum
space. Asher chose to remove these objects
from one side of the symmetrical museum's
ground floor, preparing to temporarily
shift his approach from social exchanges to
material, symbolic exchanges. The latter approach culminated in Asher's contribution
to the "73rd American Exhibition" at the Art
Institute of Chicago later the same year.

100   Asher, *Writings*, 188.

101   Insofar as Asher's Fort Worth project
was promoted within the museum, however,
the participating staff members did become
associated with Asher's situation aesthetics, a view that is corroborated by Asher's
unpublished notes, which disclose that he
considered the project participatory at the
time of the exhibition. "This work . . . takes
knowledge of the staff's existence and their
relationship to their respective museums,"
Asher noted, "by explicitly participating in
the work, thereby bringing into question
their function beyond their specific job."
Asher, "Fort Worth" project notes, November 5, 1977, Asher papers.

102   The structure of Asher's participatory
projects does, however, resemble LeWitt's
wall drawings, which were also based on a
set of instructions the artist gave to participants, who then independently executed
the work. Both Asher and LeWitt embrace
openness and assign responsibility for their
participants in the completion of the work.
LeWitt and Asher differ from each other,
though, in the nature of the participatory
activity. The labor of LeWitt's participants
results in a fairly traditional object of art: a
wall drawing. Asher's participants, on the
other hand, tend to engage in professionally appropriate forms of labor in their own
institutional context. LeWitt's focus is on
the resulting work; Asher's product is the
process of labor.

103   Because the participants' labor in
Asher's work resembles their everyday
activities, these insider participants are not
likely to treat their involvement in Asher's

work as unimplicated or disinterested. Although comparing Asher's participatory oeuvre to recent practices of participatory "relational aesthetics"—which tend to engage viewers rather than specifically contracted individuals—falls outside the scope of this book, I want to note that the restrictions (but also the particular epistemological rewards) of the contracted status of Asher's participants challenge some of the central premises of recent theorization of relational aesthetics, which focuses on the liberatory effects of participation for any museum or gallery visitor rather than the social specificity of their experience. See, for example, Nicolas Bourriaud, *Relational Aesthetics* (Paris: Les Presses du Réel, 2002). Claire Bishop criticizes Bourriaud's approach for its neutralization of the social differences that structure the exhibition situation in contemporary participatory work in her "Antagonism and Relational Aesthetics," *October*, no. 110 (Fall 2004): 51–79, and Anna Dezeuze questions Bourriaud's universalization of everyday experience in her "Everyday Life, 'Relational Aesthetics' and the 'Transfiguration of the Commonplace,'" *Journal of Visual Art Practice* 5, no. 3 (2006): 143–152.

104 Kristin Ross, "On Jacques Rancière," *Artforum* 45, no. 7 (March 2007): 255.

105 Rancière critiques assumptions regarding the spectator's passivity in "The Emancipated Spectator," 279.

106 Asher, *Writings*, 101.

3 In The Name of the Artist

1 Robert Morris, "The Art of Existence—Three Extra-Visual Artists: Works in Process," *Artforum* 9, no. 5 (January 1971): 29. The article's illustrations included Nauman's 1969 *Acoustic Wall* and Asher's 1970 Pomona College installation.

2 Maurice Berger, *Labyrinths: Robert Morris, Minimalism, and the 1960s* (New York: Harper & Row, 1989), 103.

3 Morris, "The Art of Existence," 28. Morris's list of established artists does not include James Turrell, whose work, Adcock argues, was in fact the model for the projects Morris ascribed to the fictional artists in his essay. According to Adcock, Morris had visited Turrell during the summer of 1969, some eighteen months before he published "The Art of Existence." Morris does mention Turrell's work later in the article in relation to one of his fictional artists. Craig E. Adcock, *James Turrell: The Art of Light and Space* (Berkeley: University of California Press, 1990), 111–113.

4 Morris, "The Art of Existence," 28.

5 Morris must have encountered Asher's work at least in the context of "Spaces," a 1969–1970 exhibition at the Museum of Modern Art, in which both artists participated.

6 Morris, "The Art of Existence," 32.

7 Morris's listing of Asher among the benchmarks of this particular style or movement followed Tate Gallery curator Michael Compton's mention of Asher's work in relation to that of Bell, Irwin, and Wheeler in a catalogue essay. Compton, "Three Artists from Los Angeles," in *The Tate Gallery: Larry Bell, Robert Irwin, Doug Wheeler* (London: Tate Gallery, 1970), 7.

8 In a similar manner, documentation of Asher's work has been included in exhibitions in lieu of new work. Exhibitions such as "LA Hot and Cool" at the MIT List Art Center (1987) and "Sunshine & Noir: Art in L.A., 1960–1997" at the Louisiana Museum of Modern Art in Humlebaek, Denmark (1997), for example, have included Asher via a presentation of pages from his book *Writings 1973–1983 on Works 1969–1979*.

9 I do not mean to imply, however, that any individual usage of a name would necessarily settle or fix the meaning of these broader categories.

10   Asher made a connection between the Otis piece and the 1974 Claire Copley and Anna Leonowens exhibitions, noting that "these works circumscribed the production, distribution, and reception of the artwork." Michael Asher, *Writings 1973–1983 on Works 1969–1979*, ed. Benjamin H. D. Buchloh, Nova Scotia Series 15 (Halifax: Press of the Nova Scotia College of Art and Design; Los Angeles: Los Angeles Museum of Contemporary Art, 1983), 105.

11   Asher, project notes on Otis Institute, n.d., Asher papers. In his published account of the Otis project, Asher alluded to these early ideas by noting that the realized version of the work "implied that the author was not separate from his own manifestation and that his work had developed from and was integral to his experience." Asher, *Writings*, 105.

12   Asher, project notes on Otis Institute. The realized Otis project is described in Asher, *Writings*, 105–106.

13   Asher's proposal to meet with gallery visitors would have extended his current role at Otis, where he was teaching a semester-long critique class at the time of his exhibition. Asher, telephone interview with author, August 5, 2008.

14   The location of Asher's exhibition was specified in the announcement card as the gallery foyer, rather than the gallery itself.

15   Emile Benveniste, "The Nature of Pronouns," in *Problems in General Linguistics*, trans. Mary Elizabeth Meek (Coral Gables: University of Miami Press, 1971), 218–219.

16   Benveniste notes that "these 'pronominal' forms do not refer to 'reality' or to 'objective' positions in space or time but to the utterance, unique each time, that contains them, and thus they reflect their proper use." Ibid., 219.

17   Benveniste attributes language with constitutive power by arguing that "[i]t is in and through language that man constitutes himself as a *subject*." Emile Benveniste,

"Subjectivity in Language," in *Problems in General Linguistics*, 224 (italics in original).

18   Benveniste, "The Nature of Pronouns," 219.

19   Asher, *Writings*, 105.

20   Ibid., 106.

21   Ibid.

22   Asher, project notes for "Audio by Artists," n.d., Asher papers.

23   The series was conceived by Ian Murray in the late 1970s and first exhibited (without Asher's work) at A Space, an artist-run exhibition space in Toronto, in 1980. Asher's work ran in the seventh, eighth, and tenth program installments in the second showing of the series at the Walter Phillips Gallery in 1983.

24   The museum's in-house designers helped Asher with the poster project.

25   The size of Asher's posters, twenty-five by thirty-four inches, was designed to mimic film posters placed outside movie theaters. Asher, telephone interview with author, November 17, 2008.

26   Ibid.

27   "Matrix" curator Constance Lewallen made this point in the exhibition brochure, arguing, "[a]ccording to Asher's point of view, the identity of the individuals responsible for making a documentary film is especially significant, because documentaries are often believed to be factual and objective." Lewallen, *Michael Asher: Matrix/Berkeley 67* (Berkeley: University Art Museum, 1983), n.p.

28   LACE Gallery Artists to Friends of LACE Gallery, February 10, 1978, Asher papers.

29   Asher, LACE project notes, March 7, 1978, Asher papers.

30   Asher, "L.A.C.E./Michael Asher," exhibition proposal, April 11, 1978, Asher papers.

31   More specifically, Asher's contract stipulated that he would have retained the right to participate in making decisions about exhibiting at LACE any work that "involve[d] a direct comment upon [his] work." Ibid.

32 Asher, LACE project notes.

33 Asher, "L.A.C.E./Michael Asher." The quotations in the following paragraphs are from this source.

34 Asher's 1977 LAICA, Claire Copley/Morgan Thomas, and Fort Worth projects are discussed in detail in chapter 2.

35 Asher's proposals for the Van Abbemuseum's permanent collection were preceded by some initial ideas that were not documented. Although Asher's two formal proposals are undated, their dating can be approximated from correspondence between Asher and Fuchs. The first formal proposal was first raised by Asher in his correspondence with Fuchs in February 1978, when Asher mentioned that he was "working on another proposal for the permanent collection." Asher to Rudi Fuchs, February 15, 1978, the Van Abbemuseum Archives, VAM SSA inv.nr. 345. Asher reiterated his involvement in a letter to Fuchs in April 1978: "I am doing a new proposal for the collection as I have mentioned in the past." Asher to Fuchs, April 12, 1978, the Van Abbemuseum Archives, VAM SSA inv.nr. 345. Asher's project notes in the Van Abbemuseum folder in his papers, dated May 21, 1978, and May 30, 1978, make repeated references to the conceptual implications of "rentals." Asher first wrote to Fuchs to inquire about the status of his (then already submitted) proposal in June 1978. Michael Asher to Rudi Fuchs, June 11, 1978, the Van Abbemuseum Archives, VAM SSA inv.nr. 345

36 Drafts of Asher's LACE and Van Abbemuseum proposals in his papers indicate that the "rental" format of the LACE project proposal preceded his use of similar elements in his Van Abbemuseum proposal.

37 Asher, "Michael Asher Permanent Collection Van Abbemuseum Eindhoven Holland," n.d., Asher papers and the archives of the Van Abbemuseum, VAM Beheersarchief 1980–1989 inv.nr. 206.

38 Ibid.

39 Ibid.

40 Asher, Van Abbemuseum project notes, May 21, 1978, Asher papers.

41 Ibid.

42 Asher, "Michael Asher Permanent Collection."

43 Ibid.

44 Correspondence between Asher and Fuchs indicates that this proposal was submitted to the museum in 1978 and considered by the museum between 1978 and early 1980. The proposal's status is documented in the Van Abbemuseum's archives and Asher papers. Asher inquired about its status in several letters to Fuchs between 1978 and 1979. These letters are dated June 11, 1978; July 20, 1978; September 21, 1978; October 11, 1978; and March 6, 1979; the Van Abbemuseum Archives, VAM SSA inv.nr. 345.

45 Fuchs indicated in a 1979 postcard that the museum's committee on acquisitions had accepted Asher's proposal. Fuchs to Asher, postcard, October 19, 1979, Asher papers. In two more postcards to Asher, dated March 4, 1980, and March 10, 1980, Fuchs again informed Asher that his proposal had been accepted. Van Abbemuseum archives, VAM Beheersarchief 1980–1989 inv.nr. 205.

46 Fuchs to Asher, postcard, October 19, 1979.

47 Burgemeester en wethouders van Eindhoven (Lord Mayor and Councilors of Eindhoven) to the director of Stedelijk Van Abbemuseum, January 6, 1981. Van Abbemuseum archives, VAM Beheersarchief 1980–1989 inv.nr. 205. This document refers to Asher's work only as "Installation."

48 Rudi Fuchs to Het college van burgemeester en wethouders van Eindhoven (The Council of the Lord Mayor and Councilors of Eindhoven), March 4, 1981. Van Abbemuseum archives, VAM Beheersarchief 1980–1989 inv.nr. 205.

49 Gehry had also participated in the architectural competition for the design of the museum's flagship building, but he did not receive the commission. Instead, the Bunker Hill commission went to Arata Isozaki.

See Pilar Viladas, "The 1980s," in *The Architecture of Frank Gehry*, ed. Mildred Friedman (New York: Rizzoli, 1986), 184; Mildred Friedman, "The Reluctant Master," in *Gehry Talks: Architecture + Process*, ed. Friedman, rev. ed. (New York: Universe Publishing, 2002), 21–22. For a comparison between Gehry's and Isozaki's museum buildings, see Herbert Muschamp, "The L.A. Museum of Contemporary Art: What's in a Name?" *Architectural Record* 175 (May 1987): 83–89, and Rowan Moore, "Frank Gehry: Temporary Contemporary," *Architectural Review* 182, no. 1090 (December 1987): 68–72.

50 Strictly speaking, the first event in the Temporary Contemporary space was the performance *Available Light*, a MOCA-commissioned collaboration between dancer/choreographer Lucinda Childs, composer John Adams, and Gehry, who designed the set for the performance.

51 The collectors who lent works to "The First Show: Painting and Sculpture from Eight Collections, 1940–1980" were Dominique de Menil, Howard and Jean Lipman, Peter and Irene Ludwig, Giuseppe and Giovanna Panza di Biumo, Robert A. Rowan, Charles and Doris Saatchi, Taft and Rita Schreiber, and the Weisman family. De Menil, Panza, Rowan, and Weisman were also founding trustees of MOCA. Julia Brown and Bridget Johnson, eds., *The First Show: Painting and Sculpture from Eight Collections, 1940–1980* (Los Angeles: Los Angeles Museum of Contemporary Art, 1983).

52 Asher had also been involved in the process of designing MOCA's warehouse space, meeting with Gehry once to consult about the renovation. Asher, interview with author, June 20, 2006; Julia Brown to Asher, June 3, 1982, Asher papers. Asher and Gehry also had some previous connections. Asher had briefly worked for Gehry's studio designing models for the surface texture of his cardboard furniture in the early 1970s. Gehry and Asher had also both served on the advisory board of FAR, or the

Foundation for Art Resources, a Los Angeles nonprofit art organization that organizes exhibitions and public lectures.

53 "Michael Asher—Museum of Contemporary Art Proposal 3/23/83," Asher papers.

54 Ibid.

55 Ibid.

56 Asher, "L.A.C.E./Michael Asher."

57 Ibid.

58 "Michael Asher—Museum of Contemporary Art Proposal 3/23/83."

59 David E. James made this observation in his review of Asher's MOCA work. James, "A Pre-Occupation of Space," *Artweek* 15 (September 22, 1984): 3.

60 The contract between Asher and MOCA was drafted by MOCA's Vice-Chairman of the Board of Trustees, Frederick M. Nicholas.

61 "Aesthetic control" is a term Asher used in the folded business card, placed on the admissions desk in the MOCA lobby, that explained the arrangement between Asher and the museum.

62 Asher, telephone interview with author, August 31, 2008.

63 The folded card included the following text:

I have proposed to The Museum of Contemporary Art in Los Angeles that an agreement be made which will give me a license for the aesthetic control of the lobby area of the Museum. In so doing, the Museum will then sublicense this area making it possible to be rented from me on a monthly basis.

As part of the installation my name will identify the lobby area along with a description of the work. The Museum will have my name appear on all reception cards which refer to the lobby as a place for public assembly or as an area for the display of cultural objects.

During the license period, however, maintenance, insurance, and taxes will be at the Museum's expense, a responsibility generally assumed by the Museum for works that they house. I have requested that they regulate all day-to-day functions and operations of the lobby area without my intervention. M.A.

64 Asher, "Michael Asher—Museum of Contemporary Art Proposal 3/23/1983."

65 Ibid.

66 Asher wrote to MOCA curator Julia Brown in February 1984, inquiring after rent from the previous four months. Asher to Julia Brown, February 23, 1984, Asher papers.

67 J. L. Austin, *How to Do Things with Words*, ed. J. O. Urmson and Marina Sbisà, 2nd ed. (Cambridge, Mass.: Harvard University Press, 1975), 13–16.

68 Ibid., 5.

69 Ibid., 14–15.

70 Ibid., 14.

71 Ibid., 24.

72 For artists such as Asher who produce site-specific work without material residue or byproduct, the question of compensation for the work performed becomes critical. Andrea Fraser has explored the critical implications of compensating artists for contemporary project-oriented work when they are contracted by institutions to produce non-object-based, often temporary work. See, for example, Andrea Fraser, "*Services*: A Working-Group Exhibition," in *Games Fights Collaborations: Das Spiel von Grenze und Überschreitung*, ed. Beatrice von Bismarck, Diethelm Stoller, and Ulf Wuggenig (Ostfildern: Cantz, 1996), 210–213; and Andrea Fraser, "What's Intangible, Transitory, Mediating, Participatory, and Rendered in the Public Sphere?" *October*, no. 80 (Spring 1997): 111–116.

73 Austin, *How to Do Things*, 44.

74 Ibid., 18. Judith Butler, one of Austin's most forceful interlocutors, addresses the division of limit conditions to external and internal, conventional and intentional, in her theorization of the cultural constructedness of identity—and the constitutive force of cultural conventions—against the voluntarism of unlimited choices. Judith Butler, *Excitable Speech: A Politics of the Performative* (New York: Routledge, 1997).

75 Austin, *How to Do Things*, 40–44.

76 Ibid., 22 (italics removed from original). When reading Austin's reference to theater, Michael Fried's evocation of theatricality in his analysis of minimalist art comes to mind: for both Austin and Fried, theater stands in for a superficial, external relation to (artistic or linguistic) representation that is devoid of the kind of internal commitment that Austin grants to ordinary performative speech acts and Fried assigns to late modernist painting. Michael Fried, "Art and Objecthood," in *Minimal Art: A Critical Anthology*, ed. Gregory Battcock (New York: E. P. Dutton, 1968), 116–147.

77 Butler, *Excitable Speech*, 5, 27–29.

78 Ibid., 28, 89–90.

79 Ibid., 89.

80 "Affective economy" is a term Ahmed uses to discuss the ways in which emotions build social relations. See Sara Ahmed, "Affective Economies," *Social Text* 22, no. 2 (Summer 2004): 117–139.

81 At that time, Fuchs wrote that he still held Asher's proposal for the museum's permanent collection in high regard. Rudi Fuchs to Asher, postcard, May 25, 1985, the Van Abbemuseum Archives, VAM SSA inv. nr. 345. Asher mentions working on a new proposal before his visit in his letter to Fuchs dated June 29, 1985. Asher to Fuchs, June 29, 1985, the Van Abbemuseum archives, VAM Beheersarchief 1980–1989 inv. nr. 206.

82 Asher, telephone interview with author, August 14, 2008. After his visit, Asher wrote to Fuchs that he had submitted the proposal to Jan Debbaut, incoming director, during his visit. Asher to Fuchs, January 6,

1986, the Van Abbemuseum archives, VAM Beheersarchief 1980–1989 inv.nr. 206.

83 Asher, "Working Title: 'The Michael Asher Trust Fund,'" n.d. [1985], Asher papers and the Van Abbemuseum archives, VAM Beheersarchief 1980–1989 inv.nr. 206.

84 Asher's proposal does not specify what portion of the interest would be remitted to Asher and what portion would fund museum purchases. Ibid.

85 "Questions Regarding Bank Trust," ibid. Asher's subsequent letters to Van Abbemuseum staff repeatedly ask for legal definitions of "permanence" in the Dutch context, indicating that the question of permanence in the context of the museum's "permanent collection" was a crucial part of his proposal.

86 Ibid.

87 At the same time as he made his trust fund proposal to the Van Abbemuseum, Asher completed another work that sought donations to a local nonprofit in 1986. In this project, on display in the group exhibition called "A Southern California Collection" at the Cirrus Gallery in Los Angeles, Asher asked gallery visitors to consider donating money to a local nonprofit arts organization, the Foundation for Art Resources, or F.A.R. The work contained the text, "Influence your culture/Donate to F.A.R.," in large painted letters above a wall-mounted shelf. On the shelf, Asher had placed F.A.R. handouts containing information about the organization's history and purpose, future plans, board of directors, and a statement of revenues and expenditures. The work resulted in at least one donation to F.A.R. from a local art collector.

88 Asher to Piet de Jonge, December 28, 1985; Asher to Jan Debbaut, May 12, 1986; Asher to Debbaut, May 19, 1986; Asher to de Jonge, October 1, 1986; all from the Van Abbemuseum archives, VAM Beheersarchief 1980–1989 inv.nr. 206. A letter from de Jonge to Asher, dated May 23, 1986, stated that de Jonge had discussed The Michael

Asher Trust Fund project with Fuchs, but that Fuchs had not made a decision about the project yet. De Jonge to Asher, May 23, 1986, the Van Abbemuseum archives, VAM Beheersarchief 1980–1989 inv.nr. 206.

89 De Jonge to Asher, February 12, 1987, Asher papers and the Van Abbemuseum archives, VAM Beheersarchief 1980–1989 inv.nr. 206.

90 Michel Foucault, "Nietzsche, Genealogy, History," in *The Foucault Reader*, ed. Paul Rabinow, trans. Donald F. Bouchard and Sherry Simon (New York: Pantheon Books, 1984), 82.

91 Ibid., 88.

92 During the intervening period between 1983 and 2007, Asher had also participated in the MOCA exhibitions "Reconsidering the Object of Art, 1965–1975" in 1995–1996 and "A Minimal Future? Art as Object, 1958–1968" in 2004.

93 Exhibition statement, "Artists' Gifts: Michael Asher" at the Museum of Contemporary Art, Los Angeles, September 9, 2007–January 7, 2008.

94 Ibid.

95 Benjamin H. D. Buchloh, "Conceptual Art 1962–1969: From the Aesthetic of Administration to the Critique of Institutions," *October*, no. 55 (Winter 1990): 106–143. This essay was a revised version of his "From the Aesthetic of Administration to Institutional Critique (Some Aspects of Conceptual Art 1962–1969)," in *L'art conceptuel, une perspective*, ed. Claude Gintz (Paris: Musée d'art moderne de la Ville de Paris, 1989), 41–53.

96 Buchloh, "Conceptual Art," 142.

97 Ibid., 143.

98 Ibid.

99 Ibid.

4 Institutional Support

1 Asher's sculptural proposal for the Stuart Collection eventually developed into the drinking fountain discussed in chapter 1.

2 Anne Rorimer, "Michael Asher: Recent Work," *Artforum* 18, no. 8 (April 1980): 50 (italics in original). See also Anne Rorimer, "Reevaluating the Object of Collecting and Display," *Art Bulletin* 77, no. 1 (March 1995): 23, where she argues that Asher's work "addresses institutional support structures in order to demonstrate that objects are beholden to their physical and social context."

3 Kasper Koenig had approached Asher with the idea for a book project in 1973 when he was the editor of the Press of the Nova Scotia College of Art and Design. Koenig also organized Asher's exhibition at the Anna Leonowens Gallery at the Nova Scotia College of Art and Design in 1974. After Koenig left the Nova Scotia Press in 1976, his successor, Benjamin H. D. Buchloh, continued the editing process and collaborated with Asher on writing the book. Asher, "Author's Introduction," in *Writings 1973–1983 on Works 1969–1979*, ed. Benjamin H. D. Buchloh, Nova Scotia Series 15 (Halifax: Press of the Nova Scotia College of Art and Design; Los Angeles: Los Angeles Museum of Contemporary Art, 1983), ix.

4 Grace Glueck, "Art People: Cologne's Vast Postwar Show," *New York Times*, December 12, 1980. The subtitle of the "Heute" section was "37 Künstler der jungen Generation."

5 According to Koenig, "We had to make a compromise . . . either cut down by about one-third of the historical survey to accommodate the new work, or change the structure of 'Today.'" Koenig in Glueck, "Art People: The Summer in Europe," *New York Times*, July 31, 1981.

6 The organization and funding structure of "Heute" is detailed in Glueck, "Art People: The Summer in Europe."

7 Glueck noted that "Heute" artists included "Kim MacConnel and Robert Kushner—artists not originally tapped by Mr. Koenig—[who were] represented [both] by the Zwirner Gallery in Cologne and the Holly Solomon Gallery in New York." Ibid.

8 Glueck, "Art View: An Ambitious Showing of Modern Art; Cologne, West Germany," *New York Times*, August 9, 1981.

9 Kasper Koenig, ed., *Heute, Westkunst* (Cologne: Museen der Stadt Köln, 1981). The artists exhibiting in "Heute" were John Ahearn, Michael Asher, Barbara Bloom, Jonathan Borofsky, Troy Brauntuch, Luciano Castelli, Sandro Chia, Francesco Clemente, Enzo Cucchi, René Daniels, Nicola de Maria, Felix Droese, Isa Genzken, Jack Goldstein, Franz Graf, Jenny Holzer, Anselm Kiefer, Juergen Klauke, Brigitte Kowanz, Robert Kushner, Robert Longo, Andrew Lord, Urs Lüthi, Kim MacConnel, Gerhard Merz, Peter Nadin, Mimmo Paladino, Judith Pfaff, David Salle, Salome, Hubert Schmalix, Julian Schnabel, Horst Schuler, Thomas Schütte, Jeff Wall, Franz West, and Robin Winters.

10 The main exhibition is documented in Laszlo Glozer, *Westkunst: Zeitgenössische Kunst seit 1939* (Cologne: DuMont Buchverlag, 1981).

11 The letter's text was also printed in the exhibition's catalogue, where it was accompanied by a photograph of chairs on display at the Department of Design and Architecture at the Museum of Modern Art in New York City. In the photograph, Modern Movement chairs by Ludwig Mies van der Rohe (Barcelona and Cantilever chairs), Marcel Breuer (Cesca and Slatted chairs), and Gerrit Rietveld (Red-Blue chair) were crowded together on a low platform under Bauhaus and Soviet constructivist posters and flanked by French art nouveau furniture at one end. *Artforum* reviewer Richard Armstrong pointed out that Asher's display of chairs resembled the modern design chairs at MoMA, stating that "Asher's hallway installation [was] modeled after the glassed-in furniture ensembles at the design collection of The Museum of Modern Art, New York." Armstrong, "'Heute,' *Westkunst*," *Artforum* 20, no. 1 (1981): 84.

12 The request to participating dealers was written by Koenig, based on informa-

tion obtained from Asher in a telephone conversation. Asher, telephone interview with author, January 6, 2009.

13 The chairs on display represented the following galleries: Galerie Hans Mayer, Düsseldorf; Galerie Konrad Fischer, Düsseldorf; Paula Cooper Gallery, New York; Galerie Arno Kohnen, Düsseldorf; Galerie Nächst St. Stephan, Wien; Galerie Rüdiger Schöttle, München; Galerie Pablo Stähli, Zürich; and Galleria Lucio Amelio, Napoli. The following participating dealers did not send in chairs: Galerie Krinzinger, Innsbruck; Metro Pictures, New York; Galleria Gian Enzo Sperone, Rome; Galerie Helen van der Meij, Amsterdam; Galerie Bruno Bischofberger, Zürich; Holly Solomon Gallery, New York.

14 Asher to critic James Meyer, January 27, 1993, Asher papers.

15 Asher's project notes indicate that he intended the work to critique the funding structure of "Westkunst 'Heute.' " Asher, project notes for "Heute," n.d., Asher papers.

16 Asher, exhibition statement, quoted in Glueck, "Art People: The Summer in Europe."

17 Fuchs's letter was dated September 1981.

18 Rudi Fuchs, in "Excerpts from a letter to the participating artists by the Director of Documenta 7, R. H. Fuchs, edited and published by Louise Lawler," quoted in Douglas Crimp, "The Art of Exhibition," in his *On the Museum's Ruins* (Cambridge, Mass.: MIT Press, 1993), 239. Fuchs's letter had been appropriated by artist Louise Lawler, who quoted sections of it on a set of stationery that she produced in an edition of one hundred for distribution before and during Documenta 7 (she was not, however, among Fuchs's Documenta invitees). During Documenta 7, Lawler's stationery was sold in Kassel in a trailer operated by Fashion Moda, an alternative Bronx art gallery whose presence had been facilitated by Jenny Holzer, one of the exhibiting artists. Crimp, "The Art of Exhibition," 238–240.

19 Crimp discusses Fuchs's letter and its reception in the New York art world in "The Art of Exhibition," 238–241. This essay was first published in *October*, no. 30 (Fall 1984).

20 Asher's work was thus not installed in the same venue for which Fuchs commissioned his walls.

21 Asher's exhibition at Museum Haus Lange in Krefeld opened on May 16, 1982, and Documenta 7 opened on June 19, 1982. In Krefeld, Asher's exhibition was paired with one by Daniel Buren, whose installation occupied Museum Haus Esters.

22 Haus Esters and Haus Lange were designed in 1927 and 1928, and their building was completed in 1930. Haus Lange had been used for exhibitions of modern and contemporary art since 1955, while Haus Esters was converted into a museum only in 1981. Kent Kleinman, Leslie Van Duzer, and Ludwig Mies van der Rohe, *Mies van der Rohe: The Krefeld Villas* (New York: Princeton Architectural Press, 2005), 22.

23 The chronology of Asher's projects in the early 1980s provides evidence of thematic connections among formally different projects. The reproduction aspect of Asher's Documenta 7 work might be analyzed in relation to his concurrent exploration of originality and mechanical reproduction in his 1981 work for "Vocation/Vacation" at the Banff Centre's Walter Phillips Gallery. Asher continued to think about reproduction in his contracted viewer piece for the "74th American Exhibition" at the Art Institute of Chicago, which opened only two weeks before Documenta 7. At the Art Institute, Asher was concerned with the reproduction of viewing relations rather than with the material support structures of exhibitions.

24 The installation of Asher's walls in the Orangerie was completed only after the opening of Documenta, when wooden Nussbaum molding was applied to the lower horizontal edges of the walls. Hence, photographs taken of the work during the opening reception show the work in its incomplete stage. Asher, interview with author, June 27, 2008.

25 The wall statement contained the following text: "This installation is a partial reconstruction of Haus Esters, located at Wilhelmshofallee 97, Krefeld, West Germany. It was designed by Mies Van der Rohe in 1927. As of 1981 it was restored to become Museum Haus Esters. This reconstruction constitutes the interior wing walls which function as the existing exhibition display system." Reprinted in *Documenta 7*, vol. 2 (Kassel: D + V Paul Dierichs, 1982), 22.

26 There are, of course, differences between the walls Fuchs called for and those that Asher provided. Fuchs's brick walls were constructed in the main Documenta venue, the Museum Fridericianum, while Asher installed his walls in the Orangerie, another exhibition site. Fuchs's walls were intended to be permanent, and constructed as such, while Asher's walls came down at the end of the exhibition.

27 Michael Asher, Benjamin H. D. Buchloh, and Rudi Fuchs, *Michael Asher: Exhibitions in Europe 1972–1977* (Eindhoven: Van Abbemuseum, 1980).

28 Here, Fuchs is describing the Asher exhibition he had organized at the Van Abbemuseum. R. H. Fuchs, "Eindhoven: Michael Asher: –1977," in *Michael Asher: Exhibitions in Europe*, 34.

29 In his account of Fuchs's press conference in New York in the spring of 1982, Crimp comments: "at least half of the artistic director's presentation [was] not about artworks but about work in progress to ready the exhibition spaces for installation. . . . It was these [permanent] walls [that Fuchs was having built in the museum], together with the lighting design and other details of museological enterprise, that he took great pains to present to his listeners." Crimp, "The Art of Exhibition," 240. Crimp also contrasts Fuchs's obsession with permanent exhibition architecture with Fashion Moda's deliberately temporary and

makeshift display and sales trailer outside the Museum Fridericianum in Kassel during Documenta 7.

30 Fuchs, "Foreword," in *Documenta 7*, vol. 2, vii.

31 Fuchs explained, "I feel the time one can show contemporary art in makeshift spaces, converted factories and so on is over. Art is a noble achievement and should be handled with dignity and with respect. Therefore we have finally built real walls." Fuchs, quoted in Coosje van Bruggen, "In the Mist Things Appear Larger," in *Documenta 7*, vol. 2, ix.

32 Fuchs, "Introduction," in *Documenta 7*, vol. 1, xv (italics in original).

33 Ibid.

34 Other works situated on or in close proximity to Asher's walls included those by Vito Acconci, Richard Long, Claude Rutault, Ettore Spalletti, and Frank Gehry.

35 Weiner's statement was inscribed on the facade in capital letters. The statement, however, had been formulated in 1979 and was used in a variety of exhibition contexts. While the repeatability of the statement does not remove site specificity from its commentary, it does mean that the statement was considered by Weiner to describe many such situations, rather than Documenta 7 exclusively.

36 Fuchs, "Introduction," xv.

37 Marcel Mauss, *The Gift: The Form and Reason for Exchange in Archaic Societies*, trans. W. D. Halls (New York: W. W. Norton, 1990), 41–42. Janet Kraynak discusses Mauss's theory in "Rirkrit Tiravanija's Liability," *Documents*, no. 13 (1998): 26–40.

38 "L'art conceptuel" was followed in the 1990s by "Reconsidering the Object of Art" at the Los Angeles Museum of Contemporary Art (1995–1996) and "Global Conceptualism: Points of Origin, 1950s–1980s" at the Queens Museum of Art (1999), among others.

39 Asher responded to Gintz's exhibition invitation (dated March 17, 1988) in a letter dated April 5, 1988. Asher to Claude Gintz, April 5, 1988, Asher papers.

40 Asher to Gintz, April 5, 1988.

41 Ibid.

42 Gintz to Asher, April 23, 1988, Asher papers.

43 Asher to Gintz, May 5, 1989, Asher papers.

44 Curator Juliette Laffon to Asher, March 15, 1989, Asher papers.

45 Asher to Gintz, May 5, 1989.

46 In a letter to Gintz, Asher expressed concerns about the reception of the work, and emphasized his interest in intervening in the art historical interpretation of conceptual art. Asher to Gintz, June 2, 1989, Asher papers.

47 Asher wrote: "Many times a retrospective of a prior art movement can serve as a means of recapturing the past, such as if members of the elder part of our art community and its institutions realize a historical need to introduce the movement's constituent issues to a younger generation in order to somehow ensure the reproduction of these issues." Asher to Gintz, May 5, 1989.

48 Ibid. In a truly appropriate manner, the exhibition "l'art conceptuel, une perspective" did turn into a critical site of problematizing the historiography of conceptual art. The exchange in the exhibition's catalogue between Buchloh and Joseph Kosuth contested the origin of the aesthetic practices executed under the name of conceptual art. Benjamin H. D. Buchloh, "From the Aesthetic of Administration to Institutional Critique (Some Aspects of Conceptual Art 1962–1969)," in *L'art conceptuel, une perspective*, ed. Claude Gintz (Paris: Musée d'art moderne de la Ville de Paris, 1989), 41–53; Joseph Kosuth, "Joseph Kosuth Responds to Benjamin Buchloh," in *L'art conceptuel*, 60. The debate continued in the journal *October*, where Buchloh's revised article received further commentary from Kosuth and Seth Siegelaub. See Benjamin H. D. Buchloh, "Conceptual Art 1962–1969: From the Aes-

thetic of Administration to the Critique of Institutions," *October*, no. 55 (Winter 1990): 106–143; Joseph Kosuth and Seth Siegelaub, "Joseph Kosuth and Seth Siegelaub Reply to Benjamin Buchloh on Conceptual Art," *October*, no. 57 (Summer 1991): 152–157; Benjamin H. D. Buchloh, "Benjamin Buchloh Replies to Joseph Kosuth and Seth Siegelaub," *October*, no. 57 (Summer 1991): 158–161.

49 Asher to Gintz, May 5, 1989.

50 In his exhibition and catalogue statement, Asher wrote: "Historical objectification ought to be accelerated while there is still a collective experience and memory which can assist in the clarity of an analysis, simultaneously opening up a space to ask fundamental questions regarding history making." Asher addressed this gesture to art historians who were to be "notified . . . that a new historical perspective is being mapped on to conceptual art practice." Asher in *L'art conceptuel*, 112.

51 Asher used the word "announcement" rather than "advertisement" in his wall label and catalogue statement.

52 Due to publishing schedules, some of the journal issues available at the bookstore at the time of the exhibition did not yet carry Asher's advertisement.

53 The November 1997 invitation came from curatorial assistant Lilian Tone on behalf of McShine. Lilian Tone to Asher, November 3, 1997, Asher papers.

54 Asher's notes queried whether MoMA had had any doubts about its own exhibitions, how its exhibitions were received internally, and how—or whether—MoMA represented its own institutional history to the public. Asher, project notes for "Museum as Muse," n.d., Asher papers.

55 Kynaston McShine to Asher, June 9, 1998, Asher papers.

56 Asher to McShine, June 14, 1998, Asher papers.

57 McShine to Asher, July 23, 1998, Asher papers.

58 Asher wrote, "the reason for a publication was in response to your information that there would be very little money for my project. I wanted to propose a work where the museum could either break even or make a profit on my project. It was my hope that proceeds from the sale of the publication could offset all production costs." Asher to McShine, August 2, 1998, Asher papers.

59 Ibid. MoMA appears to have originally agreed to make the catalogue available for free in the bookstore, as Asher had proposed. In January 1999, however, MoMA proposed to limit the catalogue's circulation to the exhibition area only. In a letter to McShine dated January 27, 1999, Asher informed the curator that he would withdraw from the exhibition if the project was modified in this manner. In this letter, Asher connected his objection to the institutional limitations this mode of distribution would have effected: "This decision places a limit upon the scope of this work since it will remain in an aesthetic context rather than allowing its use to change with each new situation. Likewise, it won't mirror an artwork which transfers from one collection to the next." Asher to McShine, January 27, 1999, Asher papers.

60 As Crow described this process, "Acquiring the handsomely slick booklet . . . required a trip to the always bustling museum store and a specific request to the cashier, who then pulled a copy from a drawer under the counter as if providing some forbidden work of heresy or pornography." Thomas Crow, "'The Museum as Muse: Artists Reflect,' Museum of Modern Art, New York," *Artforum* 37, no. 10 (Summer 1999): 146.

61 Roberta Smith, "Critic's Notebook: What's No Longer on Museum Walls," *New York Times*, May 31, 1999.

62 Although Asher was initially against allowing such a statement, he agreed to its inclusion less than a week after it was proposed. In the January 27, 1999, letter to

McShine, Asher expressed his disagreement with the museum's request to outline its policy in the catalogue. Asher explains his change of mind in "Cave Notes: Stephen Pascher and Michael Asher Examine Asher's Recent Work at the MoMA," *Merge*, no. 5 (1999): 24.

63 Kirk Varnedoe, "A Note on Deaccessioning at The Museum of Modern Art," in Michael Asher, *Painting and Sculpture from The Museum of Modern Art: Catalog of Deaccessions 1929 through 1998 by Michael Asher* (New York: Michael Asher and The Museum of Modern Art, 1999), n.p.

64 The suggestion that the entries in the catalogue lacked credibility is puzzling, because the information in the catalogue had in fact been collected and organized internally at the museum without the artist's involvement (although one might question why the project was assigned to an intern if the museum was concerned about the "accuracy" and "completeness" of the listings).

65 Freud originally developed his theory of the split ego in reference to fetishism, but later extended it to describe the general constitution of human subjectivity. Sigmund Freud, "Fetishism," in *The Standard Edition of the Complete Psychological Works of Sigmund Freud*, ed. James Strachey, vol. 21 (London: Hogarth Press, 1964), 152–157.

66 The well-known phrase, "I know very well . . . but all the same," was used by psychoanalyst Octave Mannoni to refer to a coexistence of two attitudes, acknowledgement and refusal, or recognition and disavowal, in Freud's theory of fetishism. On Mannoni's interpretation of Freud's fetishism, see, for example, Christian Metz, *The Imaginary Signifier: Psychoanalysis and the Cinema*, trans. Celia Britton, Annwyl Williams, Ben Brewster, and Alfred Guzzetti (Bloomington: Indiana University Press, 1982), 71–76.

67 Freud, "An Outline of Psycho-Analysis" (1938), in *The Standard Edition of the Complete Psychological Works of Sigmund Freud*, ed.

James Strachey, vol. 23 (London: Hogarth Press, 1964), 202–204. Freud theorized that such a splitting is a defense mechanism for the ego in order to handle threatening situations.

68 Accordingly, Freud argued that there was nothing extraordinary about the existence of such a split, rather, Freud maintained, "the two attitudes persist side by side throughout their lives without influencing each other." Freud, "An Outline," 203.

69 Daniel Buren's work for the Sixth Guggenheim International Exhibition was taken down by the museum before the exhibition opened. The removal was done at the request of some of the other exhibiting artists who felt Buren's work impinged upon the viewing of their work. Buren's motive for the interior part of the work, a large banner that descended through the central space of the museum, was to counter the dominance of the museum's architecture by installing a work that would not be visually and ideologically subordinate to it. Hans Haacke's planned solo exhibition at the Guggenheim was canceled because of the museum director's opinion that the focus on socioeconomic issues in three of Haacke's planned works—including *Shapolsky et al. Manhattan Real Estate Holdings, a Real-Time Social System, as of May 1, 1971* (1971)—was not suitable for an art museum. On Buren and the Guggenheim, see Alexander Alberro, "The Turn of the Screw: Daniel Buren, Dan Flavin, and the Sixth Guggenheim International Exhibition," *October* 80 (Spring 1997): 57–84. On Haacke and the Guggenheim, see Rosalyn Deutsche, "Property Values: Hans Haacke, Real Estate, and the Museum," in *Hans Haacke: Unfinished Business*, ed. Brian Wallis (New York: New Museum of Contemporary Art; Cambridge, Mass.: MIT Press, 1986), 20–37.

70 Asher was well aware of the critical potential involved in the inclusion of Varnedoe's note: "At first I certainly didn't want it. But when I finally read it I realized it could be quite revealing." Asher in "Cave Notes," 24.

71 Asher to McShine, February 4, 1999, Asher papers.

72 Smith, "Critic's Notebook."

73 Ibid.

74 Craig Owens, "The Allegorical Impulse: Toward a Theory of Postmodernism," in his *Beyond Recognition: Representation, Power, and Culture*, ed. Scott Bryson, Barbara Kruger, Lynne Tillman, and Jane Weinstock (Berkeley: University of California Press, 1992), 53, 63–64.